Dipped in

Nicholas Parsons has always been a fanatical reader of reviews. A one-time teacher of English at Pisa University, he spent several years working as a publishing editor in London, as well as writing occasional travel journalism and reviewing. He now lives and works in Greece.

edited by
Nicholas Parsons

Dipped in Vitriol

Pan Original
Pan Books London and Sydney

First published 1981 by Pan Books Ltd,
Cavaye Place, London SW10 9PG
© Nicholas Parsons 1981
ISBN 0 330 26556 3
Printed and bound in Great Britain by
Richard Clay (The Chaucer Press) Ltd, Bungay, Suffolk

Contents

Contents

Acknowledgements

Nicholas Parsons would especially like to thank the following for their assistance and good humour: Victoria Bott and Alison Holding of the Old Vic Press Office; Mary Parsons of the Royal Court Theatre Press Office; Nicola Shane of the Tate Gallery Press Office. Also the following, who patiently answered queries: John Amis, Edward Bond, Paul Bailey, Paul Callan, Geoffrey Gorer, Geoffrey Grigson, Lord Harewood, Raglan Squire, Alexander Walker and Auberon Waugh. Also Peta Murray, Diana Balfour, Lotte James and Souli Streatfield-Moore who typed the manuscript swiftly and accurately.

Introduction

Perception of badness, as of beauty, is in the eye of the beholder. To this welcome fact we owe the variety of critical response and wit which will be found in the following pages. Undoubtedly the best 'hatchet' reviews are composed by those with a definite vision of what is good art as opposed to incompetence, propaganda or pseudery. Consequently many of the writers featured have a strongly recognizable personality, but not, in most cases, an easily reducible ideology. 'All art is propaganda,' wrote George Orwell, 'but not all propaganda is art', and the same could be said of much critical writing. Where hostile criticism stems from a fixed ideological standpoint it degenerates into mere abuse; which is why those violent attacks on revisionist or decadent Western art by the official organs of dictatorships impress only those who write them (and possibly not even them).

This is not a book of abuse, therefore, but a humorous excursion through the realms of badness, highlighting some of its more persistent traits on the way: hagiography, self-importance in autobiography, pretentiousness and incompetence in fiction, mountebankery and shallowness in the theatre, whimsical follies in music, brain-crushing bad taste in the cinema. This is the cultural effluent of our society and is not without its lovable qualities. These are most apparent in bad movies where a total absence of a sense of the ridiculous is most satisfyingly to be found.

Our contributors write, in almost every case, out of affection for the art form at its best; which makes the desecration of it at its worst as much a pointer to excellence as an exposure of failure. The best critiques, however vitriolic, are written *con amore*: Tynan's for the theatre, Shaw's for the theatre and music, to take the two outstanding examples. They are also written by people whose tastes are not narrow but whose criteria are severe. They take their writing, not themselves, seriously; and entertainment is a serious part of writing. The tradition of frivolous profundity is seen at its best in the pieces by Wilde, Shaw, Gore Vidal and Clive James. The effects of their verbal chastisement are hard to measure; but laughter is a potent weapon and, if nothing else, they help to educate the taste of their readers so that they are better able to spot the cheap, the insincere, the second-hand, the untruthful and the morally obtuse at ten paces.

Nicholas Parsons, August 1981

The Pious, the Bad and the Ugly

The quest for best-sellerdom is perennial; like that for the philosopher's stone it has attracted some talented people and innumerable worthless plodders. Our forefathers believed the philosopher's stone was compounded of the purest sulphur and mercury, which are not unlike the pungent but elusive qualities of a literary blockbuster. Biblical stories were often the basis for these, it being easier to rehash old plots than to think up new ones. Besides, such books tended to spike the guns of the critics by virtue of their unspotted parentage, at the same time reassuring the respectable reading public. In a survey he once did of the top ten best sellers, Gore Vidal began with a biblical smash:

Let us begin with number ten on your Hit Parade of Fiction, *Two from Galilee* by Marjorie Holmes. Marjorie is also the author of *I've Got to Talk to Somebody, God* and *Who Am I, God? Two from Galilee* is subtitled significantly, 'A Love Story of Mary and Joseph'. Since the film *Love Story* really took off, what about a love story starring the Mother and the Stepfather of Our Lord? A super idea. And Marjorie has written it. We open with the thirteen-year-old Mary menstruating ('a bloody hand had smitten her in the night'). ' "I am almost fourteen, Father," she said, "and I have become nubile this day." ' She is 'mad for' Joseph, a carpenter's son; he is mad for her.

Shrewdly Marjorie has taken two young Americans of the lower middle class and placed them in old Galilee. I recognize some of the descriptions as being from the last version of *Ben Hur* to which I made a considerable contribution. 'The couches covered with a silken stuff threaded with gold. The glow from a hanging alabaster lamp . . .' Luckily, I was on the set at the beginning of the shooting and so was able to persuade the art director to remove tomatoes from Mrs Ben Hur Senior's kitchen. Otherwise, Marjorie might have had Hannah prepare a tomato and bacon sandwich for her daughter Mary.

Since Miss Holmes is not an experienced writer, it is difficult to know what, if anything, she had in mind when she decided to tell the Age-Old Story with nothing new to add. True, there are some domestic crises and folksy wrinkles like Joseph's father being a drunk. Incidentally, Joseph and Mary are known by their English names while the other characters keep their Hebrew names. Mary's mother Hannah is fun: a Jewish mother as observed by a gentile housewife in McLean, Virginia, who has seen some recent movies on the subject and heard all the jokes on television.

Hannah worries for her daughter. Will Joseph get into Mary *before* the wedding? 'Hannah had no idea what it was like to be a man – this waiting. No woman could comprehend physical passion.' Helen Gurley Brown and Germaine Greer will no doubt set Miss Holmes straight on that sexist point. But perhaps the author is reflecting her audience (Who are they, by the way? *Where* are they? Baptists in Oklahoma City? Catholics in Duluth suburbs?) when she writes that Hannah 'did not have the faintest concept of the demon-god that entered a youth's loins at puberty and gave him no peace thereafter'. Yes, I checked the last noun for spelling. Joseph, incidentally, is such a stud that when Mary is with him 'the thing that was between them chimed and quivered and lent discomfort to all'.

Suddenly between that chiming, quivering thing and Mary falls the shadow of the Holy Ghost. 'Mary's flesh sang', as she experienced 'the singing silence of God'. Miss Holmes rises to lyricism. 'The Holy Spirit came upon her, invaded her body, and her bowels stirred and her loins melted.' Obviously, entry was not made through the ear as those Renaissance painters who lacked Miss Holmes's powerful realism believed. Mary soon starts wondering why 'the blood pumps so painfully in my breast and my bowels run so thin?' She finds out in due course. Joseph has a hard time believing her story until the Holy Spirit tells him to get it together and accept his peculiar role as the antlered saint of a new cult.

At census time the young marrieds set out for Bethlehem, where the local Holiday Inn is full up or, as a passer-by says, ' "The Inn? You'll be lucky to find a corner for the ass at the Inn." ' As these quotations demonstrate, Miss Holmes's style is beyond cliché. But when it comes to scene-making, she is sometimes betrayed by the familiarity of her subject matter. If the Story is to be told truly there must be a birth scene, and so she is obliged to write, ' "Some hot water if you can get it," ' adding, ' "Go no further even to fetch a midwife." ' To which a helpful stranger replies, ' "I'll send one of them for one," ' reminding us of the Joan Crawford interview some decades ago when the living legend asked with quiet majesty, 'Whom is fooling whom?'

Use of Biblical raw material, and the dangers inherent therein, may be witnessed even more startlingly on the stage. Sir John Squire showed a similar lack of reverence for the author, if not the subject, of *Job*:

A modern writer comes across a noble story or a fine lyric passage and thinks, 'What a scandal that this should be buried away out of sight in the Old Testament! It is just the theme for me.' The lure is so strong that one contemporary poet has attempted, and failed (though not ignominiously), to rewrite David's Lament for Jonathan, and another has endeavoured to adapt the dramatic poem *Job* to the modern stage. It was a lamentable affair, redeemed only from complete inconspicuousness by a highly incongruous chorus inspired by Swinburne and by an arresting entry of Satan with the salutation:

Ho Job! How goes it?

Edmund Wilson analysed the success of another pop-Christianity epic, *The Robe* by Lloyd C. Douglas which sold in two years one million four hundred and fifty thousand copies, and was said to have been read by five times that number of people:

It is a story of the Roman Empire in the days of early Christianity, and its appeal is exactly the same as that of *The Last Days of Pompeii, Quo Vadis?* and *Ben Hur*. The surface has been brought up to date by diluting the old grandiose language of the novel of ancient Rome with a jargon which sounds as if Dr Douglas had picked it up during the years when, as the publishers' leaflet tells us, he was a counsellor of college students at the universities of Michigan and Illinois. The aristocratic Romans are always saying things like 'You're definitely drunk.' 'But what's the matter with idols? They're usually quite artistic.' 'Indeed! Well – she'd better be good!' 'I wouldn't know.' 'What do you mean – "a Christian"?' . . . Dr Douglas has woven, in *The Robe*, an almost unrivalled fabric of old clichés, in which one of the only attempts at a literary heightening of effect is the substitution for the simple 'said' of other more pretentious verbs –

so that the characters are always shrilling, barking, speculating, parrying, wailing, wheedling or grunting whatever they have to say.

When Americans weren't buying biblical blockbusters with bang-up-to-date dialogue, they often fell for a philosophical story which, if pretentious enough and sufficiently ill-written, could hit the jackpot. Dwight Macdonald wrote a long article on the phenomenally successful *By Love Possessed*, James Gould Cozzens' 1957 best seller. Most of the critics went overboard for it, so Macdonald devoted a lot of space to showing up the discrepancies in their reviews. He then settled down to exhibiting Mr Cozzens' style – of which the description 'unreadable' would be generous:

. . . the main burden of the reviewers was not doubt but affirmation. In reading their praise of Cozzens' prose, I had an uneasy feeling that perhaps we were working with different texts.

> *Every sentence has been hammered, filed and tested until it bears precisely the weight it was designed to carry, and does it with clarity and grace,*

wrote John Fischer. The sentences have been hammered all right:

> *Recollected with detachment, these self-contrived quandaries, these piffling dilemmas that young love could invent for itself were comic – too much ado about nothing much! Arthur Winner Junior was entangled laughably in his still-juvenile illogicalities and inconsistencies. Absurdly set on working contradictories and incompatibles, he showed how the world was indeed a comedy for those who think. By his unripe, all-or-nothing-at-all views, he was bound to be self confounded. By the ridiculous impracticalness of his aspirations, he was inescapably that figure of fun whose lofty professions go with quite other performances. The high endeavour's very moments of true-predominance guaranteed the little joke-on-them to follow.*

This is not a Horrible Example – we shall have some later – but a typical run-of-the-mill Cozzens paragraph, chosen at random. It seems to me about as bad as prose can get – what sensitive or even merely competent novelist would write a phrase like 'the ridiculous impracticalness of his aspirations'?

Mr Cozzens is a master of dialogue, wrote Orville Prescott. On the contrary, he has no ear for speech at all. 'You answer well, Arthur!'

says one matron. 'But, to my very point!' And another: 'They're all, or almost all, down at the boathouse, swimming, Arthur.'

He has always written with complete clarity, wrote Granville Hicks, *but here, without forsaking clarity and correctness, he achieves great eloquence and even poetic power*. On the contrary, malphony exfoliates, as our author might put it. As:

The succusive, earthquake-like throwing-over of a counted-on years-old stable state of things had opened fissures. Through one of them, Arthur Winner stared a giddying, horrifying moment down unplumbed, nameless abysses in himself. He might later deny the cognition, put thoughts of the undiscovered country away, seek to lose the memory; yet the heart's mute halt at every occasional, accidental recollection of those gulfs admitted their existence, confessed his fearful close shave.

'Successive' is cake-walking,* since it means 'violently shaking . . . as of earthquakes' and so merely duplicates the next word; a good writer wouldn't use four hyphenated expressions in a row; he would also avoid the 'occasional, accidental' rhyme, and the reference to unplumbed abysses; he would ask himself what a 'mute halt' is (as versus a noisy halt?); and he would sense that 'close shave' is stylistically an anticlimax to so elevated a passage. It's all very puzzling. Here's Richard Ellmann of Northwestern University, who has been perceptive about Joyce's prose, finding *By Love Possessed* 'so pleasant to read', while I find almost every sentence grates.

Cozzens, according to Macdonald, lived a life 'compared to which Thoreau's on Walden Pond was gregarious. "I am a hermit and have no friends," he understates.' Writing novels was not a problem despite no human contacts. You had to know yourself. Cozzens didn't go to plays, concerts or art galleries either, though he admitted to visiting a movie in 1940. 'My own literary preferences are for writers who write well,' he is recorded as saying, pleasantly adding: 'This necessarily excludes most of my contemporaries.'

The most celebrated genre of best sellers is the pulp rom-

---

* Macdonald uses 'cake-walking' as a term of abuse derived from Webster's dictionary definition of 'a cakewalk': 'A form of entertainment among American Negroes in which a prize of a cake was given for the most accomplished steps and figures.'

ance. These take various forms, one of the more entertaining being the 'kitsch Emily Brontë' novel in which everybody is rough and tough and speaks in funny dialects. H. G. Wells once reviewed Frances Hodgson Burnett's *A Lady of Quality*, a startling literary effusion from the authoress of *Little Lord Fauntleroy*. One of the (many) stock ingredients of this book was the character of Clorinda, a reckless tomboy given to using her hunting crop on those around her until Chapter 4, when she suddenly becomes 'a woman': ' "Look your last on my fine shape," she proclaimed in her high rich voice. "You will see but little of the lower part of it when it is hidden in farthingales and petticoats. Look your last before I go to don my fine lady's furbelows." ' The men in the book are all stock and all wicked. Clorinda's father is a 'bad rural Baronet, drunken, malicious, poverty-stricken, ignorant, brutal' etc. But the other males are no better. Wells takes up the story from the point at which Clorinda has struggled into her furbelows:

More than three hundred pages remain of the book after this, and about one half of them are devoted to rhapsodies about this Clorinda's beauty, wisdom, strength, daring, culture, wit, and general miraculousness. It is true that what she is represented as saying is invariably stupid, and that she never helps out by an action of her own the portrait which the author imagines is being drawn. But then it is not a portrait, but a shapeless mass of adjectives heaped against the skeleton conception of a heroine as stucco is plastered on a wall. The most sympathetic imagination could not fancy that there is such a person as Clorinda. The other marionettes make even less pretence of being alive. There is another wicked Baronet, a young man, Sir John Oxon by name, and he is very bad indeed. 'Few men there lived who were as vile as he, his power of villany lying in that he knew not the meaning of man's shame or honour.' This gentleman seems to have seduced Clorinda at some period of her infancy to win a wager, although this episode is wrapped in the profoundest mystery by the author. At any rate, he is on terms of intimacy sufficient to enable him to cut from her head without her knowing it a lock of hair five feet long, and get away with it unobserved. He intends to use this trophy with diabolical effect later on, but unhappily mislays it, and cannot remember where it is. This renders him temporarily powerless, and he is forced to stand by and see Clorinda marry another, and become the greatest lady in England, if not Christendom. Her aged husband thoughtfully dies in a fit, after there has appeared upon the scene a third person, who is usually referred to in awed fashion as his Grace of Osmonde, whose palace was at Camylotte. This hybrid of the *Idylls of the King* and Ouida's *Othmar* surpasses both parents. "Twas said that he was the most magnificent gentleman in Europe; that there was none to compare with him in the combination of gifts given by both Nature and Fortune. His beauty both of feature and carriage was of the greatest, his mind was of the highest . . . he had no equal in polished knowledge and charm of bearing.' He had remained unmarried through a delicate feeling that no woman was up to his mark; but to see Clorinda was to abandon that notion. 'He was too high and fine in all his thoughts to say to himself that in her he saw for the first time the woman who was his peer, but this was very truth.'

But at this point the depraved Sir John suddenly recalls where he put that lock of hair, and after several chapters of ostentatious lurking about the premises, muttering and shaking his fist, he says so, and the lady faints. The only clue to her excessive perturbation seems to lie in the fact that, whereas on page 108, when Clorinda finds that her tresses have been rifled, the lock of hair is described as five feet long, on page 229 we find Sir John declaring, after a lapse of years, that it is now 'like a raven's wing, and six feet long'.

Naturally in the end she got her Duke, and clearly this incident-packed novel gave much entertainment, most of it intentional, to its many readers. But overwriting was not a pitfall into which these lady authors fell lightly. James Agate gives another irresistible example:

If *Death of Felicity Taverner* by Mary Butts is high art, which it is, write me down a Philistine, which I will consent to become. I say this because Miss Butts, who obviously has a mind out of the ordinary, has wilfully chosen to wrap her story in a wholly pretentious and sometimes wholly unintelligible jargon. 'Felix had said that a sonata could be written on the room's tempo, whose finale should be a demonstration of relativity . . .' 'She was how I have tried to describe her to you, everywhere, so that the hills were her body laid-down, and "Felicity" was said, over and over again, in each bud and leaf . . . Think of a shape of bright darkness, blowing out flowers . . .' 'Picus whistled his bird call, Mozart-whistler through the impediment of a last sob . . .'

Miss Butts cannot describe a housemaid's activities without overwriting: 'But when even the rugs, after a tea-leaf massage and a sun-bath on the dew-heavy grass, were replaced, when pillars of new wax stood in the sconces and a pyramid of dry sticks had been built in the grate, she felt none of the housewife's satisfaction.' And what on earth is 'the hour of spiritual angularity'? Can it be first cousin to that oasis of futurity on whose bosom Irene Iddesleigh cast her buried scorn? Of one character one reads that she 'crouches like a hare in its form', and of another that 'into this distorted lucidity she had been dropped like a fowl trussed up'. This last passage alone proves that the author is without vestige of humour.

The most successful proponent of pulp romance is Barbara Cartland who was reported as having written 285 novels by 1980, besides some forty-five other books. Bernard Levin reviewed *Love at the Helm*, a fatuous tale of wicked lords, a pantingly innocent heroine, an inheritance and a glamorous sea captain. But she had enlisted expert help to get the maritime detail right:

Miss Cartland makes much of the fact that part of the proceeds of the book are going to the Mountbatten Memorial Trust, and indeed insists that Earl Mountbatten helped her with the writing, and had done as much for her previously, with other novels set at sea; she draws conspicuous attention to the connection on the front of the jacket (twice), in the blurb, on the back of the jacket (photographically), on the title-page, on the half-title and in an Author's Note. All that expert help, however, has still not managed to correct her apparent belief that Trafalgar came very shortly before Waterloo; perhaps she has confused English history with the London Underground system.

Another famous name in the pulp fiction ratings was Benito Mussolini who at the age of twenty-six wrote *Claudia Particella, L'Amante del Cardinale: Grande Romanzo dei Tempi del Cardinale Emanuel Madruzzo*. 'If *The Cardinal's Mistress* is a *grande romanzo*,' wrote Dorothy Parker, 'I am Alexandre Dumas, *père et fils*.' She found the Mussolini masterpiece unreadable, one of those books that 'should not be tossed aside lightly. It should be thrown with force.'

But there is probably a lot of pleasure to be missed by adopting such a course of action. One feels, notwithstanding Agate's denouncement of it, that a quiet hour with Eleanor Turton's *Virgin Soil* could certainly not have been boring:

Having explained what one kind of good writing is, let us have a look at some of the other sort. I shall take my examples from Miss Eleanor Turton's *Virgin Soil*, a novel about a young woman, born on a farm in Somerset, who tries to educate herself. She asks a young farmer whether he thinks she is silly, and he replies: ' "No, not silly, but I don't think you realize what are you trying to do!" ' I don't think Miss Turton does, either. I propose to give you some extracts taken at random showing that this writer cannot have the faintest notion of what words mean: 'The homage paid to her mother and father, even though in the coin of flattery, was wine to their old blood.' 'Lady Bland descended on Ursula from behind an azalea bush, her draperies in danger of becoming entangled in their wild flight from her ample person.' 'Clothes were nonentities in Crane's life.' 'A brewer's dray with a pair of strapping dray-horses trotted past.' 'Side by side they would run and drop down among the sweet-smelling flowers when they were out of breath.' 'The fiddle ceased and the couples remained where they stood for a moment, then gradually broke apart and began to wander away, and even the cuckoo had become silent when he took her in his arms.' Coins which are wine, draperies in flight, trousers which are nonentities, trotting drays, breathless flowers, cuckoos taking young women in their arms – this is writing which just won't do.

'Ernie Haemorrhoid, the Poor Man's Pile'

The reputation of Ernest Hemingway became rather inflated in his lifetime, not least as a result of the generous puffs he was able to give it himself. But of his posthumously published *Across the River and into the Trees* Cyril Connolly wrote:

To my sorrow, *Across the River* can be summed up in one word, lamentable.

Despite an excellent beginning, the Colonel soon emerges as one of the most unlikeable, drink-sodden and maundering old bores ever to have inflicted an interior monologue on those who can't answer back. His ladylove is a whimsical waxwork whose love scenes punctuate the book like a pneumatic drill on a hot afternoon, while the Colonel's fuddled war-reminiscences reveal a blind grudge against Generals, brass-hats, war correspondents and the British, but very little of the campaign. Bitter, sentimental and facetious, he mulls along from bar to bar like a mixture of Bloom and Soames Forsyte.

James Agate had never been all that impressed with Hemingway. It was he who came up with the novel idea that Hemingway was a woman all along. That was why he wrote so tough:

George Eliot, the author of *Adam Bede*, was in private life Mary Ann Evans. John Strange Winter, the author of *Bootle's Baby*, was Mrs Stannard. John Oliver Hobbes, the author of *Some Emotions and a Moral*, was Mrs Craigie. In each of these cases the news that the author was a woman came as a surprise, and it is an old story how Thackeray was astonished to discover that Currer Bell, the author of *Jane Eyre*, was a Yorkshire spinster of the name of Charlotte Brontë.

This week I am to make the startling suggestion that 'Ernest Hemingway' is the nom-de-plume of a maiden lady of the most rigid respectability. I propose to prove this by internal evidence drawn from the volume of short stories before me.

There is a well-known tale of an American cowboy who went into a saloon carrying under his arm a small grizzly bear. Flinging the bear into a corner and planking a brace of pistols on the counter, he called for a bottle of whisky, broke off the neck of the bottle with his teeth, swallowed the contents at a gulp, fired both pistols, picked up the grizzly, and was about to leave the saloon when he was hailed by another customer. 'Say, cowboy! Tell us where you come from!' 'Red Gulch,' growled the cowboy. 'They must be a pretty tough lot there!' 'You're telling me!' said the cowboy. 'They kicked me out for being a nance!'

The prose of Mr Hemingway corresponds to the grizzly bear, the pistols, and the broken bottle. It lays so much stress on the author's masculinity that one suspects femininity's cloak. It is an old dodge. 'We'll have a swashing and a martial outside!' said Rosalind, preparing to put on doublet and hose. I suggest that something of the sort lies beneath Mr Hemingway's literary swashbuckling.

Here is the beginning of a story about a bartender and two toughs:

> 'What's yours?' the bartender said.
> 'Beer,' I said, and before he drew the beer he uncovered both the free-lunch bowls.
> 'Your goddam pigs' feet stink,' Tom said, and spit what he had in his mouth on the floor.
> 'You stink yourself,' the bartender said. 'All you punks stink.'
> 'He says we're punks,' Tommy said to me.
> 'Listen,' I said. 'Let's get out.'
> 'You punks clear the hell out of here,' the bartender said.

Only an old maid with ringlets could have written this.

'Joysprick'

The reception given to the various instalments of James Joyce's *Work in Progress* varied from the enthusiastic, to the bewildered, to the outraged. Several critics felt that the author had left the reader out of his calculations altogether, apparently indifferent to his presence; as G. K. Chesterton put it: ' . . . Joyce is rather inaudible, because he is talking to himself . . .' and Oliver Gogarty observed that 'Joyce talked to himself in his sleep: hence *Finnegans Wake.*'

In the flesh Joyce seemed reluctant to talk at all, even to his guests. Dwight Macdonald, four years out of Yale, went to see him in 1932 with a friend, George Morris, and has left us this account of the uphill struggle to extract words from the great man:

Nervous, overflowing with awe and questions, we presented ourselves at his door. He opened it himself – although he was wearing a gray dressing gown, I remember an impression of jaunty elegance – and led us down an interminable corridor to his study, where he sank exhaustedly into a chair. The next twenty minutes were hell. We thanked him for letting us come, we hoped we weren't disturbing him, we said we greatly admired his work. He said nothing. Every now and then he passed a limp hand over his face, a gesture that became more and more unnerving. We began to ask direct questions; he would answer yes or no, and then relapse into silence. Typical dialogues were:

    G.L.K.M.: *What do you think of Gertrude Stein, Mr Joyce?*
    J.J.: *Who?*
    G.L.K.M.: *Gertrude Stein – the writer. Do you know her work?*
    J.J.: *No.*
    Myself (brightly): *You know, Mr Joyce, I'm very much interested in the movies.* (Pause) *And I've always thought* Ulysses *would make a great movie.* (Pause) *Eisenstein ought to do it, really.* (Pause) *Do you know his films?*

J.J.: *Mmmmmmmmmm.*
Myself: *Have you ever thought of* Ulysses *as a movie, Mr Joyce?*
J.J.: *Mmmmmmmmmm.*

It was like trying to open a safe without the combination. At one point the subject of language came up – or, rather, we hauled it up – and I observed, desperately, that Mr Joyce must know all there was to know about words, a gambit to which Morris assented with an enthusiastic giggle. The effect was frightening; a look of pain came over Joyce's face, and he slowly raised his hands, as if to ward off evil. We dropped the subject. There were, however, three lively – or not wholly unlively – moments. One came when either Morris or I, in a context I've forgotten, said something about people not knowing what to do with their lives. Joyce, his face flushed with animosity, gestured toward the window: 'There are people who go walkin' up and down the street and they don't know what they want.' We were impressed – his voice had an epic ring – but neither of us could think of anything more to say. The second moment came when Morris chanced to say he had an apartment in Paris. For the first time, Joyce took the initiative. 'Where is your apartment, Mr Morris?' he asked; he sounded almost interested. Later, as we were trying to get him to make a pronouncement on the Revolution of the Word his disciple Eugene Jolas had recently proclaimed, he broke in: 'How many rooms are there in your apartment, Mr Morris?' And still later: 'Ah, Mr Morris, how much do you pay for your apartment?' Presently one of us cleared his throat and said, nervously but resolutely, that we must be going. We all rose instantly. 'Mr Macdonald,' said Joyce, addressing me for the first time, 'I understand you are on *Fortune* magazine.' 'Yes.' (It was nice to be in the monosyllabic position.) 'An old school friend of mine is shortly going to New York. His name is Brian O'Leary [or some such] and he is a writer and he needs a job.' At this point I must admit to a flash of suspicion about why Mr Joyce had agreed to receive us. 'I wonder if you could put in a word for him at *Fortune*, Mr Macdonald?' he continued. I said, untruthfully, that I would be glad to. There was another long pause. Then we put on our coats, Joyce helping us cordially, and left. Outside the door, we turned to each other. 'Well!' From Mr Ellmann's biography, I gather this was a typical conversation with Joyce – parakeets was his sole topic with Le Corbusier, headaches and truffles with Proust. But we didn't know this in 1932.

Harold Nicolson was a little more successful in that Joyce told him a story about a man who had taken 'Oolissays' to the Vatican and had 'hidden it in a prayer book and that it had been blessed by the Pope'. 'He saw,' wrote Nicolson, 'that I would think it funny and at the same time he did not think it wholly funny himself.'

Encountering Joyce in print seems to have been more alarming than meeting him in person – at least for D. H. Lawrence:

My God, what a clumsy *olla putrida* James Joyce is! Nothing but old fags and cabbage-stumps of quotations from the Bible and the rest stewed in the juice of deliberate, journalistic dirty-mindedness – what old and hard-worked staleness, masquerading as the all-new! Gertrude Stein is more amusing. . .

Gertrude Stein herself was characteristically ambiguous. Besides, the public had overlooked an important fact of chronology:

He is a good writer. People like him because he is incomprehensible and anybody can understand him. But who came first, Gertrude Stein or James Joyce? Do not forget that my first great book *Three Lives* was published in 1908. . .

(It is a little unfortunate that she should have cited this particular work in view of Wyndham Lewis's description of it; he represents it as competing closely with Joyce for unreadability:

It is a cold suet-roll of fabulously reptilian length. Cut it at any point, it is the same thing; the same heavy, sticky, opaque mass all through, and all along . . . it is mournful and monstrous, composed of dead inanimate material. It is all fat, without nerve . . . its life is a low-grade, if tenacious one; of the sausage, by-the-yard variety.

Lewis's attacks on Stein's work became increasingly vitriolic over the years as he raved on about her 'gargantuan mental stutter'. They culminated in the startling demand that 'Miss Stein should get out of English.')

Elevation of what appeared to be rambling gibberish to the status of multifaceted profundity was a complaint often made against Joyce; expressed for instance by Gerald Gould in the *Observer*:

. . . a little language is a dangerous thing. When broadcast, it is apt to trickle exiguously. Mr James Joyce says with commendable firmness: 'Icis on us! Seints of light! Zezere! Subdue your noise, you hamble creature! What is but a blackburry growth or the dwyer-gray ass them four old codgers owns? Are you meanam Tarpey and Lyons and Gregory? I meyne now, thank all, the four of them, and the roar of them. . .' But I don't know what he meynes, nor what he is meanam. It looks as if he had a spelling bee in his bonnet, and had got confused by the buzz.

Carl Jung records a feeling of almost physical pain caused by an attempt to read *Ulysses*, which he nevertheless regarded as a 'positively brilliant and hellish monster-birth':

I had an old uncle whose thinking was always to the point. One day he stopped me on the street and asked, 'Do you know how the devil tortures the souls in hell?' When I said no, he declared, 'He keeps them waiting.' This remark occurred to me when I was ploughing through *Ulysses* for the first time. Every sentence raises an expectation which is not fulfilled; finally, out of sheer resignation, you come to expect nothing any longer. Then bit by bit, again to your horror, it dawns upon you that in all truth you have hit the nail on the head. It is actual fact that nothing happens and nothing comes of it, and yet a secret expectation at war with hopeless resignation drags the reader from page to page. The seven hundred and thirty-five pages that contain nothing by no means consist of blank paper, but are closely printed. You read and read and read and you pretend to understand what you read. Occasionally you drop through an air pocket into another sentence, but when once the proper degree of resignation has been reached you accustom yourself to anything. So I, too, read to page one hundred and thirty-five with despair in my heart, falling asleep twice on the way.

When it came to *Finnegans Wake* the critic in the *Tablet* took up the twin themes of pretentiousness and filth:

The *flabella* are the great fans used in papal processions; and it makes petty-minded persons feel quite learned when they can puzzle out 'flabelled his eyes, vaticanated his ears, and palliumed his throats'. To have written 'carburetted his eyes, rolls-royced his ears and six-cylindered his throats' would have just as much or as little sense. . .

Joyce's works, declared the *Tablet*, were 'aesthetically monstrous' as well as being 'morally unclean', a judgement in which Virginia Woolf surprisingly seemed to concur, at least as far as Chapters 3, 4, and 5 of *Ulysses* were concerned: '. . . merely the scratching of pimples on the body of the bootboy at Claridges'.

All of which echoes the opinion of an anonymous reviewer who observed after reading *Portrait of an Artist as a Young Man*: 'Mr Joyce is a clever novelist but we feel he would really be at his best in a treatise on drains. . .'

A rearguard action on behalf of other writers whose reputations he felt were threatened by critical acceptance of Joyce was undertaken by the poet Alfred Noyes. In his lecture to the Royal Society of Literature he clutched rather wildly at any available support in his campaign to give Joyce the heave-ho:

The only sound analysis of the book in this country was made by the *Sporting Times* which described it as 'the work of a madman' and said it was 'couched in language that would make a Hottentot sick'.

The signs were that Joyce couldn't give a monkey's what pious or impious critics thought about his masterpiece. 'The demand that I make of my reader,' he was once heard to murmur, 'is that he devote his life to a study of my work.' Those pressed for time and unable to meet Joyce's exacting standards of application could avail themselves of Brendan Behan's tip on how to tackle the Master: 'The key to reading *Ulysses* is to treat it like a comedian would – as a sort of gag book.'

Behan also obligingly condensed the recommended reading list of world-authors to three, pointing out that 'Shakespeare said pretty well everything, and what he left out, James Joyce, with a nudge from meself, put in.'

With reassuring support like this Joyce hardly needed to

mount a defence. But he did write a letter to Grant Richards as early as 1906 which was unanswerable in its logic:

It is not my fault that the odor of armpits and old weeds and offal hangs round my stories. I seriously believe that you will retard the course of civilization in Ireland by preventing the Irish people from having a good look at themselves in my nicely polished looking-glass.

This didn't persuade Richards to publish *Dubliners*; neither was it an attitude likely to win friends and influence people in his native Ireland. People are notoriously ungrateful for having their shortcomings pointed out so candidly. Bernard Shaw, in a famous letter to Sylvia Beach praising *Ulysses*, mischievously summed up Joyce's looking-glass technique:

In Ireland they try to make a cat cleanly by rubbing its nose in its own filth. Mr Joyce has tried the same treatment on the human subject. I hope it may prove successful.

'The Stanchless Flux'

Henry Miller elevated self-promotion to the status of an art form. Gore Vidal was quick to pay tribute to this achievement:

Right off, it must be noted that only a total egotist could have written a book which has no subject other than Henry Miller in all his sweet monotony. Like shadows in a solipsist's daydream, the other characters flit through the narrative, playing straight to the relentless old exhibitionist whose routine has not changed in nearly half a century. Pose one: Henry Miller, sexual athlete. Pose two: Henry Miller, literary genius and life force. Pose three: Henry Miller and the cosmos (they have an understanding). The narrative is haphazard. Things usually get going when Miller meets a New Person at a party. New Person immediately realizes that this is no ordinary man. In fact, New Person's whole life is often changed after exposure to the hot radiance of Henry Miller. For opening the door to Feeling, Miller is then praised by New Person in terms which might turn the head of God – but not the head of Henry Miller, who notes each compliment with the gravity of the recording angel. If New Person is a woman, then she is due for a double thrill. As a lover, Henry Miller is a national resource, on the order of Yosemite National Park. Later, exhausted by his unearthly potency, she realizes that for the first time she has met Man . . . one for whom *post coitum* is not *triste* but rhetorical. When lesser men sleep, Miller talks about the cosmos, the artist, the sterility of modern life. Or in his own words: . . . our conversations were like passages out of *The Magic Mountain*, only more virulent, more exalted, more sustained, more provocative, more inflammable, more dangerous, more menacing, and much more, ever so much more, exhausting'.

Everyone he meets either likes or admires him, while not once in the course of Sexus does he fail in bed. Hour after hour, orgasm after orgasm, the great man goes about his priapic task. Yet from Rousseau to Gide the true confessors have been aware that not only is life mostly failure, but that in one's failure or pettiness or wrongness exists the living drama of the self. Henry Miller, by his own account, is never less than superb, in life, in art, in bed. Not since the memoirs of Frank Harris has there been such a record of success in the sack. Nor does Miller provide us with any sort of relief. One could always skip Frank Harris's erotic scenes in favor of literary and political gossip. But Miller is much too important for gossip. People do not interest him. Why should they? They are mere wedding guests: he is Ancient Mariner.

. . . Miller is particularly irresistible to Jews: 'You're no Goy. You're a black Jew. You're one of those fascinating Gentiles that every Jew wants to shine up to.'

. . . For a man who boasts of writing nothing but the truth, I find it more than odd that not once in the course of a long narrative does anyone say, 'Henry, you're full of shit.' It is possible, of course, that no one ever did, but I doubt it. Interlarded with sexual bouts and testimonials are a series of prose poems in which the author works the cosmos for all it's worth. The style changes noticeably during these arias. Usually Miller's writing is old-fashioned American demotic, rather like the prose of one of those magazines Theodore Dreiser used to edit. But when Miller climbs onto the old cracker barrel, he gets very fancy indeed. Sentences swell and billow, engulfing syntax. Arcane words are put to use, often accurately: ectoplasmic, mandibular, anthropophagous, terrene, volupt, occipital, fatidical. Not since H. P. Lovecraft has there been such a lover of language. Then, lurking pale and wan in this jungle of rich prose, are the Thoughts: 'Joy is founded on something too profound to be understood and communicated: To be joyous is to be a madman in a world of sad ghosts.' Or: 'Only the great, the truly distinctive individuals resemble one another. Brotherhood doesn't start at the bottom, but at the top.' Or: 'Sex and poverty go hand in hand.' The interesting thing about the Thoughts is that they can be turned inside out and the effect is precisely the same: 'Sex and affluence go hand in hand,' and so on . . .

The monotony of Miller's 'hydraulic approach to sex', as one of his detractors put it, deprives his books of the sexiness that is the ostensible reason for their popularity, at least for Brigid Brophy:

He is no sensualist: He might have made a mechanical engineer. He sees the female body as an assembly of knobs, pipes and slots. The connecting passages of flesh mean nothing to him except as containing a wall on which he might well chalk . . . 'Miller was here'.

Neither is Miller the more readable for his apparent belief that he has made unique discoveries in human physiology; Brophy refers to:

. . . Miller's . . . persistent image of human excrement, which he relies on to shock and soil our minds at each repetitive encounter, quite as though he didn't know it is a substance we all produce every day. (Perhaps he believes this, too, is an originality on his part.)

Miller is amply compensated for his detractors in the devotion of his admirers. One of these is Lawrence Durrell, and in 1966 their private correspondence was published. D. J. Enright got to work on it:

PUBLIC FAECES:
THE CORRESPONDENCE OF LAWRENCE DURRELL
AND HENRY MILLER

Lawrence Durrell and Henry Miller: A Private Correspondence, edited by George Wickes: or the transactions, over 400 pages and twenty-five years, of a small but active mutual admiration society. It must be granted that this is not a case of you-scratch-my-back-I'll-scratch-yours. For the partners are quite disinterested; they are utterly sincere, alas. It can only be supposed that the ungrateful publisher has some enormous grudge against the two of them, since the making public of this 'private correspondence' will hardly enhance the reputations which they have so painstakingly built up with the collaboration of an unnerved and gullible international public. Even gullibility, even international gullibility, has its limits.

    The correspondence opens in August 1935 with a fan letter from Durrell. *Tropic of Cancer*, recently published, 'strikes me as being the only really man-size piece of work which this century can really boast of . . . It's the final copy of all those feeble, smudgy rough drafts – *Chatterley, Ulysses, Tarr*, etc.' The outburst has the captivating enthusiasm of youth: Durrell was only twenty-three. Miller's reply is short and to the point. 'I particularly prize your letter because it's the kind of letter I would have written myself had I not been the author of the book.' Miller was only forty-three. Durrell then confesses to being a writer himself, and Miller asks, 'Why don't you send me something of yours so that I can return some of the audacious compliments you pay me?' Which shows a nice nature. . .

A little later and Miller is writing a huge book on Hamlet but can't bring himself to read Shakespeare's version and asks Durrell to 'give me the low-down on it'. He writes to T. S. Eliot (a minor but engaging character in this correspondence) to tell him about Durrell, but complains that Eliot 'seems to treat me very gingerly and cavalierly. . .'

The fastidious Eliot was perhaps terrified of unleashing the tidal wave of Miller's 'Stanchless Flux' as Durrell called it, bowling along with a detritus of blood, wombs and bowels. There wasn't time to pick and choose between words and ideas if you were busy being a real man. Geoffrey Grigson reviewing the Durrell–Miller letters quotes Miller on Balzac:

> Do you know what he said to that prick Georges Sand? He said, 'Literature! but my dear lady, literature doesn't exist. There is life of which politics and art are part. And I am a man that's alive, that's all – a man living his life, nothing more.'

That is the Miller line about writing, and though diminished by a little later sense and caution as the correspondence proceeds, the Durrell line. What you eat, you digest and evacuate, slackening the sphincter . . . Although by Bruegel's proverb those who eat fire shit sparks; in general the pat – cow-pat or man-pat, or in particular the Miller-pat – isn't much of a shape, even when it grows cold and hardens.

Writer at Work

Frank Zappa has described rock journalism as: 'people who can't write interviewing people who can't talk for people who can't read'. It might be thought that journalists interviewing writers would make for more edifying copy. Not so; especially when the writer mumbles pretentiously and incoherently to an over-reverential interviewer. One particularly self-indulgent series of publications over the years have been *The Paris Review Interviews*. In these, modern writers go on (and on) about their work to platitudinous hacks. When the fourth series emerged, edited by George Plimpton, Auberon Waugh was ready for it, pen poised: 'It is not a writer's job to gabble into a tape-recorder and call it art,' he began crisply. 'If he has something to say, he should write it down.'

That said, he proceeds to write something down himself, in an unflattering Cook's tour of some of the interviews:

If Isherwood appears the most odious of those interviewed, Kerouac (who died seven years ago) is undoubtedly the most absurd. What is terrifying about the Kerouac phenomenon is not that one drunken, doped-out, unintelligent exhibitionist could be found to spout such drivel, but that a whole generation of earnest young students and lecturers in English could be found to take him seriously. He is the original exploiter of the American obsession with art and genius. If an artist farts, that is important. Better still, it is a work of art. 'By not revising what you've already written, you simply give the readers the actual workings of your mind during the writing itself.' Big deal, as they say. The terrifying thing is that this apparently is what the pathetic Americans want. Of his friend Cassady he says: 'Cassady also began his early, youthful writing with attempts at slow, painstaking and all-that-crap craft business, but got sick of it like I did, seeing it wasn't getting out his guts and heart the way it *felt* coming out.' Why can't they keep their miserable guts to themselves? But, as I say, the worst part of the interview is the way the interviewer is taken in by him:

> **Interviewer:** *Allen [Ginsberg] once said . . . that he never did understand Shakespeare until he heard you read Shakespeare to him.*
> **Kerouac:** *Because in a previous lifetime, that's who I was.* [Groan. Groan. But worse is to come.]
> **Interviewer:** *What do you think about the hippies and the LSD scene?*
> **Kerouac:** *As for LSD, it's bad for people with incidence of heart disease in the family.* [Knocks microphone off footstool . . . recovers it.] *Is there any reason why you can see anything good in this here mortality?*
> **Interviewer:** *Excuse me, would you mind repeating that?*
> **Kerouac:** *You said you had a little white beard in your belly. Why is there a little white beard in your mortality belly?*
> **Interviewer:** *Let me think about it. Actually it's a little white pill.*
> **Kerouac:** *Give me.*
> **Interviewer:** *We should wait till the scene cools a little.*
> **Kerouac:** *Right. This little white pill is a little white beard in your mortality which advises you and advertises to you that you will be growing long fingernails in the graves of Peru.*
> **2nd Interviewer:** *Do you feel middle aged?*
> **Kerouac:** *No . . .*

Waugh is not at all kind about Isherwood either:

A few blanks in the abject career of this worthless man are filled in. Since settling in the United States for pacifist reasons in 1939, Isherwood has not moved far. 'I've lived in eleven places in America and all of them are within sight of this window.' He is still boyishly enthusiastic about Hinduism and now, rather late in the day, perhaps, is equally committed to the Gay Liberation Movement.

> **Interviewer:** *Would you write more about homosexuality if you were starting out now as a writer?*
> **Isherwood:** *Yes, I'd write about it a good deal. It is an exceedingly interesting subject and I couldn't or thought I couldn't go into it.*

Now at a time when few people in American artistic circles dare admit to the slightest heterosexual urge, our Christopher is being *tewwifically* brave and outspoken about it. 'A thing that seems to me almost worse than hatred and active opposition is the indifference that most people have towards minorities. Let them rot, they don't care, they don't care a bit! Also they're hypocritical. They pretend to be much more shocked than they are. I often feel that worse than the most fiendish Nazis were the Germans who went along with the persecution of the Jews not because they really disliked them but because it *was the thing*.'

Oh, put a sock in it! How does this septuagenarian, Hindu expatriate suppose he has earned the right to tell us about the Nazis? Listen to him on Stravinsky: 'I always think of Stravinsky in a very physical way. He was physically adorable, he was cuddly – so little, you wanted to protect him.' I am not sure that I would have chosen Isherwood as my protector, had I been Stravinsky. But everything he says is phony, everything he says is banal.

But Waugh is actually enthusiastic about Nabokov, a pseud-spotter after his own unregenerate heart:

> Interviewer: *E. M. Forster speaks of his major characters sometimes taking over and dictating the course of his novels. Has this ever been a problem for you, or are you in complete command?*
> Nabokov: *My knowledge of Mr Forster's works is limited to one novel which I dislike, and anyway it was not he who fathered that trite little whimsy about characters getting out of hand, it is as old as the quills, although, of course, one sympathizes with* his *people if they try to wriggle out of that trip to India or wherever he takes them. My characters are galley-slaves.* [Bless his heart. Nabokov makes fools of us all.]
> Interviewer: *What have you learned from Joyce?*
> Nabokov: Nothing.

Critical Warfare

Quite a lot of energy and ink is expended by critics attacking other critics. Gore Vidal, a literary piranha who is always able to make an appetizing meal out of self-important academics, has launched more than one attack on those he called 'The Hacks of Academe'. Here he is getting his teeth into one of those thick and solemn symposiums on the nature of the novel:

The first essay is called 'What is Exposition?' This subject plainly troubles Professor Sternberg. At a loss for the right words, he resorts to graphics. An inverted 'V' occupies the top of one page. At the foot of the left leg is the word 'introduction'; then 'exciting force'; then 'rise'. The apex of the inverted 'V' is labelled 'climax'. Partway down the right leg is the word 'fall', while at the base occurs the sombre word 'catastrophe'. This treasure-seeker's map to tragedy is something called 'Freytag's pyramid', which the eponymous architect set up in the desert of novel-theory to show how 'time-honoured' exposition works in tragedy.

Professor Sternberg then adds his own markings to the sand. 'Suppose an author wishes to compose a narrative which is to consist of three motifs: a1, a2, a3. These motifs, arranged in an order in which a2 follows a1 in a time and a3 follows a2, will form the *fabula* of his story.' The sequence of numbered a's is then arranged vertically on the page, and casts almost as minatory a shadow as Freytag's pyramid. Later Professor Sternberg assembles a positively Cheopsean structure with such parallel headings as 'story', '*fabula*', 'plot', '*sujet*', a monster Rosetta stone with which to confound strawman Freytag. The resulting *agon* (or duel or *lutte*) in the desert is very elaborate and not easy to follow. Occasionally there is a simple sentence like: 'A work of fiction presents characters in action during a certain period of time.' But, by and large, sentences are as elaborate as the ideas that they wish to express are simple. And so, as the sun sinks behind the last tautology, our guide sums up: 'As my definition of it clearly implies, exposition is a time problem par excellence.' (Instructor's note: Transpose 'it' and 'exposition'.)

. . . In general, [these] novel-theorists have nothing very urgent or interesting to say about literature. Why then do they write when they have nothing to say? Because the ambitious teacher can only rise in the academic bureaucracy by writing at complicated length about writing that has already been much written about. The result of all this book-chat cannot interest anyone who knows literature while those who would like to learn something about books can only be mystified and discouraged by these commentaries. Certainly it is no accident that the number of students taking English courses has been in decline for some years. But that is beside the point. What matters is that the efforts of the teachers now under review add up to at least a half millennium of academic tenure.

Elsewhere Vidal, in an article entitled 'Literary Gangsters', attacked Richard Gilman's collection of literary articles published under the title *The Confusion of Realms*:

Mr Gilman has his idols – somewhat. He thinks Miss Sontag 'one of the most interesting and valuable critics we possess, a writer from whom it's continually possible to learn, even when you're most dissatisfied with what she's saying, or perhaps especially at those times'. Mr Gilman relies heavily on the 'or perhapses' that let him off those critical hooks he has a tendency to get himself hung on as his slow, bumbling sentences unfold like bolts of wet wool. Here are two hooks in one sentence: 'We might call her a critic of ideas, except that she has always wished to treat ideas sensuously, aesthetically; or decide that she is a philosopher of cultural forms, except that philosophy for her has always been a drama rather than a method.' Reading this, one realizes that Mr Gilman is a serious literary critic even though he does not actually write criticism; a profound thinker were his mind not shallow.

Throughout *The Confusion of Realms*, Mr Gilman reminds us that the writers he admires (Gass and Barthelme) are making new things, and the ones he cannot endorse, like Mailer, are simply repeating old forms. But again let us listen to his very own voice: '*The Naked and the Dead* remains at bottom a conventional work of literature. As it shapes itself into a tale, it proceeds along predictable lines, creates no convincingly new style, and offers no new purchase on imaginative reality, nothing that can be used by other writers as a model of a way of seeing, or as incontrovertible vision by anyone else' . . . This is a startling approach to literature. Apparently books are valuable only to the extent that they will help other writers to make newer and newer books to be added as links to some sort of Hegelian chain. . .

Reading *The Confusion of Realms* (with some continence I have refrained from making any play on the title) I find myself wondering who reads this sort of writing and what pleasure and revelation they get from it. Is there a public I know nothing of? Quite possibly. After all, I am often away from the United States. For all I know there are students of education who carefully read (with lips moving?) these long confusions. But I doubt it. With the exception of one piece, there is no ease, no joy, no light in Mr Gilman's writing. Every sentence seems to have been an effort for him to make, as though he knew he had nothing to say but was impelled for career reasons to set down something. Certainly he has no talent at all for our difficult and various language – by no means a deterrent, let me quickly say, to a literary career in America. Yet it must be a terrible strain to have to keep on doing something one does not do easily or well.

This backbiting seems to bear out some remarks made by Raymond Mortimer when he reviewed new literary criticism designed for students:

. . . learned critics devote much of their energy to contradicting one another; and nobody can want to read Mortimer's view of David Lodge's view of Hough's view of Leavis's view of *Emma*.

Ah, *Dr Leavis*'s view of *Emma*! The name of Leavis is at once associated with columns of epistolary anger and aggrieved scholarship; the literary Savonarola from Downing has attracted some tart responses over the years. J. B. Priestley, for example, objected to being hectored by the good doctor:

It seems that Dr Leavis gave a lecture at Nottingham University on 'Literature In My Time' and declared that apart from D. H. Lawrence there has been no literature in his time. He knocked hell out of everybody, and no doubt had all the Lucky Jims rolling down the aisles. Like Groucho Marx on another academic occasion, whatever it was he was against it. Virginia Woolf was a 'slender talent'; Lytton Strachey 'irresponsible and unscrupulous'; W. H. Auden 'the career type', fixed at 'the undergraduate stage'; Spender 'no talent whatsoever'; Day-Lewis 'Book Society author'; the whole age 'dismal', and outlook 'very poor'. By the time Dr Leavis caught his train back to Cambridge, there was hardly anything left to read in Nottingham. I have not the pleasure of the doctor's acquaintance – he was up at Cambridge just after me – but I have a vague but impressive vision of him, pale and glittering-eyed, shining with integrity, marching out of Downing to close whole departments of libraries, to snatch books out of people's hands, to proclaim the bitter truth that nobody writes anything worth reading. There is Lawrence; there is Leavis on Lawrence; perhaps a disciple, Jones, is writing something – let us say, Jones on Leavis on Lawrence; after that, nothing.

Years ago, just after he was appointed Chief Controller of Literary Passports, Dr Leavis announced one morning – playing for a laugh, for the boys and girls love this sort of thing – that no time need be wasted on Priestley. He was quite right too. Suppose a man said to me: 'My boy's up at Cambridge doing English. It's a bit of a struggle for us to keep him there – that's why I've stopped smoking – so I don't want him to waste a minute of his time. Now, honestly, old man, do you think he ought to read your stuff?' I would reply without hesitation: 'No, old man, he oughtn't. Leavis is quite right. If your boy's committed to Eng. Lit., and at such a sacrifice too, he must be careful what he reads. But as we're being honest, old man, I must add one thing. For my part I wouldn't swap a pound of tobacco for all the Eng. Lit. courses in the country. If it's not too late, take your boy out of that mournful little racket, let him learn something while he has a chance.'

It was about this time that Dr Leavis, with one quick turn of the wrist, dropped most of the eighteenth century into the ash-can. No time need be wasted reading Fielding, Sterne, Goldsmith, Smollett. This seemed to some of us dabblers in letters to be rather severe. . .

Further on in his article Priestley poses the $64,000 question which is the logical conclusion of Leavisite exclusivity:

If our time is so precious that we should not waste it reading a hundred reputable authors from Fielding to Day-Lewis, then why should we waste any time reading or listening to Dr Leavis?

Being told what not to read by critics may be tiresome but being told what *to* read can be tiring; and impressive lists of writers often make a nice casserole that can be served up as illustrative of trends in culture or literature. One of the most celebrated recent examples of this was Colin Wilson's book *The Outsider* which greatly excited Cyril Connolly and others. Dwight Macdonald, however, in his article 'Inside *The Outsider*', was irreverent about what he called 'the cement mixer of Mr Wilson's mind' and iconoclastic about the work's vulgarity and pretentiousness:

. . . [Here] is Mr Wilson's evaluation of Hermann Hesse, a minor German novelist to whose work he devotes many pages: 'Considered as a whole, Hesse's achievement can hardly be matched in modern literature. . . Hesse has little imagination in the sense that Shakespeare or Tolstoy can be said to have imagination, but his ideas have a vitality that more than makes up for it.' In a novelist, nothing makes up for imagination (nothing 'makes up for' anything anyway), and certainly not 'ideas'. But 'ideas' that can be botched into the jerry-built structure of his argument are all that Mr Wilson wants from the poets, novelists, mystics, and philosophers he exploits; he reduces their work to fragments with his rough-and-ready summaries and erects his thesis with the rubble. At times, one has the impression that the masters of modern literature were Mr Wilson's research assistants. '*The Brothers Daramazov* is Dostoevsky's biggest attack on the *Outsider* theme,' he writes. And: 'To facilitate his [William Blake's] analysis of *Outsider* problems, he divided man into the same three divisions that we arrived at in Chapter IV. . . His system . . . provides a skeleton key to every Outsider in this book.' Many hands make light work.

J. B. Priestley, who praised the book overall, also objected to very different writers being shovelled into categories to suit an academic thesis. And he protested at a strain of intolerance in the author:

Like most clever young men, hurrying home with a pile of books and glowering at the passers-by, he magnifies the gulf between men of genius and ordinary stupid people . . . he cannot believe that stockbrokers may have strange dreams, that butchers cutting off chops may be touched with intimations of immortality, that the grocer, even as he hesitates over the sugar, may yet see the world in a grain of sand.

Of course this sort of idea can be taken too far. It may tempt the critic into a beery patronizing of philosophical grocers on the one hand and a blowing into the reputations of authors, as if they were vast balloons, on the other. This seems to be the objection of Geoffrey Grigson to the Anthony Burgess approach.

Mr Anthony Burgess has collected his reviews. (*Urgent Copy*, published in 1968.) Of this I do not complain altogether, things being what they are. Yet dog proceeding to eat dog, I shall ask: How does one review reviews?

Perhaps, to begin with, by abstracting sentences, to get at the mind of the reviewing writer, at his mental style; which I shall do, with one or two comments.

Page 11. Writing books 'engenders tobacco-addiction, an over-reliance on caffeine and dexedrine, piles, dyspepsia, chronic anxiety, sexual impotence'. Not in everyone. And not all of them, I hope, in Mr Burgess.

Page 22. 'Mere authors will continue to despair of their ability to approach that prose perfection' – of the books of Evelyn Waugh.

Page 23. 'He is as welcome as is Apethorpe.' Style.

Page 31. 'It is right for the European novel to be interested in disease, since Europe itself is a disease – exquisitely but treacherously mined with fistulas.' – No comment.

Page 63. 'With the general acceptance of Yeats's greatness, a lot of life has gone out of Yeats criticism.' This is too bad.

Page 66. Taking Yeats's verse seriously 'means not poring over it in the study, but declaiming it to the waves and over pints of draught Guinness'. This is very masculine.

Page 89. 'Dylan was the great lyric poet of the twentieth century.'

Page 91. 'Look for a parallel to him' – Dylan Thomas again – 'in the literature of the past, and you won't go far wrong if you adduce Virgil.' A contradiction?

Page 99. 'Lament for a Maker'. Novel title for an obituary piece on T. S. Eliot.

These fair samples bring one about a third of the way through. I have quoted them less because they are silly (but some of them are surely a trifle bizarre?) than because the words do exhibit a quality – unlike the blue in Cézanne – which no one will find other than coarse and unattractive, I should think, or hope.

George S. Kaufman, playwright and wit, took revenge on

another critic, Joseph Wood Krutch. Krutch didn't like Kaufman's plays, and wrote disparagingly of them. Then he published a book himself – which was a foolhardy thing to do while Kaufman was still alive:

MY BOOK AND I

To tell the truth, I am just a little bit behind in my reading. My friends tell me there is a new one out in the Graustark series, called *Beverly of Graustark*, but, what with one thing and another, I haven't got around to it yet. I began the first Lanny Budd book bravely enough, intending to shoot right through the series, but for some reason I let Upton Sinclair get nine volumes ahead of me, and now it's a little hard to catch up. I notice, by the way, that Mr Sinclair has given up on that series. I knew I'd get him sooner or later.

But in many years I do not recall having quite the fight with any book that I have had – and am still having – with *Samuel Johnson*, by Joseph Wood Krutch. My usual procedure with a book is, roughly, as follows: I hear about a book or read a notice of it. I say to myself, 'Now, there is a book that is just my dish. I have always been interested in books of that sort. I must read it.' So I buy it. It stays in the wrapper for two or three days after it arrives, because a lot of things have a habit of coming up. I open it, finally, with great pleasure. 'Ah!' I say to myself. 'Just the kind of book I like!' I put it prominently on my desk, right on top of a pile of books that I am just crazy to read.

The next few months pass quietly, what with playing bridge, and going out to dinner, and talking to people, and things like that. Then comes an important moment. Flushed with energy, I move the book from my desk to my bed table. Now I am really ready to start.

Several weeks pass and I don't start. I can explain this. I have a habit of reading all the newspapers every day, and there is nothing quite so luxurious as reading newspapers in bed. Then, there are the magazines – *Time*, and *Life* and even *The New Yorker*. These come out every week, and once you settle down to them, you will be surprised how quickly Thursday and Friday come around.

Along about this time, the book begins to get in the way of the newspapers and things, so I move it back to the desk for a couple of months. Then the publishers bring out another book, and it's just my dish, so I buy it. In this way, one thing leads to another, and pretty soon it's later than you think.

If there is one subject I am completely fascinated by it's Samuel Johnson, and when I heard that Mr Krutch was taking a sabbatical year in which to write a book about him, I didn't even wait for the publication date. I ordered the book at once. Little did I think at that time that whereas Mr Krutch would be on the book for one year, I would be on it for seven, and only up to page 9 at that.

In these seven years, *Samuel Johnson* has piled up the following history with me: It has made three round trips to Hollywood, staying twice at the Garden of Allah, and once at the Beverly Hills Hotel, where the dust jacket was slightly spotted by a highball glass; it has gone twice to Florida and got quite a little sand on it, some of which I am still shaking out; and last summer it visited England and the French Riviera.

On each occasion, I took it with me in the firm conviction that I was finally going to get somewhere with it, and I still feel that it is exactly my dish. I was fascinated by the very opening sentence, and remember it as though it were only six years ago: 'Samuel Johnson was a pessimist with an enormous zest for living.' You must admit that this is an intriguing sentence, one that will catch the reader up and hold him. It has held me for seven years.

Also, I have enormous respect for Mr Joseph Wood Krutch, a scholar and a gentleman. The fact that I have carried his book halfway around the world with me is certainly proof of that. I'll bet he hasn't got another reader who has shown such loyalty. I don't deserve any particular credit for this; *Samuel Johnson* just happens to be my kind of book.

In Hollywood, someone wanted to borrow it once, but I felt that I would get at it any minute, so I refused to lend it. In Florida, as I have already implied, I used to carry it with me to the beach. I remember that it got buried in the sand one day, and I was frantic until I found it again. I lost the dust jacket four or five years ago, but the book itself is in splendid condition. Why shouldn't it be?

The place where I left off, on page 9, was absolutely enthralling: 'The father was proud of his son – foolishly so, in that son's opinion – but he showed his pride in clumsy ways which humiliated an intelligent child.' Think of the heartbreaking stories that will illustrate the child's humiliation, the sufferings of his sensitive soul! I can hardly wait for page 10.

And I mean to read it, I promise you. I am taking it with me to California soon, and, if necessary, to Europe again in the summer. It is exactly my dish.

Poetic Gems

The enormous services rendered to poetry in English by William McGonagall, of whom *Chambers Biographical Dictionary* says, 'His poems are uniformly bad, but possess a disarming *naïveté* and a calypso-like disregard for metre which still never fail to entertain', have been emulated by others, unjustly neglected. Criticism has been described as 'cutting a skylark's throat to see what makes him sing', but some 'poetry' sounds more like a skylark's throat being cut. At any one time a lot of people are writing poetry, which inevitably results in an awful lot of badness. ('What do you think of so-and-so?' someone asked Charles Lamb, naming the latest fashionable poet. 'I don't know him,' stuttered Lamb, 'b-b-but d-d-damn him at a venture!') Oscar Wilde at least ploughed through some of the stuff pouring off the presses in 1885. He recorded his reactions to it in the *Pall Mall Gazette*:

This spring the little singers are out before the little sparrows and have already begun chirruping. Here are four volumes already, and who knows how many more will be given to us before the laburnums blossom? The best-bound volume must of course have precedence. It is called *Echoes of Memory* by Atherton Furlong, and is cased in creamy vellum and tied with ribbons of yellow silk. Mr Furlong's charm is the unsullied sweetness of his simplicity. Indeed, we can strongly recommend to the School-Board the *Lines on the Old Town Pump* as eminently suitable for recitation by children. Such a verse, for instance, as:

> *I hear the little children say*
> *(For the tale will never die)*
> *How the old pump flowed both night and day*
> *When the brooks and the wells ran dry*

has all the ring of Macaulay in it, and is a form of poetry which cannot possibly harm anybody, even if translated into French. Any inaccurate ideas of the laws of nature which the children might get from the passage in question could easily be corrected afterwards by a lecture on hydrostatics. The poem, however, which gives us most pleasure is the one called *The Dear Old Knocker on the Door*. It is appropriately illustrated by Mr Tristram Ellis. We quote the concluding verses of the first and last stanzas:

> *Blithe voices then so dear*
> *Send up their shouts once more,*
> *Then sounds again on memory's ear*
> *The dear old knocker on the door.*

> *When mem'ry turns the key*
> *Where time has placed my score,*
> *Encased 'mid treasured thoughts must be*
> *The dear old knocker on the door.*

The cynic may mock at the subject of these verses, but we do not. Why not an ode on a knocker? Does not Victor Hugo's tragedy of *Lucrèce Borgia* turn on the defacement of a door-plate? Mr Furlong must not be discouraged. Perhaps he will write poetry some day. If he does we would earnestly appeal to him to give up calling a cock 'proud chanticleer'. . .

And again, in 1887, Oscar Wilde did his best for a poet with the nom de plume of 'Glenessa':

Such a pseudonym as 'Glenessa' reminds us of the good old days of the Della Cruscans, but it would not be fair to attribute Glenessa's poetry to any known school of literature, either past or present. Whatever qualities it possesses are entirely its own. Glenessa's most ambitious work, and the one that gives the title to his book, is a poetic drama about the Garden of Eden. The subject is undoubtedly interesting, but the execution can hardly be said to be quite worthy of it. Devils, on account of their inherent wickedness, may be excused for singing:

> *Then we'll rally-rally-rally-*
> *Yes, we'll rally-rally O!*

But such scenes as:

> Enter *Adam*
> *Adam* (excitedly): *Eve, where art thou?*
> *Eve* (surprised): *Oh!*

Adam (in astonishment): *Eve! My God, she's there beside that fatal tree;*

or:

Enter *Adam and Eve*
Eve (in astonishment): *Well, is not this surprising?*
Adam (distractedly): *It is*

seem to belong rather to the sphere of comedy than to that of serious verse. Poor Glenessa! the gods have not made him poetical, and we hope he will abandon his wooing of the muse. He is fitted, not for better, but for other things.

Usually Wilde's natural love of fun overcame his critical seriousness:

The Chronicle of Mites is a mock-heroic poem about the inhabitants of a decaying cheese who speculate about the origin of their species and hold learned discussions upon the meaning of evolution and the Gospel according to Darwin. This cheese-epic is a rather unsavoury production and the style is at times so monstrous and so realistic that the author should be called the Gorgon-Zola of literature.

But not all poets are as bad as their critics. They too need exposing. Henry James, in a devastating review of George Barnett Smith's *Poets and Novelists* published in New York in 1875, went to work on what he clearly regarded as a compendium of critical obtuseness:

For Mrs Browning Mr Smith has a boundless admiration. He devotes some space to considering the question whether it better describes her to say that she is 'Tennyson's sister' or 'Shakespeare's daughter'. It is impossible to withold the suggestion that it might do to try 'Wordsworth's niece' or 'Swinburne's aunt'. There was a chance to say a great many discriminating things about Mrs Browning, but Mr Smith has utterly missed it. Mrs Browning possessed the real poetic heat in a high degree; but it is not too much to say that her sense of the poetic form was an absolute muddle. Mr Smith, however, has no eye for the niceties of diction (his own is often decidedly erratic) and he swallows everything whole. 'And Burns with pungent passionings set in his eyes' and 'poor proud Byron, sad as the grave and salt as life' – Mr Smith thinks those are 'excellent touches'. . .

Mr Smith says in his preface that he has collected his essays in compliance with the importunities of his friends. He would have done better bravely to make up his mind to seem ill-natured and resist them.

Henry James's attitude that too uncritical an approach to the glamorous names of poetry is as useless as an incapacity to respond to beautiful writing is echoed in William Plomer's delicious demonstration of a great man on an off day:

Imaginery lines by great poets sometimes form themselves in minds with a satirical bent. A friend of mine used to recite with glee a line which he said could be found in the *Idylls of the King*:

> *Adown the glade a-jumpt the harlot.*

It was a little difficult to swallow 'a-jumpt', though I thought it *ben trovato*. In fact the last four lines of *Merlin and Vivien*, which might well be part of a parody, run as follows:

> *Then crying, 'I have made his glory mine,'*
> *And shrieking out 'O fool!' the harlot leapt*
> *Adown the forest, and the thicket closed*
> *Behind her, and the forest echo'd 'fool'.*

Sir John Squire made a speciality of collecting bad verse. Like bad movies, the best of it is memorably bad:

There is, for instance, a gentleman (at one time a distinguished scholar of Balliol) who describes himself as 'The Modern Homer', and has written a number of epics, including *The Human Epic*, *The Epic of London*, *The Epic of Charlemagne*, and *The Epic of God and the Devil*. Preoccupation with his matter leads him to such phrases as:

> *When Murder is on the* tapis
> *Then the Devil is happy*

But he perhaps is not so interesting as Mr William Nathan Stedman, who used to live in London, and now, I believe, is settled in Australia. This gentleman is addicted to prefaces proving that Mr Gladstone, 'this DIRTY OLD DEVIL', 'this sly old wizard, a protoplasm from the abyss of nowhere', was the Beast of the Revelations, and he has an aversion from Mr R. J. Campbell, whom he calls 'moo-cow, kid-gloved Campbell'. It is well worthwhile buying his *Sonnets, Lays and Lyrics*. The poems themselves are not so amusing, though we sometimes came across such ambiguous phrases as:

> *And when upon your dainty breast I lay*
> *My wearied head – more soft than eiderdown.*

But the illustrations – wood-blocks from eminent artists like Albert Dürer and Louis Wain – are charmingly irrelevant, and the prose passages are unique.

Difficult to place in either class are the poets who have some technical faculty, who are not necessarily cranks, but who endeavour to put such extraordinarily prosy things into verse that the result is as comic as though they were. I have, for example, a book containing 'a lyrical romance in verse', which tells a story, that might have gone quite well in prose, of a man who falls in love with a girl and has long discussions with her about politics. The author's choice of a metrical form leads him to pages and pages of this sort of thing:

> *I ceased, and somewhat eagerly she asked:*
> *'Then you would justify the Socialist,*
> *Or Anarchist, the brute assassin, masked*
> *As a reformer, him who has dismissed*
> *All scruples, and himself or others tasked*
> *To murder innocence? Can there exist*
> *A reason to excuse Luccheni's action,*
> *Of life's great rights most dastardly infraction?'*
>
> *'Excuse it, no!' I said; 'nor justify it;*
> *But understand it yes! – I find confusion*
> *In both your questions; and, your words imply it,*
> *They have their base in popular illusion.*
> *In Socialism and Anarchism, deny it*
> *Who will, there's no imperative inclusion*
> *Of violence. Each, aiming at reform,*
> *Would lay life's ever-raging life and storm.'*

The growth of the Socialist and Suffragist movements has led to a great increase in this kind of argumentative verse. . . But most of the best bad verse is not propagandist. Amongst the classics of the kind the works of Johnston-Smith rank high. These have been published complete in one volume, but the best of them are to be found in a smaller book entitled *The Captain of the Dolphin*. Mr Johnston-Smith had a great vocabulary and peculiar gifts of metaphor and of abrupt conclusion. . . One of his nicest surprises is the ending of:

> *Where the sun circles round for the half of the year*
>   *And is cold – like a yellow balloon.*

The kind of thrill produced by this unexpected ending is, of course, common in verse. Some readers will be acquainted with the epitaph:

> *Here beneath this stone at rest*
> *Lies the dear dog who loved us best.*
> *Within his heart was nothing mean,*
> *He seemed just like a human being.*

But a university poet's anticlimax on *Actaeon* may not be so generally known:

> *His hands were changed to feet, and he in short*
> *Became a stag. . .*

An equal bathos is sometimes produced by inappropriate metaphor. The worst instance I know is found in the poems of quite a well-known writer who describes roses:

> *Aft before and fore behind*
> *Swung upon the summer wind.*

The chase after the unusual almost always means disaster. This is another recent example:

> *I have found thee there, in a world of rest,*
> *In the fair sweet gardens of sunlit bliss,*
> *Where the sibilant sound of an Angel's kiss*
> *Is the sanctioned seal of a Holy quest.*

But nothing produced in this manner is so attractive as the merely commonplace can be when carried to its farthest pitch. A year or two ago a young American published a volume with a preface ending: 'He was apprised of the death of his invalid brother, whose remaining portion of his grandfather's legacy accruing to him facilitated the publication of this book.' The epilogue ran as follows:

> *Oh, the rain, rain, rain!*
> *All the day it doth complain.*
> *On the window-pane, just near me,*
> *How it sputters, oh, how dreary!*
> *One becomes so awful weary*
> *With the rain, rain, rain.*

The difference between this and Verlaine's *Il pleut sur la ville* would be hard to define, but there certainly is a marked difference.

Spilling the Beans

Biographies often reveal as much about their authors as about their subjects. Two examples are Beaverbrook's life of Christ, entitled *The Divine Propagandist*, and Lord Longford's book on *Nixon*. Malcolm Muggeridge reviewed the Beaverbrook work, demonstrating hilariously how the 'success story' of Jesus Christ had been ruthlessly reduced by the author to propaganda for the *Daily Express* viewpoint: a unique blend of uplift, lunacy and untruthfulness:

Jesus Christ, in any case, is a Name Which Makes News. During his lifetime he would not, perhaps, have rated the attention of William Hickey, but his subsequent fame, and the wealth and eminence of many of those associated with it, qualified him for a place in any gossip-column. From Lord Beaverbrook's point of view, his was essentially a success story. From humble origins (though, as the Son of God, he might be considered to have exalted connections) he achieved a position of outstanding power and influence. The Crucifixion was a set-back, certainly, but the Resurrection more than compensated for it. Thenceforth, the movement he founded progressed almost as fast as the circulation of the *Daily Express*. Though his earthly estate was negligible, and far below the level at which death duties become payable, his posthumous circumstances put him in the multi-millionaire class. His astonishing career, from carpenter's son to an accepted position on God's right hand, exemplified Lord Beaverbrook's favourite proposition that dazzling opportunities await whoever has the shrewdness, energy and pertinacity to see and seize them. Not even the sky was the limit.

It was as a successful propagandist that Jesus Christ won Lord Beaverbrook's particular admiration. Without the advantages of a chain of newspapers, lacking financial resources and powerful earthly connections, he still managed to put across his ideas so effectively that nearly two thousand years later they are still ringing in mankind's ears. Is is surprising that so outstanding a feat should have impressed another operator in the field of propaganda who, with so many additional advantages, saw every cause he espoused founder, every individual he attacked thrive, and most of those he praised fall in public esteem?

No doubt, too, Jesus Christ would have made, in Lord Beaverbrook's estimation, an admirable columnist: a sort of super-Godfrey Winn, felicitously reminding his readers of life's deeper purposes and truer values. His evangel might well have been advanced by editorial support such as the Express newspapers could have afforded, but the fact remains that, by mere word of mouth, he did surprisingly well. Lord Beaverbrook attributes this success, in the first place to his choice of disciples. He eschewed 'intellectuals who would have spread the doctrine quickly', and went 'for simple men of tenacious character who will obey and bear witness'. 'Almost any twelve honest men selected at random,' Lord Beaverbrook considers, would have been as serviceable as the actual apostles. It was not for them to 'theorize and embroider on the teaching as men of greater intellectual force would certainly have done', but just to report what they saw and heard. Like good *Daily Express* correspondents, their function was to be on the spot, and first with the news.

After the Sermon on the Mount, Lord Beaverbrook tells us, Jesus Christ embarked upon his 'great campaign', in the conduct of which he appears 'simply and nakedly as the greatest propagandist the world has ever known'. The main propagandist weapons he used were 'personality, example and oratory'. It is significant that so old a hand at the game as Lord Beaverbrook should have omitted any reference to the truth of what was being propagated as a factor in its successful propagation. Here, he was following his own practice. In his own essays as a propagandist he always concentrated on presentation rather than content, and assumed that Jesus Christ would necessarily have done likewise.

If Christ was not exactly in need of an apologist in the shape of Lord Beaverbrook, Richard Nixon was certainly in need of one in any shape or form by 1980. Lord Longford galloped to the rescue, and Hugh Brogan reviewed his rehabilitation job in the *Listener*:

I cannot like the practice of publishers writing books about their authors. For one thing, it is flagrant puffery: thus Lord Longford misses no opportunity of reminding us that his firm offers two books by Richard Nixon for sale, just as he misses no opportunity of reminding us that he once had dinner with the great man. For another, it opens vistas of infinite recession: I suppose the next thing will be a biography of Lord Longford by Lord Weidenfeld. Let us hope that the chain will break there, or it will become even more difficult than it is already for real authors to get into print.

This is a curious work. As a study of Richard Nixon it is wholly without value, except that, unintentionally, the author's own mental and moral confusion enables him to convey the dark fog in which Mr Nixon passed his public career. Lord Longford's notion of scholarship can be judged by the fact that, instead of listening to the famous Watergate tapes himself, as he could easily have done, or relying upon an official transcript, he takes his account of what is in them from the Nixon memoirs. Indeed, he has built his entire book out of the more noticeably vapid, self-serving and unconvincing passages in that enormous volume, which may save at least some of his readers from having to wade through it. His solution to the extraordinarily difficult problems of interpretation which Nixon's career presents, from the first race for Congress to the end, is consistent: he adopts the former President's account every time. To be sure, he cannot quite bring himself to say that the whole Watergate affair was a conspiracy got up by the press (Nixon made some mistakes, he admits) but he seldom or never gives the President's opponents credit for intelligence or decency. Perhaps the most memorable remark in the book is: 'No honest person believes that [Nixon] knew in advance of the burglaries.' I propose to Lord Longford that he asks the next ten Americans he meets what they think: he will be surprised. Or perhaps he won't: he seems to meet Americans only at publishers' parties. That is no way to find out what ordinary honest people think of the fallen chief.

To be blunt, the book is sickeningly sycophantic: a life of Lady Catherine de Bourgh written by Mr Collins.

As an episode in the career of this eccentric nobleman the book is not without interest. It seems to signal his return to those crusted conservative spheres from which he wandered in his hot youth. How respectfully he reports the pompous flatteries which statesmen bestow on each other! How loftily he ignores the problems of the poor and oppressed which Mr Nixon's long stint in public life did so little to alleviate! How lightly he brushes aside the sufferings of

Indochina! How unctuously he praises 'Chuck' Colson for his turn to Jesus, and commends Mr Nixon's religiosity! How significantly he pats Mrs Thatcher on the back! Welcome home, my lord, as Elizabeth I said to the Earl of Oxford. We can forget the days when Frank Pakenham had better things to do with pen, ink, paper and time than compose diffuse lay sermons on subjects of which he knows little and understands less.

I must add that the proof-reading of this volume is, even by today's standards, quite dreadful.

If biography reveals its authors accidentally, autobiography does so by intention. That is the problem. Autobiographers proudly display what they take to be their best profile. Unkind critics take them at their own estimation of themselves, sometimes with lethal consequences for the subject. Poor Lord Longford was once again the victim, this time of Gore Vidal's withering fire:

In front of me now is the Seventh Earl's third volume of memoirs. On the dust jacket there is a photograph in colour of the Seventh Earl's head. He looks mighty pleased with himself – as well he ought. Beneath the picture the words *The Grain of Wheat, an Autobiography*, Frank Longford. That's all: a vivid contrast to the Seventh Earl's billing on the slender paperback *Humility*. The title *Humility* was hardly visible, modest mauve on black, while the author's name was in stark white, Frank Pakenham, Earl of Longford. But no matter how Frank wants to be known, I find his ruling passion perfectly irresistible.

In the present volume Frank brings us up to date. He admits right off to being an intellectual and a quotation from A. J. Cronin early on convinced me that the contents of Frank's mind are well worth a detour. As he says, 'My special kind of brain is well above average in literature.' After all, he produced '*Peace by Ordeal*, still the standard book on the Anglo-Irish Treaty of 1931'; as for his biography of De Valera, 'Sales were highly satisfactory . . . and the English reviews were very pleasing.' Frank tells us that his college was Christchurch, 'certainly the most aristocratic college in the world'. Frank's war was not much good; he was 'invalided out with a nervous breakdown' in May 1940. But Frank turned his misfortune to tremendous advantage:

With prisoners, ex-prisoners, outcasts generally and all those who hesitate to show their faces abroad, I have had one unfailing and unforeseen point of contact. I can say and mean and be believed – 'I also have been humiliated.' The gulf is bridged as if by magic. If my sense of compassion has been strengthened and activated from any human experience, it is from my own infirmities and the indignities I have myself undergone.

Like Henry James, Frank does not spell out those infirmities and indignities. We can only guess at his anguish. But he does share his triumphs with us: 'According to the *Economist*, I was an enormously successful amateur banker.' When Leader of the House of Lords, Frank spoke on Rhodesia and 'Harold Wilson and other leaders crowded in to listen. Next day, Harold Wilson congratulated me in front of the Cabinet.' Later, 'when I resigned I was overwhelmed with letters . . . referring in glowing terms to my leadership'. And why not? On one occasion, when Leader, Frank spoke from the back benches! 'I can't find that a Leader of the House had ever previously done what I did.'

Frank had his downs as well as his ups in politics. He was not heeded as often as he ought to have been. He might 'have swayed the issue' on devaluation, but didn't. Serenely he records that Harold Wilson is supposed to have noted, 'Frank Longford quite useless. Mental age of twelve.' Frank takes this very well (after all, any bright twelve-year-old is perfectly able to lead the Lords). But he does hope that in future Harold 'will avoid such indiscretions'. Anyway, 'nothing in any membership of the Wilson Government became me so well – it was said at the time – as the manner of my leaving it'. He left it on a Point of Principle. He 'most treasures' a letter he got from someone mysteriously called 'Bobbity Salisbury'. Truly great men like Clem Attlee thought the world of Frank who also treasures more than one of his letters running like this: 'My dear Frank, I will look into the point you mentioned as soon as possible. Yours ever, Clem.'

Yet for all the wonderful letters and compliments from his peers, 'I felt, and still feel, that I was largely wasted in the Cabinet.' But Frank, that's the point isn't it? To be humiliated in order that you may be able to grow as a human being, to learn compassion so that you can help us outcasts across that awful gulf.

Frank writes a lot about sinners (loves them, hates the sin). He got to know the gangster brothers Kray: 'talking to me that afternoon, I am sure that they had made a resolution: never again'. He befriended Ian Brady and Myra Hindley, of the Moors murders fame: 'their agony is never far from my mind'. Frank admits that he is sometimes criticized for his Christian treatment of murderers: 'psychologists and other men assess my motives as they wish'. But Frank is, simply, good. There is not other word. Best of all, he wants us to share with him through his many testaments his many good actions. That's why he writes books and appears on television programmes. By reading Frank and looking at Frank people will want to be as good as he is. Of course, he can be stern. Although Frank doesn't want to put homosexuals in jail, he doesn't want people to forget that 'homosexual conduct . . . remains wrongful'. Pornography, on the other hand, is not only wrongful but must be rooted out and the makers and dispensers of it punished.

Frank reports on his still unfinished crusade against pornography. All in all, he has been having a super time even though he is a bit miffed that the press has not so far acknowledged that 'I had an experience of inquiries which no one in politics could equal.' Unfortunately, 'these rather striking qualifications . . . were never mentioned'. But more fortunately,

> I was featured in the Evening Standard as 'British worthy No. 4', my predecessors being the Duke of Norfolk, the Archbishop of Canterbury and Mick Jagger. I was interviewed times without number and was chosen by the Sunday Times as the most caricatured figure of 1972. . . My citation as 'Man of the Year' referred to me as Crusader Extraordinary.

Then came The Garter, 'a clear reminder that I was not without recognition'. And so, gartered as well as belted, on to Copenhagen. TV cameras. Strippers. Porn. Jesus. Love. Compassion. Outrage. Filth. Human decency. Where will it end, Frank?

I think I know, because Frank let a bit of the cat's whisker out of the bag when he quoted a journalist who wrote:

> Lord Longford is clearly a good man. If he is not actually a saint, he is certainly the most saintly member of the Upper Chamber, and. I do not overlook the Bishops.

That's it. After the humiliation of the bad war, the failed career in politics, the eccentric attempt to regulate England's morals, now comes the halo, the nimbus, the mandala, the translation to Paradise by special arrangement with Telstar. And so at God's right hand, for ever and ever stands the Seventh Earl of Longford, peering happily into an eternal television monitor. Pray for us, Saint Frank. Intercede for us, and teach us to love ourselves as you loved you.

Aristocratic memoirs quite often have this quality of sublime innocence. Lord Drogheda ventured out into the literary jungle where he promptly got stuck all over with poisoned darts from John Mortimer lurking in the undergrowth of the columns of the *Observer*:

THE MAN WITH TWO STRINGS TO HIS BOW

Lord Drogheda, as surely no one will need to be told after the publication of this definitive work, has led a double life as chairman both of the *Financial Times* and Covent Garden (perhaps these worlds are not so absolutely opposed; it may need a close study of the *Financial Times* to be able to afford to go to Covent Garden in the future). He has now written a book of 367 pages dealing with his life in these and various other activities (he has also been chairman of the Newspaper Publishers Association and a governor of the Royal Ballet).

His book, a snip at £10, might be entitled 'All You Need to Know About Lord Drogheda But Were Too Shy To Ask'. It is clear that in writing it Lord Drogheda has found a most congenial subject. Indeed, no detail of his life has escaped his industrious research; witness the index which includes such entries as 'takes up still photography' and 'golf outings with father'.

Early in the story Lord Drogheda met Brendan Bracken who offered him work in the financial Press. Bracken overshadows the book, an enigmatic figure, who hinted that he was Winston Churchill's illegitimate son, and arrived from nowhere at Sedbergh School at the age of eighteen, where he pretended to be fifteen and wrote out a cheque for his first year's fees. It strikes me as so bizarre that anyone should go to an English public school of his own free will that I wanted Lord Drogheda to tell us a great deal more about Mr Bracken. However, as he has reminded us sharply in a letter to *The Times*, 'My book is not primarily about Brendan Bracken, but about myself.'

Lord Drogheda leaves us in no doubt that 'myself' is a worthy subject for his labours and he quotes many letters from those who, throughout his life, have spoken of him in the highest terms. 'He is top of my mathematical division,' wrote his prep. school masters, 'Like Alexander he is never happy unless conquering new worlds.' His tutor at Eton found that he was 'good company in the pupil room', and that 'the addition of House Colours will help to establish him in his own and others' estimation as a good mixture of aesthetics and masculinity'.

Lord Drogheda, as the twenty-one excellent pictures of himself included in the book show, is extremely personable, with the sort of good looks which could be thought of in fiction as going with tiger-skin rugs and riding boots being polished below stairs.

. . . No doubt Lord Drogheda was an enthusiastic chairman of Covent Garden, and I share his preference for opera in its original language. Under his, and David Webster's, regime the Royal Opera House became a huge international success.

All was not plain sailing however. Peter Hall, undoubtedly the country's best opera director, grew weary at the thought of directing endless revivals and Visconti decided to do *Traviata* in black and white like Beardsley drawings. Lord Drogheda and the Board were appalled. 'Where is the colour?' he asked, feeling very 'let down', and David Webster was sent off to Algiers to protest to the great director who merely shrugged and said the Italian equivalent of 'Take it or leave it', although he did agree to introduce 'a little colour in some of the accessories'.

Difficulties with the artistes were amply compensated for, however, by the Royal Visits. On one such occasion Lord Drogheda was able to refer to Princess Margaret, President of the Ballet, as 'Queen of the Dance', and to have switched on a row of candelabra which had been bought with the help of a contribution from the Queen Mother. As the theatre glowed rosily we can feel the happy chairman glowing with it; both Visconti and the wretched Aubrey Beardsley being mercifully forgotten.

One of the royal visits that compensated so well for 'troubles with the artistes' is described by Richard Buckle, who was feeling a bit under-dressed:

Received by Lord Drogheda in his new Garter, amid a crowd of towering Coldstreamers and several dishy servicemen from the Nine Countries in interesting uniforms, the Queen and the Duke of Edinburgh appeared a few minutes later in the centrally contrived Royal Box, with Mr Heath, to be greeted by a very odd version of the National Anthem arranged by Carl Davis. Nearest to the royal party on its left was the Archbishop of Canterbury in magenta, and on the right were the organizers, Lords Goodman and Mancroft.

The house was festooned prettily with pink artificial roses. The Duchess of Bedford had the biggest tiara. I saw three Directors, past or present, of the Edinburgh International Festival. Unable to compete with all the orders and medals around me, I wished I had followed the example of Prince Felix Yusupov on another gaudy night, and come wearing nothing but my Rembrandt, removed from its frame and stretcher, secured neatly on one shoulder with a safety-pin.

A splendid occasion and a delightful image of old England this must have been. But there is another, very different England from that of dukes and earls, and even impoverished ballet critics. Its increasingly *louche* atmosphere in the 1960s struck terror into the heart of an irascible thriller writer who finally could contain himself no longer. His autobiographical outburst against the decadent islanders and their incorrigible ways was reviewed with some amusement by an Australian, Robert Hughes, as James Barlow left in high dudgeon for the Antipodes:

Gore Vidal once remarked that the Puritans left England 'not because they were persecuted for their religious beliefs, but because they were forbidden to persecute others for their beliefs'.

One is apt, at first, to guess that Mr Barlow (author of several gripping adventure novels) has now written the fictional memoirs of an eponymous hero James Barlow, who – obsessed with sexuality and tortured by his conviction that England is in the grip of a Communist conspiracy – flees to Tasmania to find a society which fits his phantasies.

James (as I call this character, to distinguish him from his creator, Mr Barlow) utters a monologue of clinical vividness. The fats of the Puritan ethic boil and curdle in him. Fear of impotence ('How absurd is the man with an erection . . . he looks at once like the village idiot') mingles with a vision of sex by class: 'I would say it was the middle class that held morality together . . . a working-class boy expected his girls to have sexual intercourse (often standing up!)'.

London, great wen or bubo, teems with 'fools who want girls to wear mini-skirts and become sexy'. Ths *città dolente*, full of wailing and the gnashing of diaphragms, is populated by incubi and succubi. The former, with 'rotten teeth and pale, undernourished, sexually exhausted faces' devote themselves to 'sniggering at anything tender, worthwhile or intellectual, sneering at the police, God, law, morality and parents'; the latter customarily 'walks along King's Road, Chelsea, in a topless dress, collecting dust and flies and bits of bus tickets on her breasts'. In creating such allegories of James's neuroses, Mr Barlow joins Bosch: the ticket-encrusted mammary is as authentic a paranoid invention as anything in the Temptations of St Anthony.

But every Inferno has its Paradiso and James finds his in Australia; it is 'like moving back to the better, if simpler, standards of my youth . . . Boys, here, are still shy and nervous about meeting girls.'

Mr Barlow is novelist enough to realize that nobody as profoundly disturbed as James will restrict his dreamworld to sex. It extends to politics too: for if the priapic savage must be restrained in bed, so must he be at the polls. Saving Us from Them is known as saving People from Themselves; and James, in a long paean of praise to those societies which he regards as misunderstood utopias (Rhodesia, South Africa and Portuguese Angola), makes clear how this may be done. 'Freedom in the liberal sense is rubbish,' and the West is so corrupted by liberalism that 'Tyranny might seem to some preferable to democracy; after all, suffering ennobles us and brings us closer to God'.

The first step, however, is to be brought closer to Ian Smith and Vorster. James recoils with disgust from the concept of equality. Like some of his real-life equivalents, he read some books once. One of them was *Animal Farm*, in which Napoleon the Pig's dictum 'All animals are equal, but some are more equal than others' impressed him so deeply that he took it to be Orwell's own view and cites it as authority. But he has evidence too. 'Even President Nkrumah didn't feel his personal airliner should have an African pilot. He hurriedly brought in a white pilot.' Besides, 'No Asian or African has invented a steam turbine. . .'

Who is to blame for our decadence? In the interests of art, Mr Barlow leaves the matter vague and James leads the reader to a *Walpurgisnacht* of 'Commie subversion', with unnamed agitators flitting like bats between Whitehall, Westminster, El Vino's and Portland Place. James knows that 'Left-wing liberal racialists [sic] have a complete monopoly of the BBC,' but little can be done about it because of the 'liberal press' – a term for nearly every journal to the Left of the *Rhodesia Herald*. James distrusts the liberal press, for (can this be Mr Barlow's oblique tribute to 'Herzog'?) he bombards it with letters in praise of UDI, none of which get printed.

Beside this conspiracy 'the jollities of Dr Goebbels and the Third Reich assume the innocence of children's homework'.

But truth is stranger than fiction, and *Goodbye England* is not, in fact, a novel. James, unlike jolly Dr Goebbels, is alive and living in Tasmania; he is James Barlow. As an Australian, what can I do but wish him well? I am sure that, in whatever dingly dell this new ornament to my native culture may have parked his swag, boiling his billy on the land fertilized by Tasmania's long-exterminated blacks, he will be happy.

Hagiography

Political hagiography is an all too flourishing genre. There are two broad categories: professional sycophancy to advance the careers of journalists or young politicians and written while the subject is still alive; and posthumous monuments of stupefying banality and untruthfulness. The latter are designed to obscure as much as possible the venality and incompetence of a recently dead politician. There are also books by people who were on the fringes of politics written to show that they were in fact at the centre. These are often exercises in egomania.

Dorothy Parker was impressed by the pleasure Margot Asquith took in the subject matter of her 'autobiography': 'The affair between Margot Asquith and Margot Asquith will live as one of the prettiest love stories in all literature,' she wrote. After the autobiography ('four volumes, neatly boxed, suitable for throwing purposes') came *Lay Sermons*, succinctly described by Miss Parker as 'tripe'. 'I'm not sure that my ultimate choice for the title of this modest work is altogether happy,' the author had written; to which Miss Parker responded: 'Happier I think it would have been if, instead of the word "Sermons" she had selected the word "off" ':

In this book of essays, which has all the depth and glitter of a worn dime, the Countess walks right up to such subjects as Health, Human Nature, Fame, Character, Marriage, Politics, and Opportunities. A rather large order, you might say, but it leaves the lady with unturned hair. Successively, she knocks down and drags out each topic. And there is something vastly stirring in the way in which, no matter where she takes off from, she brings the discourse back to Margot Asquith. Such singleness of purpose is met but infrequently.

When she does get around to less personal matters, it turns out that her conclusions are soothingly far from startling. A compilation of her sentiments, suitably engraved upon a nice, big calendar, would make an ideal Christmas gift for your pastor, your dentist, or Junior's music teacher. Here, for instance, are a few ingots lifted from her golden treasury: 'The artistic temperament has been known to land people in every kind of dilemma'. . . Pleasure will always make a stronger appeal that Wisdom'. . . 'It is only the fine natures that profit by Experience'. . . 'It is better to be a pioneer than a passenger, and best of all to try and create'. . . 'It is not only what you See but what you Feel that kindles appreciation and gives life to Beauty'. . . 'Quite apart from the question of sex, some of the greatest rascals have been loved'. . . 'I think it is a duty women owe not only to themselves, but to everyone else, to dress well.'

The Thames, I hear, remains as damp as ever in the face of these observations.

Through the pages of *Lay Sermons* walk the great. I don't say that Margot Asquith actually permits us to rub elbows with them ourselves, but she willingly shows us her own elbow, which has been, so to say, honed on the mighty. 'I remember President Wilson saying to me'; 'John Addington Symonds once said to me'; 'The Master of Balliol told me' – thus does she introduce her anecdotes. And you know those anecdotes that begin that way; me, I find them more efficacious than sheep-counting, rain on a tin roof, or alanol tablets. Just begin a story with such a phrase as 'I remember Disraeli – poor old Dizzy! – once saying to me, in answer to my poke in the eye,' and you will find me and Morpheus off in a corner, necking.

Margot Asquith knew the great and capitalized on this in her books. But what of the literature of leaders themselves? Norman Mailer found Lyndon Johnson's effort *My Hope For America* pretty dreadful: 'It is even not impossible that it is the worst book ever written by any political leader anywhere.' This certainly gives it some competition. Its most notable defect was a prose 'whose waters are so brackish that a spoonful is enough to sicken the mind for hours':

Examine it: 127 pages, a little more than 200 words to a page, most of the pages half pages or blank pages so that in bulk there are 17,000 words collected in thirteen short chapters; they have titles like this – 'President of All the People', 'A President's Faith and Vision', 'Building the Atlantic Partnership', 'This Developing World', 'Creative Federalism'. Each page of each chapter is divided into paragraphs. Page 8 has twelve paragraphs; the average page has four or five with a generous space between each paragraph. This is not because the remarks have the resonant echo of Pascal's *Pensées*, rather one idea does not lead to another. So the space must be there. It is useful for burying whichever infinitesimal part of the brain died in the gas of the preceding phrase.

Yet every altruistic idea and every well-tuned moderation which Lyndon Johnson's political experience has put together over the years is somehow worked into the organum of his credo. It is impossible to disagree with a single of its humanistic desires ('We know that we can learn from the culture, the arts, and the traditions of other countries'); it is equally impossible to feel the least pleasure at the thought these goods may yet come to be – just so bad and disheartening is the style of this book:

> *Reality rarely matches dream. But only dreams give nobility to purpose. This is the star I hope to follow – which I know most of you have seen, and which I first glimpsed many years ago in the Texas night.*

> *When the helpless call for help – the hearing must hear, the seeing must see, and the able must act.*

> *It is in America where every man has an equal chance for the well-being that is essential to the enjoyment of the freedom that we brag about.*

> *The Gulf of Tonkin may be distant Asian waters, but none can be detached about what happened there.*

High-school students will be writing essays on these paragraphs. One's stomach turns over. It is certain that if Barry Goldwater had written the same book, everyone would be agreed his style was a menace. Still, what is quoted up to here is still English, English more or less. It is in the depth of the real prose articulated by Johnson and his corps of ghost writers that the heart of the darkness resides. For Johnson is not a writer and has no wish to be. He is a communications engineer. He uses words in interlocking aggregates which fence in thought like cattle.

My Hope For America sounds as if it is, well, turgid. This seems to be a feature of political apologia. Harold Wilson's *The Labour Government 1964–1970 – A Personal Record* was also long – 790 pages to cover a period of less than six years.

'Why on earth did he do it?' wondered Enoch Powell in the *Spectator*, and, moreover, 'How did he do it?'

The book was a ragbag of self-justification laced with gob-bets of speeches and official documents, and spiced with

records of sentimental moments. ('Readers interested in displays of sentimentality,' wrote Paul Foot, 'should refer to Wilson's visit to the Pope and, particularly, to Mr Wilson's acquisition of Manchester United buttons for General Gowon, Prime Minister of Nigeria.') A number of critics pointed out the author's attacks of amnesia about various episodes in his period of government, and his inability to squeeze in relevant detail elsewhere – though 836 pages of course cramp an author somewhat. But the *Personal Record* did seem a faithful reflection of the Prime Minister all had known and loved when in office. It appeared that other people were to blame for most of the failures. At the same time, the most abject of these were hailed as magnificent victories in the book. This was a point that did not escape Alasdair MacIntyre in the *Listener* who was particularly acid about the record on *In Place of Strife* and the climbdown on industrial relations:

The true reason why Conservative policies were pursued is that the Labour Government's vision of the limits of political possibility was a Conservative vision. The key concept which determined what was perceived was that of 'the national interest': the national interest, thus understood, is served by collaboration between a Labour Government and the City and it is endangered by strikes. Hence the Labour Government's continuous attack on the only weapon available to the working class in its struggle with rising prices and unemployment – the strike.

Mr Wilson's attempt to rewrite the record on the Industrial Relations Bill is so blatant that it underlines this point very well. He claims that the sentences from his speech to the Parliamentary Labour Party on 17 April 1969, in which he asserted that the passing of the Bill was essential for the Labour Government's economic policy and its continuance in office, only give the impression that they mean what they seem to mean when they are quoted out of context as part of a legend 'unscrupulously fostered by Opposition leaders and Opposition press' and helped on by at least one television interviewer. In fact, a reading of Mr Wilson's actual words makes it plain that what he is taking on is not the Conservative Party or Mr Robert Kee, but the English language.

Other reviewers complained more generally of the 'turgid'

and 'vapid' nature of Mr Wilson's prose and the uneven manner. ('The tone is mainly good-humoured, but a vitriolic antipathy to Mr Heath wrecks the effect.')

After his third term of office, Mr Wilson launched into print again. Exhausted reviewers were relieved to find that this volume let them off with 322 pages, but pointed out that the price had risen from £4.80 for the 836-page book to £8.95 for a book under half its size. Economies of scale being what they are in publishing, it might be conjectured that the anticipated market for Wilson II had declined disastrously, thus forcing the publishers to shorten the run and up the price. Or was it merely, as Bernard Crick drily observed in his *Guardian* review, 'a measure of course, as the author would argue, of the inflation that began in the intervening Heath administration'. Crick referred to the work as being in the 'pietistic tradition of theology'. What appeared to the uninitiated to be an incredibly boring, trivial and egocentric narrative was a 'hymn to God's creation' for the believer. 'By and large,' said the reviewer in the *Diplomatist*, whom you would expect to exercise tact, 'Sir Harold is charitable in his description of others, and even more charitable in his description of himself.' Amnesia seemed to have set in again however: 'Carefully ignored in the memoirs,' said the *Morning Star* unpleasantly, 'are many of the shadier happenings of the final Wilson years,' i.e. no mention of slag-heaps in passages about the industrial regeneration of Britain. No matter; as John Vincent observed in *New Society*, 'Truth is one of the great inflation-proof assets. If Sir Harold's memory becomes clearer, as often happens, in old age, it will provide ample recompense for his failure to remember much now.'

Sir Harold published a further work on politics after his amnesic sagas. This was called *The Governance of Britain*, an impressive title with an archaic and portentous ring about it. The critics weren't much kinder to that work either. Bernard Crick pointed out that the preface was remarkable in that there were no thanks to anyone – 'Mr Toad did it all on his own.' 'Failure,' observed Crick, 'appeared to have gone to

Harold Wilson's head.' And he ended his piece with a fierce blast of Wilsonophobia:

Never has a man wielded more power, made so little effective use of it and appeared in such an indecent haste to blow his own trumpet before. . . A reaction will set in and will begin with this fascinating but intellectually disgraceful book on mis-government.

A far more vitriolic review came from Robert Rhodes James in the *Sunday Telegraph* who combined an attack on Wilson the inept Prime Minister with Wilson the grotesque self-hagiographer:

There is a strong temptation to remark that only Sir Harold Wilson would have the sheer gall to impose upon us a self-congratulatory and superficial book entitled *The Governance of Britain*, and to publish it at this precise moment of deep national misfortune. Furthermore, it turns out – not altogether surprisingly – to be a book about Sir Harold Wilson, somewhat thinly dressed up as an analysis of 'the powers of the Prime Minister as an essential part of Cabinet Government within our parliamentary democracy'.

. . . Bold Sir Harold inhabits a self-created fantasy world in which, single-handedly, he slays dragons, rescues sobbing damsels in distress, wields the sword without fear but with compassion, stands fearlessly against all storms, and bestrides the world and inspirits its inhabitants like a new Churchill. This romantic vision of himself would be touching, and is certainly very human, were it not for the grim fact that we, the British people, have only been given the role of admiring audience in the drama of Sir Harold's dreams, and are now left to pay the bill.

Getting into his stride Rhodes James described the book as an irrelevant, 'conceited and shallow lecture', and ended in a peroration that likened Mr Wilson to the Flying Dutchman of politics, 'a phantom vessel floating about on the wide seas, without an anchor and without a port. . . Behind the far-off murmur of the great world where he was once the hero, now lost to him for ever; before the waste of lonely waters and the engulfing night.'

Rhodes James was a political opponent of Wilson. But as usual this ex-prime minister got even more carved up by people on the Left of the political spectrum. Anthony Howard in the *New Statesman* summed up what seemed to be the view of several writers who felt that the book was a mine of non-information:

Sir Harold Wilson's *The Governance of Britain* is my own leading candidate for this season's non-book championship. Only its pretentious title and its imposing dust jacket serve to disguise what it really is – a spiced-up Central Office of Information hand-out on British political and constitutional practice. One politician I know who served in both Sir Harold's administrations managed to get that message both economically and painlessly. Leafing through the book he discovered a chapter entitled 'The Prime Minister and National Security'. 'Ah,' he thought to himself, 'there's something I know absolutely nothing about, let's see what I can learn.' He found himself confronted with a chapter of 189 words beginning with the paragraph:

> The prime minister has the ultimate responsibility for the national security authorities at home and abroad, though the home and overseas organizations concerned come departmentally under the Home Office and the Foreign and Commonwealth Office responsibility

and ending some 130 words later with the paragraph:

> There is no further information that can usefully or properly be added before bringing this chapter to an end.

If by no means a wiser, he is at least not a poorer man. He hung on to his £5. So should you.

The ultimate in fatuous books on politics, however, must surely be the enormous empty tomes of hagiography and trivia that were part of the myth-making industry centred on the late John F. Kennedy. In these volumes the worst aspects of royalty fetishism familiar to British readers in saccharine biographies about members of the Royal Family, were combined with disingenuous attempts to put the President's political record in the most favourable light. Malcolm Muggeridge surveyed the examples of this gloomy sub-species of literature with characteristic acerbity:

The same unhappy parallel with our degraded monarchy-worship is apparent in *The Kennedy Wit*, a lavishly illustrated paperback which has already run through numerous editions. The Duke of Edinburgh himself could scarcely be expected to improve on:

> **Question:** *Senator, you were promised military intelligence briefing from the President. Have you received that?*
> **Mr Kennedy:** *Yes. I talked on Thursday morning to General Wheeler from the Defence Department.*
> **Question:** *What was his first name?*
> **Mr Kennedy:** *He didn't brief me on that.*

Or:

> *President Kennedy enlivened the ceremony for signing of a housing bill with a touch of Shakespeare. Noting the absence of two Alabama Democrats, Representative Albert Rains and Senator John J. Sparkman, who had manoeuvred the bill through Congress, the President declared: 'Having this bill signed without them is somewhat like having Hamlet played without the Prince.'*

Even an ex-editor of *Punch* winces at such an exercise in wit, more mayoral than Voltairean, surely. Years ago when I was a gossip-writer on a London newspaper, and as such expected to retail the witticisms of the great, I used to toy with the idea of producing an anthology of Royal Humour. As a basic anecdote I treasured one about King Alphonso of Spain which actually appeared in a gossip-column. One hot summer day the King was out walking in Madrid, and happened to notice a workman engaged in digging a hole in the road. ' "Hot work, eh!" ' our gossip-columnist quotes His Majesty as remarking, to which observation, the columnist goes on, 'the workman laughingly assented'. Now, having thumbed through *The Kennedy Wit*, I feel that I should have to extend the range of my anthology to take in heads of state.

Of the poetic compositions in honour of the late President I feel less competent to speak. They have been collected together in a volume (*Of Poetry and Power*) with a foreword, alas, by Arthur Schlesinger, Jr. There may, for all I know, be some hidden excellence and profundity in:

> The talk is of Johnson and a Congress
> Which has done nothing. The accents are
> Of Virginia, Maryland, the whining
> South. I sit in the back booth of a Chinese restaurant,
> Washington, 1963. Before me lie
> *The New York Times . . .*

Or:

> He sort
> of embodied
> the air he sort
> of embodied the
> air where democracy
> stood tall, Jefferson
> and Robert Frost were
> his advisers, he sort
> of clearly gave evidence of
> wit and democracy . . .

Of the political record rewrites, Muggeridge wrote:

The highly glamorized reconstruction of the late President's nomination, campaigning and election by Theodore H. White (*The Making of the President 1960*) reads like an account of a successful Woolworth's store in which no mention is made of the till.

Muggeridge also pondered the decline of scholarly minds when set to work in the vineyard of political sycophancy:

What, then, has happened to turn this luminous and critical intelligence [Arthur Schlesinger] into a slobbering apologist for the late President; an undiscriminating adulator of the whole turn-out, Bobby and Teddy and all, down to the very Hyannis Port dogs? For more than a thousand pages he sustains a tribute to the late President's sagacity, charm, wit, resolution, virtue, erudition and enlightened handling of America's business. His plaster pyramid is even larger than Theodore Sorensen's. Looking back on all the literature of obsequiousness through the ages, taking in even the Victorians and the poetasters of Oriental courts, I find it difficult to match their two efforts in sheer fulsome idiocy. To a brief interlude in American history, to a rather exceptionally lightweight President, they accord honours which a combination of Bismarck, Talleyrand, Metternich, Gladstone, Disraeli, Lincoln and Cromwell would scarcely have deserved. Whatever has happened to these two men, and to America?

It is almost refreshing to turn from the glutinous pages of Kennedy-worship to a Crawfie-like effort on Winston Churchill which appeared in the *Daily Mail* in the 1950s. As the anonymous reviewer in the *Spectator* pointed out, inability to accumulate facts need never be a bar to the practice of journalism.

CHURCHILLIAN FANTASY

In Monday's *Daily Mail* there began the publication of a series of articles on Sir Winston Churchill entitled 'Life Begins at Eighty'. The series is written by an American journalist, Mr George W. Herald. I am always suspicious of articles which purport to tell one about the private lives of well-known people, unless it is also well known that the subject of such articles courts such publicity, and provides facilities, as do, for instance, Lord and Lady Mountbatten, for their private lives to be made known. But this series of Mr Herald's does not prompt suspicion; it evokes incredulity and can only be branded as an impudent piece of fabrication.

Here are some examples of Mr Herald's inventions: *His valet, John, who accompanies him on all his trips, will invariably call him over the phone at 7 a.m. in the summer-time and 8 in winter-time.* Sir Winston has no valet called John, and is never called over the telephone. *Thereupon Churchill dons a scarlet dressing-gown. . .* Sir Winston, like all sensible men, never wears a dressing-gown in bed. He has not lived to eighty without discovering that a dressing-gown gets wrinkled up in bed. In fact, he wears a bed-jacket. *Sir Winston has a theory about breakfast . . . served by Edward, his personal cook, which consists of porridge . . .* Sir Winston has never had a personal cook named Edward or anything else, and never eats porridge at breakfast or any other time. *After coffee Sir Winston lights one of his daily six to eight cigarettes. That's correct: cigarettes.* It is incorrect. Sir Winston has not smoked a cigarette for a quarter of a century. *Since last May the man who has done more for the world's cigar trade than any other living human being has given up Havanas for good.* As everyone except Mr Herald knows, Sir Winston still smokes ten or twelve cigars a day. *While Sir Winston looks through the morning papers John* (sic) *prepares his first bath for him. . . From the bathroom Churchill goes right back to bed.* In fact, when Sir Winston has had his bath he always gets dressed. *Ritual No. 4 is a catnap after lunch. He only has to stretch out on the couch in his study and put a black satin bandage over his eyes to drop off to sleep like a baby.* There is no couch in Sir Winston's study; when he has a rest he invariably goes to bed. *By 11 o'clock, after his third and final bath of the day, he goes to bed. . .* Sir Winston has never been known to take more than two baths a day, and has never indulged in the eccentricity of having one after his dinner.

Monday's *Daily Mail* announced: 'Tomorrow – His Homes: his family and his animals'. It seems that by Tuesday the *Daily Mail* had lost confidence in the authenticity of Mr Herald's account, for without a word of explanation the series was abandoned. I only hope that the words 'world copyright' do not mean that this stuff is going to be spattered by Mr Herald all over the world.

The ERG

One of the more unlikely successful authors of the 1970s was ex-prime minister Edward Heath who first hit the jackpot with *Sailing* and followed it up with *Music: A Joy for Life*. Public enthusiasm for these artful mixtures of autobiography and instruction was encouraged to express itself in terms of hard cash by Mr Heath's tireless campaign of promotion and publicity. After his fourth book had been published, a train was hired by Mr Heath's publishers and trundled round the countryside stopping at likely venues for signing sessions that began to look increasingly like a mass inoculation campaign. *Punch* was moved to suggest that Mr Heath's next title should be *Trains*:

Extracts from the new best-selling, fantastic, incredible, smash-hit success from the author of *Boats*, *Records*, *Carols*, *Socks*, *Book Tokens*, *Christmas Cards* and *Ties and Hankies* . . .

TRAINS
by Edward Heath

'Sometimes, alas, people try to get me to sign books they haven't paid for, and I have no option but to lock them up and hand them over to the railway police. . .

'You know, some of the happiest hours of my life have been spent on trains. Perhaps looking out of the window at the "landscape" passing by, with its typical cows and grass. Perhaps standing in the mini-buffet with a couple of Scottish football supporters, discussing life an' that. Or maybe even just signing copies of my latest world best seller at some charming main-line station and swapping a good hearty laugh with folk over such old jokes as "The valuable ones are the unsigned ones. . ."

'But when I look back at a lifetime of travelling by train, I can't help thinking of the little steam train that used to take me from Broadstairs to Oxford for another term at Balliol. Little did the passengers on that far-off, pre-war "Southern" Rail think that the

'It's a book about my train trip around Britain autographing books.'

shy, bookish youth in their midst would one day become a
"block-busting" author! Little did I think, either, that one day I
would write a book about trains. If I had, I would have taken some
notes. . .

'I seem to have given the impression that there was a direct train
service from Broadstairs to Oxford. But, you know, memory plays
funny tricks, and I see now from a map of England that it is most
unlikely that such a service existed, unless it ran across Hyde
Park. . . !

'I must ask one of the many charming "research" assistants whom
I have helped to "write" my books to look up pre-war train sched-
ules between Broadstairs and Oxford, and if possible to find a
photograph of an engine of the time. . .

'I think the most memorable Christmas I have ever enjoyed was
that of 1969, which was spent simply aboard a Western Region 4–
6–0 in the company of André Previn, Michael Parkinson, Oscar
Peterson, the Broadstairs Church Choir, half a dozen American
publishers, several visiting statesmen and "Lord" Longford, as he
then was. I can imagine nothing more natural and beautiful than
sharing Christmas with your friends, singing carols, signing each
other's books, and having a "nightcap" in the dining car. How
lucky that there was a TV crew on hand to record it all for posterity,
and perhaps some of you may have seen "Edward Heath's Christmas
Party Show" on the "television set". . .

'I found when writing my book about "music" that it does not
do to become too technical in trying to talk to laymen, who after all
can appreciate the beauty of the great composers without being
confused by talk of "notes" or "beats". So I do not intend to explain
in great detail the mysteries behind the marvellous spectacle of a
railway train in full cry. . .

'However, I feel I should tell my readers that an engine is basically
driven by energy derived from fuel which is then converted into
direct drive which makes the "wheels" go round. This round-and-
round motion, or circular revolution, is then applied to the "rails"
and the train then moves. It has been traditional for many years to
use coal and steam to run trains, though I am told by younger
friends that electricity and oil are now very popular. . .

'I suppose that deep inside every one of us is the desire to own
his own train, and I can still remember the intense thrill of excite-
ment when I became the proud owner of *Morning Steam 1*. It was
only a small ex-GWR 0–6–0 pannier tank, and not much good for

anything except autographing a few paperbacks at a time, but I shall never love another train as much. Today I am lucky to be the owner of *Morning Express III*, a glittering monster with five coaches run by a crack team of crewmen who have helped me to victory in such great events as the Round Britain Bookshops Race, the Foyles-to-Blackwells Freestyle Event and the Harold Wilson Handicap. If you should happen to see it passing your neighbourhood, just wave and I will stop to sell you a copy of my book, whichever it is by then. . .

'This is no longer, of course, the "Golden" age of railways and there are fewer lines now open in Britain than at any time since the last century. Why is this? I suspect it is because down many small branch lines there simply are not enough book readers to supply the demand for book signings and "personal visits" by celebrities. It is a sad but inevitable fact that if a railway line is not worth visiting by a publisher, then there is little justification for its staying open. Even at some big stations there doesn't seem to be very much demand. I just can't understand this. What on earth is the point of laying on a big display of one's books and me waiting ready there if people simply can't be bothered to turn up and buy a copy? Goodness, it makes one so angry at the lack of initiative and cooperation in Britain today, and I shall have a lot of tough talking to say about this in my next book, *Books*.'

Mr Heath was, of course, no stranger to travelling. His thoughts on the subject, however, failed to excite the enthusiasm of the *Sunday Times* reviewer, Paul Theroux:

ROUND THE WORLD IN 80 CLICHÉS

Ever since he left office, Mr Heath has subjected his public to a kind of relentless reminiscence about his pastimes. Bachelors are such singleminded hobbyists. After *Sailing* and *Music* we have *Travels*, and before long no doubt we will be privileged to witness Mr Heath signing even more titles about other chaste recreations.

He is strong on scrapbook memorabilia – this present book contains the newspaper articles he wrote decades ago for the *Advertiser & Echo* (Broadstairs), tourist brochures, holiday snaps ('The picnic we had on our way from Warsaw to Lodz'), a forty-year-old Spanish letter of authorization, and ancient Press cuttings. But he is weak on detail of other sorts. For a man whose second favourite word is 'particularly' he is highly unparticular. The word most favoured in this book is 'agreeable': Bamberg was 'an agreeable place', Nairobi was 'pleasant and agreeable', and The Forbidden City? Mr Heath does not equivocate: 'agreeable'.

This is almost entirely a record of happy days abroad, for however exotic or distant the place, what Mr Heath requires is a good meal, a hot bath, a night's sleep, solid comfort – no crowds, no awkward temperatures (he always reports whether a place was hot or cold). His time in Venice is typical: he spends his time 'exploring different churches' – the churches are not named; he eats 'meals' – no dishes are listed; he stays at a 'hotel' – he doesn't say which one. And, 'I was captivated by Venice.' I was not captivated by Mr Heath's Venice.

But travel writing is a funny thing. The worst trips, in retrospect, make the best reading, which is why Graham Greene's The Lawless Roads and Kinglake's Eothen are so superb; and the most comfortable travel ('There was invariably split-second timing and exact positioning as they drew up at the steps leading to the red carpet and the welcoming party') becomes in the telling little more than chatting or, in Mr Heath's Travels, smug boasting. 'I wonder how many people in Europe know about the Caprivi Strip,' Mr Heath inquires, and lest anyone mistake this for a Dutch fandango, he adds, 'and how many people have been there?' Apart from the fact that he is saying 'I have and you haven't' he says practically nothing about the place itself. Like so many of his destinations – like Venice, for goodness sake – it is merely a name.

Mr Heath has been promoted as a man with wide interests. You name it, and he has sung it, or sailed in it or been there. He is a statesmanly combination of Toscanini and Joshua Slocum, and now he is an indefatigable traveller. He laments that as an official visitor he has been unable to see much of 'the day-to-day life of the people'. And yet here he is in Kenya at the time of the Mau Mau troubles. He praises the chintzes at Nairobi's Norfolk Hotel, the carved doorways in the old Arab Quarter in Mombasa ('The only attractive part of the town') and the coconut trees. In a twinkling he has had enough of the day-to-day life of the people and he is up the coast: 'I enjoyed excellent bathing.' In Miramer on the Mediterranean, 'I could swim and sunbathe all day,' and on the little island of Gan, which has been the undoing of many an RAF man, Mr Heath spends 'a few hours bathing in the translucent light-green water'. I would be willing to wager anything that his next book is called Swimming.

But is this travel at all? The Arab Quarter is attractive because it has carved doorways, and worthy of mention because it is attractive. If you can have a swim and a good snooze, yes, Mr Heath says, that's travel. And here is Aden: 'Aden was quite different. The colony existed largely to meet the maritime need for oil, as it had originally done for bunkering coal. I can remember little attractive about it.' Sometimes his bathing mania is spatch-cocked into a political judgement, as in this baffling and ungrammatical sentence: 'Durban was a fine city, though the purity of its beaches and the joys of its bathing were exaggerated, but the conditions of the workers in the sugar-growing area to the north were far from attractive.

And you thought only his French was bad!

The *New Statesman* (Jonathan Keats) was particularly hard on our travel-stained hero:

Rifling through the pages of *Travels*, a naked piece of book-production, recalls those floppy cartoon books sold during the days of *Brumas the Baby Polar Bear*, which, if you flipped them over quickly enough, created the illusion that the cuddly cub was actually diving off a Mappin terrace into a pool below. In the present work the effect is more like *Dorian Gray*: the familiar face, at first youthfully bovine above a belted mac and a rather unlikely pair of plus-fours at Le Bourget, takes on spectacles, loses them, fills out and gradually becomes the big, dented mangel-wurzel emerging at the top of the Great Wall of China or poking itself out of a Rhine Army tank. . .

The accompanying text artfully smears slabs of autobiography with a smooth margarine or travelogue. As the exotic locales whirr round after each other in anodyne home-movie style, the work swells into an unconscious threnody for vanished voyages, and as the goodwill missions, epoch-making handshakes, press-conference attitudinizing and general peace-in-our-time-ishness increase, we pine for a real traveller. Mungo Park ransoming his way across the African bush with his waistcoat buttons, Gertrude Ball kipping in the desert sandwiched between two Bedouin – anything to counter the staleness with which Heath greets a world compelled to welcome and flatter him. Here's a sample:

> Most interesting of all is Persepolis, the ancient city of Darius, the remains of which have been well protected by the climate. It is an awe-inspring experience to move around the foundation of the great halls, to see the noble pillars, and in particular, to look at the

impressive engravings on the walls; awe-inspiring to think that 4,000 years ago men were capable of such construction and decoration; and quite remarkable to think that so much should have survived.

Heath does not mention the Sahara. Anyone familiar with that desert will know about the Erg. The Erg is a high inland plateau, intensely dry, hot and shingly, more or less inimical to any form of life. The fact that the author's initials are E. R. G. proved fatally intrusive on my powers of free association, and the analogy ∴ . . offered irresistible proof that *le style c'est l'homme*. That this wretched, drivelling affair, its impressions fuzzy with jetlag and neutral-flavoured as an airline meal, should have been made into a best seller, with all the attendant flimflam of the hired train and 8.2 autographed copies per minute, is a signpost towards the gap between those who buy books and those who read them.

This review might effectively have done for Mr Heath's *Travels* – if anyone read the *New Statesman*. More people read the *Observer* where Christopher Wordsworth simply observed that the book was a reminder that '*Morning Cloud*'s skipper was no stranger to platitude and longitude'.

Mr Heath's book on *Music* fared rather better at the hands of the reviewers, but Alexander Chancellor ended his review of the book in the *Spectator* on a far from encouraging note for the author:

Thank God Mrs Thatcher has (household painting apart) no known hobbies.

Propaganda

Quite a lot of books are written with the express object of misleading readers. Controversial periods of history like the Spanish Civil War give rise to much literature that appears to have been written by parrots. George Orwell was rather good at reviewing these:

Mr Arnold Lunn writes as a supporter of General Franco and believes life in 'red' Spain (which he has not visited) to be one continuous massacre. On the authority of Mr Arthur Bryant, who, 'as an historian, is well accustomed to weigh evidence', he puts the number of non-combatants massacred by the 'reds' since the beginning of the war as 350,000. It would appear, also, that 'the burning of a nun in petrol or the sawing off of a Conservative tradesman's legs' are 'the commonplaces of "democratic" Spain'.

Now, I was about six months in Spain, almost exclusively among Socialists, Anarchists and Communists, and if I remember rightly I never even once sawed off a Conservative tradesman's legs. I am almost certain I should remember doing such a thing. . .

Orwell's wintry asides could sometimes be interpreted as humour. Elsewhere he tells the story of the incident in the House of Commons when Lloyd George pointed out that if official communiqués were added together, they showed that the British had killed more Boers in the South African war than the Boer nation contained. A. J. Balfour replied to this by rising to his feet and shouting: 'Cad!' 'Very few people,' observed Orwell, 'are proof against lapses of this type.'

Political smearing is fertile ground for the industrious hack. A. J. P. Taylor reviewed an entertaining book of the genre in the *Observer* in 1979. It was called *The British Connection* and was by an author (Richard Deacon) who had made a speciality of picking up fag-ends about the secret service:

REDS UNDER BEDS

Some books are funny in parts. This book is unique in being funny all through. No more preposterous book has ever been written. It purports to show the operations of Bolshevik espionage in Great Britain from 1889, a somewhat surprising date, to the present day.

The technique is simple: left-wing politicians, financiers and acknowledged agents are cooked together in a single pie, from which plums are pulled out at random. Usually only those safely dead are mentioned by name. Others are anonymously dismissed with some such harmless phrase as 'now living quietly in the country' or 'retired from government service with a high honour'.

The prize exhibit is Professor Pigou, a Cambridge economist of the greatest distinction and, it seems, 'the most secret and in many respects one of the most effective Russian agents in Britain for fifty years'.

. . . Similar treatment is accorded to other victims. The Apostles, a private discussion group at Cambridge, emerge as a Communist cell. Stalin was involved in the Battle of Sidney Street in 1911. The 'enigmatic' G. M. Trevelyan secured the appointment of Guy Burgess at the BBC by telephoning the Director. Deacon is adroit in having things both ways. If a man was or ever had been a member of the Communist Party, this proves that he was a Russian agent. If he had never been a member of the Communist Party, this proves that he was an undercover Russian agent. Thus Bernal comes into the first category, Patrick Blackett into the second:

> By far the most shifty and ambivalent pro-Soviet journalists were Kingsley Martin and Alexander Werth. They are still held in high regard by the literary, as distinct from the journalistic, establishment.

Maurice Dobb comes out strongly – 'one of the ablest, shrewdest and most convincing propagandists of the Soviet cause'. At Cambridge he organized 'a left-wing cult', which included Dr Roy Pascal, H. J. Habbakuk, Piero Sraffa, Professor Eric Hobsbawm, Hugh Sykes Davies and William Empson. Anyone acquainted with academic life will relish the nonsense of this list.

The Oxford connection, it seems, was 'not only slighter than that at Cambridge, but certainly subtler and far more ambivalent'. Many of the Oxford fellow-travellers 'live on as members of the Establishment, supremely confident they can never be faulted'. They include Denis Healey, Christopher Hill, Professor Hyman Levy and, of course, Tom Driberg.

I am deeply hurt at having been left out. Tom Driberg and I were the entire Communist Party in Oxford during the mid-twenties. I went to Russia for a month in 1925 and visited the horse fair at Nijni Novgorod. In 1929 the Austrian police impounded my passport at the request of the British consul; though I received an apology, I never received an explanation. In 1945 the BBC Board of Governors held a special meeting to consider a talk I had given on 'The Return of Russia as a Great Power'. In 1947 I was denounced in Zagreb as a premature Titoist. My diplomatic history is used as a textbook in Soviet and satellite universities. I have played solo whist with Harry Pollitt. In 1951 I spent a weekend with Donald Maclean at the house of, as he now is, Sir Nicholas Henderson. I was a prominent member of the Campaign for Nuclear Disarmament. I opposed British entry into the EEC. Surely I deserved a few words of smear.

In the sixties uplift and propaganda often came from the disciples of fashionable academics – Marshall Mcluhan, Herbert Marcuse, and the guru of drug culture, Dr Timothy Leary. It seemed that his verbal broadsides (*The Politics of Ecstasy*) had a counter-productive effect on one reviewer, however, Peter Lomas in the *New Statesman*:

I am in a room, alone with a man who is shouting at me. He goes on and on, incessantly, sometimes raising his voice to a scream, never giving me time to think or answer. He regards me as a poor, misguided creature, who lives in darkness and confusion, and he is determined to do something about this, to offer me a remedy that will bring me wisdom and happiness for the rest of my days.

For a moment I think I understand what he's about: he's trying to sell me an encyclopedia. But, no, it seems he's not very keen on books and old-fashioned stuff like that. Moreover, what he is trying to give me is, in fact, very small and he is – literally – attempting to shove it down my throat. It is a pill (though not, apparently, The Pill). What puzzles me most, when I can summon up enough resistance to think, is why he believes this pill will be so good for me when it appears to have been so bad for him. If it gives peace and happiness, why is he screeching? If it induces love, why does he not love me, instead of shouting at and through me in this way? I begin to feel more and more ill and look for ways of escape.

No, the acid didn't go sour on me. I'm just trying to convey the experience of reading a book by Timothy Leary.

By the end of the sixties veteran swingers were beginning to write their memoirs – masterpieces of trendiness such as Jeff Nuttall's *Performance Art* and Richard Neville's *Playpower*. These contained scenic effects akin to watching a skin flick in a bad print:

I ask her home, she rolls a joint and we begin to watch the mid-week TV movie. . . Comes the Heinz Souperday commercial, a hurricane fuck, another joint. . .

Mervyn Jones didn't take to this sort of thing when he ploughed through *Playpower* for the *New Statesman*:

This coarse, shallow and nasty book is not, I repeat, the voice of a generation. There used to be a crack about nations that go from barbarism to decadence and skip civilization. Mr Neville is now twenty-nine and it may also be possible to pass from childishness (of which marked effects remain) to cynical and bad-tempered middle age without being young.

Propaganda from another quarter was provided by the ubiquitous Arianna Stassinopoulos whose book Alan Watkins reviewed in the *Spectator* under the heading 'Windbagging', finishing thus:

This is a vulgar, trivial, pretentious and inaccurate book. It is also profoundly offensive morally. The late Anthony Crosland once memorably wrote that, while a puritan governance of one's own life was admirable, a pharisaical attitude to the lives of others was abominable. I know nothing of the state of Miss Stass's soul, but I do know that she is famous (though for what precisely is less certain), is considered attractive by many, has numerous friends, appears frequently on television and resides in comfort in a large flat near Sloane Square. She received an expensive education; generally life has treated her well. There is something disgusting in her sneers at those housewives who consider a washing-machine a necessity. By the way: the entire thrust of R. H. Tawney's socialism was opposed to Fabian managerialism. And the Northcote–Trevelyan reforms were certainly not implemented by Gladstone in 1833, when the lad had just left Oxford.

Punching a windbag is a good way for journalists to work out.

Useless Information

Much energy is expended in writing books whose purpose is obscure and whose likely audience can only be guessed at. Dorothy Parker once looked at a book of useless information which was pitched at a market that would have had to combine two incompatibles; snobbery and a sense of humour:

I got a book called *Favourite Jokes of Famous People* and settled down to read it, memorize its gems, and repeat them at select gatherings. And from the time of the world première of my recital until this very living moment, I haven't had an evening off my hands.

It was doubtless ill-advised for me, a very tyro – or, at least, a pretty tyro – as a raconteuse to start off with the selection given in the book as the favourite of Mr Bruce Barton, a selection which, by the way, could scarcely be classified as 'The Joke Nobody Knows'. Thus does Mr Barton begin his chosen story:

In the pre-prohibition days two young men set forth one evening from Detroit in an automobile. Awakening the next morning, after a somewhat tempestuous night, they found themselves parked in front of a large building which they assumed to be a hotel but was in fact a sanitarium. The proprietor of the institution was not only a vegetarian, but a zealous member of a religious order.

That, you will admit, is a rough start for the amateur storyteller. You have to remember practically everything except your stance. Pre-prohibition, Detroit, two young men, automobile, next morning, hotel which wasn't a hotel, proprietor who was not only a vegetarian but a member of a religious order – that's advanced stuff. It is perhaps sufficient to say that I made a fool of the anecdote. I represented the two young men as coming from Fort Wayne.

In the USA there has also been a torrent of books on How To Do Things. America, wrote Dwight Macdonald in the 1950s, was 'in the grip of a how to mania comparable to the dancing mania that swept over Europe in the fourteenth century'. In his survey of the field he frivolously observed that no one had yet written *How To Do Time: A Handbook for Prospective Convicts*, but was immediately corrected by a reader who wrote to say that a pamphlet of that nature was the first thing you were given on entering a federal penitentiary. It contained guidance on how to do your time 'in a constructive manner'.

Works of reassurance and self-improvement always constitute a vast category. Macdonald examined some of those aimed at the teenage market:

Betty Cornell leads the way – at least for the recent crop – with *Betty Cornell's Teen-Age Popularity Guide*, which starts, '*Hi!* I'm Betty Cornell,' and, like many of these how-to-be-a-woman books, is common sense chromium-plated with charm. In a resolutely bright and chatty way, it covers topics like skin problems, money, and personality ('First of all, let me say that every girl can be attractive'). Whether following Miss Cornell's precepts would make an adolescent girl popular, I don't know, but I suspect that she would become a terrible prig (an up-to-date prig, of course), all glamorized and personalized and adjusted, gay (but not frivolous), serious (but not too), intelligent (but not 'intellectual'), and with a pasteurized smile that would curdle your blood as Miss Cornell's on the jacket of her book curdles mine. . .

A compendium by Hill Edwards called *Personality Pointers* is now available – over-priced at thirty-five cents – and it seems to have everything, including 'Pointers to the Light Touch', which begins, 'The third field in which we desire to develop a daily rhythm of habits pertains to those qualities which make us different from everyone else.' It also contains a four-page list of 'Important Paintings Worthy of Study', and 'The Self-Searcher', a twenty-three page list of questions to ask oneself, which, with some omissions, runs like this: 'Do I know what *my* colors are? Do I make my vowels sing? Am I direct, sincere, and simple? Do I know the proper way to sit in and rise from a chair? Am I lovable? Am I original? Am I valiant? Have I made a legal will? Do I know where it is? Do I hang up my clothes as soon as I take them off? Do I sew a snap-fastener onto each end of a piece of tape about an inch and half long, and sew these tapes in the center of all shoulder seams? Am I so poised, so on my center, so innately joyous that life cannot sway me this way and that? Do I always keep my feet close together?

Progressing through the age-groups, Macdonald also examined the enormous body of marriage Howto's, mostly, he observed, devoted to the achievement of 'Success'. This seemed to take as much of a material form as an emotional one, or, in the words of one counsellor, the inimitable Dr Hirsch, his star patient is now the possessor of 'a charming lady', a wife who 'graces a pretentious home in which they entertain in style'.

'The ageing,' pursues Macdonald moving on up the scale, 'have never lacked for good advice':

Mr Giles is a veteran howto writer (one of his earlier works is *How to Retire – and Enjoy it!*, which should be carefully distinguished from Raymond P. Kaighn's *How to Retire and Like It*), and, consequently, a master of jaunty prose. Stylistically, at least, his chapters live up to their titles, some of which are 'Star Wagons', 'Shake Off Your Handcuffs'! 'For Wider Horizons, Keep Learning!', and 'There's Always Collecting!' Jerome Kaplan's *A Social Program for Older People*, a manual on organizing social activities for what are delicately termed 'senior citizens', sounds practical and authoritative. Having aged enjoyably, senior citizens face one last problem. So far, nothing has come out bluntly titled *How to Die*, but this gap will doubtless soon be filled, as others have been.* Meanwhile, we must make do with the Westminster Press's *And Peace at the Last*, described as 'the new Pastoral Aid Book to help the minister and the parishioner come to an understanding and acceptance of death', and Philosophical Library's *The Disposal of the Dead*, a British work which covers 'The Law of Burial', 'A Short History of Cremation', 'The Law and Practice of Exhumation', and other topics and which, because of the usual English gift for antiquarian anecdote, often makes lively reading.

It is indeed a varied and fascinating genre comprising everything from the amazingly specific (*Principles of Church Ushering*) to the amazingly ambitious (*How To Be A Woman*).

* Mr Alan M. Fern of Chicago has since informed me that the gap was filled five centuries ago with *Ars Moriendi*, or *The Art of Dying*, which ran through some eight editions in the fifteenth century.

Perhaps the most promising title for those requiring a short cut to fame and fortune was Ludwig Borne's *The Art of Becoming An Original Writer in Three Days*. His recipe was so simple that it is surprising nobody had thought of it before. 'Take several sheets of paper and for three days in succession. . . . write down everything that comes to your mind.' 'There is no evidence that [James] Joyce ever read' Borne's little essay, says Macdonald, 'but its spirit is his.'

The Problem and the Probe

The gathering of useless information to be enshrined in socio-logical tomes pregnant with statistics has attracted a certain amount of mockery from sceptical reviewers. 'Strix' in the *Spectator* was once puzzled by the aims of a work by Dr Dennis Chapman:

POUFFES DON'T COUNT

'The ultimate disadvantage [of the results of quantitative social research] is that they have little appeal to the popular reader and are thus unsaleable.' This somewhat wistful note is struck by Dr Dennis Chapman in the preface to *The Home and Social Status*. The words acted as a challenge. One has read prefaces in which authors described their books as humble, modest, inconsequential or un-pretentious; in many cases it would have been much nearer the truth to call them unsaleable, but I never remember this term actually being used. Earlier in the preface Dr Chapman quotes the view of 'many influential sociologists' that 'in no science is the pursuit of objective knowledge more futile than in social science'. This is presumably done to make sure that nobody will be such a fool as to suppose that the book, though perhaps rather heavy going, is worthwhile.

Dr Chapman's object, as I imperfectly understand it, is to express social status in terms of linoleum, or possibly the other way round. Sometimes he is quite easy to follow; nothing could be more lucid and less controversial than such statements as 'the house is built primarily to provide shelter from the elements' or 'there appears to be a sharp contrast between the provision made for the child in the first year of its life and afterwards'. Passages like these build up suspense, causing us to wonder what is coming next.

What does come next is apt to be a bit abstruse, e.g., 'The procedures involve the assumption that social status is measurable and can be regarded as a continuous variate. If this can be at least tentatively accepted, the method provides for a study of the effect of postulating a different distribution for "resultant status". For example, research may show that, in the present economy, the distribution of status is positively skewed rather than normal.' As far as I can see, it is anybody's guess what this means. It is a relief to get back to *terra firma* and be told that 'horse riding has become an essential accomplishment for the girl in the upper middle classes, an interesting example of the process whereby the successful city dweller seeks to acquire status by adopting obsolete rural pursuits'. It is clear that Dr Chapman does not give a damn what kind of review he gets in *Horse and Hound*.

Occasionally his pages throb with human interest. In Table 69, for instance ('The Proportions of Middlesbrough People who would Choose to live amongst the Same and Different Groups of People to Those amongst whom they at Present Live'), it is heart-warming to discover that those who wish to live among the same kind of people vastly outnumber those who yearn for a change of milieu, and that far and away the commonest reason given for this wish was 'I like them, etc.' (May one venture to hope that in any future edition the 'etc.' will be omitted? It makes the revelation somehow less luminous.)

Dr Chapman has evolved a clever, but to me incomprehensible, system of giving marks for social status and also – to chattels and furnishings – for performance, display and culture. This is what you score if you have the following objects in your living-room:

Object	Performance	Display	Culture	Total Score
A Dining Suite	4	0	0	4
No Dining Suite*	7	0	0	7
A Television Set	4	2	3	9
No Radio	0	0	0	0
A Grand Piano	4	0	6	10
Any Other Piano or none	4	0	0	4
Flowers and Plants	3	1	2	6
No Flowers or Plants	3	0	0	3

* 'The absence of a dining-room suite in the living-room implies a separate room for eating, an arrangement of living associated with higher social status.' But it may also, surely, imply that you have flogged the stuff.

There are a lot of things that puzzle me about these extracts from Table 44. Why does a grand piano get 0 for Display and why does no piano at all get 4 for Performance, which is the same as a television set gets? Why – but there is no time to ask questions while we still have the social gradations of curtains to consider; here, starting with straight-and-pelmet (*très snob*, total score 8), we descend through straight-only-or-straight-and-valance and net-and-straight-and-valance-or-pelmet   to   net-only-or-net-and-straight. Already we have (have we not?) the feeling that we are getting somewhere.

Here and there one gains the impression that some of the occupants of the dwellings whose social status Dr Chapman and his devoted field-workers were evaluating attempted to offer a resistance as vain as it was ill coordinated. In a series of tables showing a comparison of the Different Types of Sewing Machine (also Sideboard, Fireplace, Occasional Furniture, Radio, and so on) in the Main Living-Room, we come suddenly on a laconic footnote to the table dealing with Ashtrays. In as many as 19 per cent of the smallest houses this vital information 'proved impossible to obtain from the informants' description *in cases where access to the dwelling was not obtained*'. (My italics.) And in Liverpool, for no stated reasons, forty-one families 'moved house during the survey'. They were tracked down and given a Mean Indices Score.

There is no record of any field-workers either becoming casualties or going native. Their standing orders (which Dr Chapman has wisely printed in an appendix) lay down the detailed and rigid rules under which they may allot marks for social status. Books, for instance, are very properly 'classified by the width of shelf space occupied' and not by what sort of books they are. 'If only a few books (three or more) are to be found lying about the room, this counts as under six feet.' So don't fool yourself that you will improve your position in society by having a single copy of *War and Peace* negligently disposed upon the pouffe (or pouffé, as Dr Chapman calls it in a stern warning to his minions that it does not count as Occasional Furniture).

Absorbing though in many ways it is, this book makes heavy demands upon the reader, and after grappling with it I must confess to feeling (if I may borrow one of the author's happiest phrases) 'positively skewed rather than normal'. Before going out to restore my energies at one of those Food Supplement Distribution Centres of which Table 93 gives us a tempting glimpse, it remains only to note one odd coincidence. If Beachcomber, or some other anti-social wag, had invented the researches of which I have attempted to give some account, it is at least an even chance that he would have described them as having been carried out in Bootle. A lot of Dr Chapman's were.

Of course many of the best probes are sexual. By far the best publicized and most humorous in the seventies was Lord Longford's report on pornography. Bernard Levin had a few comments on it:

The mountains have laboured, and brought forth – well, not a mouse, though it amounts to very little, nor an elephant, though it is extremely large and shortsighted, nor a donkey, though it makes more noise than sense, nor a flatworm, though it does not seem to be sure in which direction it is going, nor a cat, though it will not take advice, nor a tortoise, though it is slow, nor a parrot, though it repeats what it does not understand, nor a hippopotamus, though it excites mirth.

What the mountains have brought forth is a Tigger, which was much given, as I recall, to pulling the tablecloth to the ground, wrapping itself up in it amid the broken crockery, rolling about the room going 'Worra-worra-worra', and finally sticking its head out and asking, 'Have I won?'

Far from it. This vast brantub, the contents of which are a thousand parts chaff to one part wheat, is not only useless; it has effectively ruined the market for a serious study, by some such means as an academic team or a Royal Commission, of the problem (if there is one) of pornography. It is also dangerous, in that whatever the good intentions of those responsible for it, it will be used by the unthinking, the demagogic, the freedom-hating and the malevolent, to bolster their demands for further restrictions on publication, exhibition and performance.

The book has many faults, but two are crucial; one is methodological, the other conceptual. The first is the almost total absence of intellectual rigour in the way Lord Longford and his colleagues went about their work. Bits and pieces of statements, opinions, facts, misunderstandings and haphazard research, all of it desperately unscientific and hopelessly undigested, and most of it indiscriminately shovelled together by people clearly quite unskilled in such work, make up a document which at one moment can solemnly review a lot of unsolicited letters about a film (*Growing Up*) from people who had clearly not seen it; at another moment can, no less

solemnly, offer childishly elementary amateur psychology ('By nature man seeks to form a highly individualized bond. As a baby he
cries for attention, and though Freud . . .'); and at another moment
– indeed, at several other moments – can, faced with evidence
against its authors' preformed and immovable opinions, blandly
dismiss it. . .

In almost every possible way, the book is a mess. Pseudo-acad-
emic reports from sub-committees on such divisions of the group's
study as the law, sex education, broadcasting and books rub
shoulders with, for instance, one of Peregrine Worsthorne's mean-
dering Sunday essays, elegant paradoxes and all. A penetrating
comment on the erotic in literature, by Kingsley and Jane Amis (it
is pathetic to see how in other parts of the book this is several times
proudly paraded, it being almost the only thing of any genuine
distinction in the whole collection), is ruined by an addendum of
ramshackle foolishness, calling for a vast apparatus of control over
literature, in order to prevent unsuitable varieties ('Not unsuitable
because of anything, just unsuitable') from falling into the hands of
children. Pornography and obscenity are confused, distinguished,
confused again, distinguished again, until the reader's head swims
with the effort to look both ways at once. . . Statistics for venereal
disease, illegitimacy, etc. are trotted out with the unproven, and
indeed scarcely argued, assumption that they are caused by pornography. And the whole ragamadoglio ends, in a fine flourish of crazy
illogic, with a draft Obscene Publications Bill that would abolish
the defence of 'public good', thus at last making clear in so many
words what has been visible between the lines throughout, that
Lord Longford and his group are simply concerned to ban what
they find disgusting, even if what they find disgusting does more
good than evil.

Worse, however, than the muddled thinking, the slovenly organization, the rambling, confused and repeatedly untenable argument,
is the basic assumption on which the entire book rests, which is that
sexual pleasure is only obtainable, and certainly only permissible,
when accompanied by love. 'Sex only works properly,' says one of
those who wrote to the group, and whose views are quoted with
evident approval and agreement in the report, 'if the person you are
having it with is someone you care so deeply about that you will
stay around to raise the children who may come.'

. . . It is unlikely that those not professionally obliged to read the
whole book will be able to get to the end of it, but if they do (or if,

wisely, they start reading at page 460) they will find an enchanting Trojan Horse stabled there. Some of the committee's members, evidently, were troubled by the paucity of evidence one way or the other on the effects of pornography, and an expert psychologist, Mr Maurice Yaffe, from the Institute of Psychiatry, was commissioned to survey the available material. This he has done in a dispassionate, scholarly and meticulously documented forty pages, which come, after the heated amateurism of most of what has gone before, like rain upon the desert's dusty face.

His study effectively demolishes the whole of the preceding report, showing that there is very little evidence at all as to the effects of pornography, that the majority of what there is tentatively suggests that it does no harm, and that, in the final analysis, the Longford report on pornography is no more than an essay in dogmatism.

'One of the most insidious tendencies of recent years,' says Mr Jeremy Murray-Brown in a signed addendum to the report's section on sex education, 'is society's increasing reliance on so-called "expert" opinion in preference to natural common sense.' One might ask Mr Murray-Brown how he would like to have his appendix removed by a surgeon acting according to the precepts of natural common sense rather than expert knowledge, but leaving that aside, the call, implicit in his words, for more ignorance and prejudice and less knowledge and objectivity, is unmistakable. I can only say that Lord Longford and his group have responded to that call in full and generous measure.

Is Sex Necessary?

My considered opinion, after long reflection, is that whilst in many places the effect of *Ulysses* on the reader undoubtedly is somewhat emetic, nowhere does it tend to be an aphrodisiac. *Ulysses* may, therefore, be admitted to the United States.

So said John M. Woolsey, US District Judge, giving his decision after the prosecution of *Ulysses* for obscenity. It contrasts interestingly with the judgement of Justice Younger in a case where Elinor Glyn had brought an action for infringement of copyright in *Three Weeks*:

Copyright cannot exist in a work of a tendency so grossly immoral as this.

Admittedly, this was in 1915; but the bench has never been too good at interpreting the law when its susceptibilities have been upset by a book. Politicians are not much more reliable, and their pronouncements have the added ingredient which we first meet in biblical accounts of the Pharisees:

From the reports of a debate on the censorship of obscene literature in the United States Senate, March 1930. Senator Smoot of Utah: 'I did not believe there were such books printed in the world.' (Senator Smoot had brought, as exhibits, Robert Burns' *Poems* (unexpurgated edition), Balzac's *Contes Drolatiques*, Casanova's *Memoirs*, George Moore's *Story Teller's Holiday*, D. H. Lawrence's *Lady Chatterley's Lover*, *My Life and Loves*, by Frank Harris, and that Mrs Beeton's cookery book of love-making, the *Kama Sutra*.)
 'They are lower than the beasts. . . If I were a Customs Inspector, this obscene literature would only be admitted over my dead body. . . I'd rather have a child of mine use opium than read these books.' (Compare with this the yet more heroic declaration of our own Mr James Douglas. Mr Douglas would rather give a child prussic acid than allow it to read *The Well of Loneliness*. In an article

written at the time I offered to provide Mr Douglas with a child, a bottle of prussic acid, a copy of *The Well of Loneliness*, and – if he kept his word and chose to administer the acid – a handsome memorial in marble to be erected wherever he might appoint, after his execution. The offer, I regret to say, was not accepted.)

Senator Blease of South Carolina was more eloquent even than Senator Smoot. True, he was not prepared to give children opium and prussic acid in preference to improper literature, but he was quite ready to 'see the democratic and republican form of government for ever destroyed, if necessary to protect the virtue of the womanhood of America . . . The virtue of one little sixteen-year-old girl is worth more to American than every book that ever came into it from any other country . . . I love womanhood. Take from a government the purity of its womanhood and that government will be destroyed.'

Aldous Huxley was the reporter of these remarkable exhibitions of breast-beating. But attitudes of this kind are not confined to the old. Dorothy Parker found that students at Los Angeles State College, where she taught, disapproved of Steinbeck's *The Grapes of Wrath* on the grounds that it was 'too dirty'. After Steinbeck was awarded the Nobel Prize, however, Mrs Parker recalled that they 'behaved as if they had given it to him'.

Attitudes towards sexy writing usually depend on the packaging. Slick entertainments that do not question current social mores seldom attract the odium incurred by books of an aggressive social or political stance. An exception to this rule however was Paul Johnson's apopletic onslaught against James Bond in his 1958 *New Statesman* article headed 'Sex, Snobbery and Sadism'. He recounted the plot with rhetorical venom and summed up Ian Fleming's work thus:

There are three basic ingredients in *Dr No*, all unhealthy, all thoroughly English: the sadism of a schoolboy bully, the mechanical, two-dimensional sex-longings of a frustrated adolescent, and the crude snob-cravings of a suburban adult.

Johnson's critique had the flavour of a sermon on 'the end of civilization as we know it', and caused not a flicker in the onward impetus of Bond mania. His objections were, in any case, as much political and social as to do with sexual morality.

More specific yet far more limited in its appeal was a book which in 1978 was reviewed by Alan Watkins in the *Spectator*. This was *Sex Law* by Tony Honoré:

The publishers claim this is the first time the law about (or, as the lawyers would say, 'relating to') sex has been dealt with comprehensively. Maybe it is. I still find it difficult to know to whom Professor Honoré's book is addressed. Will learned counsel say to the Court of Appeal: 'There is an interesting clarification of this point, if it would assist your Lordships, in *Honoré on Sex*'? Somehow I doubt it. In his chapter 'Offenders and Trials' the Regius Professor has a marvellous flight of fancy whereby he imagines his book being earnestly consulted by accused persons: *This chapter gives a brief survey of the legal position of sex offenders, their numbers, trials, punishments and treatments. The information may be of interest, especially to those who find themselves charged with a sex offence and want to know what to expect.*

'What do you reckon's the going rate for indecent assault, Fred?'

'Three years, I reckon, squire, seeing as you're over twenty-one and she was fifteen. Looked it up in *Honoré* just now.'

And another work which might just qualify as both instructional and descriptive was Dr Alex Comfort's highly illustrated *The Joy of Sex*. Auberon Waugh reviewed it in the *New Statesman*, though, characteristically, he took the opportunity to clout some fellow journalists who had annoyed him:

SEX WITH SAUCE

Lovers who can communicate only through the agony column of a newspaper have always touched a chord. The advertisements themselves are so reticent that one longs to learn the full story, even if it is the corny old explanation of a wife sending loving messages to her husband who refuses to talk over his newspaper at breakfast. Now the *Sunday Times* has introduced what can only be seen as a refinement of this art form, where messages of a personal nature which husbands and wives are too shy to discuss together in private can be exchanged publicly in the guise of a general dissertation on sex. The pioneers in this field of human communications are that brave and admirable couple Jill Tweedie and Alan Brien.

When Brien and Tweedie married late last year, *Private Eye* ran a special cut-out wedding supplement decorated with bells and Cupids: *For a few precious moments the cares and worries of crisis-torn Britain were forgotten. Men and women everywhere put aside their differences to share the magic of what they are calling the Wedding of the Century.* Even those who could not share the *Eye*'s euphoria felt a certain quiet satisfaction that such a resolute campaigner for women's rights as Tweedie should have been brought at last to the registry office by such a one as Brien. In the words of St Paul: 'But if they cannot contain let them marry; for it is better to marry than to burn.' (I Corinthians vii, 9.) One would be less than human if one failed to wonder how they have made out since.

The answer was given through a brief editorial announcement in last week's *Sunday Times*: 'Jill Tweedie and Alan Brien give their verdict on *The Joy of Sex* as a couple for whom sex is already a joy.' In other words, they are making out very well. So far so good. The book they discuss is a rather depressing sex manual edited by Dr Alex Comfort and written in the illiterate, folksy style one associates with holiday camps and *Blue Peter*: 'Sex play with long hair is great because of its texture.' It is full of hints for 'mind-blowing turn-ons' like this suggestion for using your partner's armpit in something called *axillary intercourse*:

> *Put her left arm round your neck and hold her right hand behind her with your right hand. She will get her sensations from the pressure against her breasts, helped by your big toe pressed to her clitoris if she wants it.*

From this treasury of helpful advice, Tweedie and Brien extract whatever seems appropriate to their needs. Thus from Tweedie we hear of a section which 'frowns gently and advisedly on the forward male's "direct grab at the clitoris" and advocates, again advisedly, "a lot more attention being devoted to the breasts than the average man may deem necessary" '.

I hope that Brien has received this message loud and clear and we won't have to return to the matter again. Tweedie praises the book because the writers do not 'sternly insist on fore-play', averring that 'females, contrary to today's sexual encyclicals, do not always want to wait for it, and one of the greatest aphrodisiacs – not enough emphasized here – is the overpowering desire of the man to do what he has to do'. The message for Brien may be plain enough, but I think she does Dr Comfort an injustice. This particular propensity is covered in the section called 'Quickies'.

Tweedie's loudest complaint is at first glance an alarming one: 'The only real criticism I have of this book is its under-emphasis on sex in the head – which is where for my money it all starts and very nearly finishes.' In fact, one of the longest and most depressing passages in the book, inelegantly called 'Mouth Music', describes every reasonable aspect of this approach to sex. What else must the unfortunate Brien be expected to start on and nearly finish in order to get Tweedie's money – her ears? But on reflection I see that what she must really be saying is that sex is nicer to think about than actually do. So the final recipe for Sex With Tweedie would seem to be this: in the first place just think about it but, if you must do something, mind what you grab and get it over quickly.

Brien tells us that he likes to wash beforehand but his preference is for something 'dark and strange and frightening and unthinking and incredible'. I don't know how Tweedie measures up to his other demands, but in its *unthinking* aspect this ticket seems the exact opposite to Tweedie's cerebral approach.

None of this explains how two intelligent people like Brien and Tweedie can take a ludicrous book like Alex Comfort's *The Joy of Sex* seriously. The explanation may lie in a particular strain of metropolitan life which is well illustrated in another passage of the book under review. It describes itself as a Gourmet Guide to Love-making, elsewhere as a Cordon Bleu Guide, and is full of gastronomic imagery – sections are called *Starters*; *Main Courses*; *Sauces and Pickles*, etc. But when our lovers actually get into a restaurant they appear to have very little interest in food:

> In a restaurant, in these days of tights, one can surreptitiously remove a shoe and sock, reach over and keep her in almost continuous orgasm with all four hands in view on the table and no sign of contact . . . She has less scope, but can learn to masturbate him with her two big toes.

Yes, yes, but what about the food? Last time I saw Brien was at a *Private Eye* lunch when I am glad to say he managed to keep his big toe to himself. To judge from his later comments in the *Sunday Times* he did not enjoy the meal much, creating little pools of embarrassment all around him by asking people: 'Do you *really* think I'm boring or do you just say you do?' But the chief awkwardness came when a voice – it may have been my own, obviously late in the meal – rose above the others announcing that its owner wouldn't really mind if he never had another orgasm in his life. For the first time in our acquaintance I saw Alan Brien look shocked.

Freebie and the Freeloader

The most spectacularly non-investigative articles in the press are the so-called 'previews' of new motorcar models. Most appear to have been written by the publicity department of the car's manufacturer and simply signed by the 'reviewer' before being set up in type. Gavin Lyall's multi-purpose car review has a horrid ring of familiarity:

Over the last few days I have been privileged to test the new car which, I can confidently predict, will be the toast of this year's Motor Show: the new English Car Manufacturers' Britannicar Plebs. In this, the first of ECM's new range of 1000 cc models (it will be followed shortly by the new Midlands TiniMidget and the Valhalla Venus, built on the same engine and bodywork but each easily distinguishable by the discreet medallion behind the front bumper), the designers have, wisely I think, avoided too violently revolutionary changes and concentrated on producing a family car that is identifiably of the unique Britannicar breed.

Eschewing the use of new (and possibly untrustworthy) light alloys, the Plebs has an engine which the older motorist will recognize as a tried and true friend. It is, in fact, basically the 2500 cc side-valve engine that ECM developed not long before the war, fitted with cylinder liners to scale it down to 1000 cc.

On the actual car I drove there were a few minor roof leaks and an occasional – very occasional – back axle failure, but one must remember that this is a new model and that these little deficiencies will most probably be rectified after the first few thousand have been produced. And otherwise I found the Plebs almost impossible to fault.

On the road the steering is light and flexible, giving the comfortable impression of controlling the front wheels through sponge rubber; the car may, however, be initially a little difficult to steer accurately, since the true width is somewhat greater than it appears from the inside. The back wheels were given, on a few occasions, to breaking away sharply, but doubtless this could be corrected by a little additional weight deposited in the boot.

The acceleration is essentially gentle, so that there is no chance of the car running away with the driver, but one reaches peak revs in top at a remarkably low speed. Some owners might find an additional two notches in the seat slide useful, although this could possibly eliminate the leg-room at the back. Still, few families would use the back for other than children, since the re-styled body (by Montesi of Ostia) has necessarily meant some sacrifices in head-, hip- and foot-room at the rear. The dashboard, attractively styled of metal grained to resemble fresh pine, has no oil-pressure, dynamo-charge or light-beam indicators to distract the eye. The controls for lights, starter, choke and windscreen wipers are neatly grouped together as identical knobs, any one being easily selected at random, and the floor-mounted dipswitch is conveniently placed so that it may be used by either driver or passenger. Drivers with shorter arms than mine may have to lean a little farther than I did in reaching the gear lever, but once grasped it goes easily into most gears; there is very little movement demanded for a change from top into reverse or vice versa.

The interior styling is modishly clean, but owners who prefer a richer finish will doubtless choose the *de luxe* version with its ash-trays, stainless-steel mascot and a remarkable variety of chrome decorations. Facilities are provided for fitting an interior light, opening rear and quarter windows, a boot handle, or, indeed, any other of the extraordinary range of extras which are included as standard on the version for more self-indulgent export markets. The plastic interior trim provides an imaginative saving in weight and I found it not easy to tear accidentally.

Exterior design is always a matter of personal taste; I found the Plebs' new styling extremely attractive, being cleverly designed to give an external impression of size to contrast with the essential cosiness of the interior. The bumpers are pleasingly delicately styled without being obtrusive and, since both the head and tail lights project beyond them, they are unlikely to suffer damage in use. Under normal conditions the boot both opens and closes satisfactorily and a well-known luggage firm is shortly to market a range of suitcases that will go into it.

When confronted with so attractive and versatile a car one hesitates to carp. Nevertheless, I feel bound to point out a sad lapse on the part of the manufacturers. The firm's medallion, while small and unobtrusively placed, seems to me – and I think this is an opinion that will be shared by others – to be unfortunately ill-designed and impracticable when studied closely. However, rectifying this will make the new Britannicar Plebs what it aims to be: a comfortable, up-to-date family car of exceptional all-round ability – and well able, I believe, to re-establish British supremacy in building cars for the home market.

Is Your Journey Really Necessary?

Bogus travel writing is not as much in vogue now as in the twenties and thirties. Then, volumes of purple prose, some of which read like a demented seedsman's catalogue or outpourings of journalists after a good lunch, rolled off the presses. Italy, Greece and Spain were sitting ducks for the simile-shooting hack. The genre is not entirely dead as Kingsley Amis showed in his review of *A Rose for Winter* by Laurie Lee:

The experienced reader will know what to do with a book whose blurb announces, as if in recommendation, its author's claim to 'the enchanted eye . . . of a true poet', but the reviewer must act differently. His part is to soldier grimly on, trying not to mind too much the absence of a verb in the opening sentence, the incessant din of adjective and poetical ('the scarred and crumpled valleys', 'the oil-blue waters'), the full close of the first paragraph, mannered as any Ciceronian *esse videatur*: 'And from a steep hillside rose a column of smoke, cool as marble, pungent as pine, which hung like a signal over the landscape, obscure, imperative and motionless.' (The effect is a little marred through having been anticipated, three sentences earlier, by a cadential 'raw, sleeping and savage'.) Another item on the list of things to try not to mind too much is the prevalence of lists – cf. Mr Auden's *Spain*, which Mr Lee has perhaps been cf.-ing too – like 'the bright façades . . . the beggars . . . the vivid shapely girls . . . the tiny, delicate-stepping donkeys', and so on; and yet another one is the 'striking' image – 'fragrant as water' – which at first sight seems to mean almost nothing, and upon reflection and reconsideration is seen to mean almost nothing. One way of summing up this book would be to call it a string of failed poems – failed not-very-good-poems too, for whoever said that bad poetry is much more like poetry than good poetry is, was in the right of it there.

This kind of objection, however, though compulsory for the

reader of almost any highbrow travel book, is here purely trifling.
The really telling strictures emerge from a mulling-over of what Mr
Lee actually reveals to us about Andalusia. The figure of the narrator
himself, having terrific fun with a drum in a wedding procession,
carrying *two* guitars 'everywhere', carefully recording every pass
made at his wife, drinking like mad at a party in a telephone
exchange while the switchboard lights 'twinkled unheeded' (not too
good for people who wanted to ring the doctor), can safely be left
on one side. One might even haul to the other side the bull-fighting
question, although the author's taste for 'the sharp mystery of blood'
will remain unshared in some quarters, where, in addition, the use
of the phrase 'the moment of truth' will appear a little worse than
naïf, and to upbraid a bull for having no grace or honour or
'vocation for martyrdom' will appear a lot worse; if we enjoined
these duties upon a bull, he would not understand us. But the least
attractive part of Mr Lee's portrayal of Spain is his portrayal of
Spaniards, so far as this can be debarnacled from rhetoric, generalization and rhapsody. The effect is not what he evidently intends;
where he seeks to show us gaiety, mere instability or hooliganism
emerges, unselfconsciousness is detectable as coxcombry or self-
pity, while the gift attributed to Andalusians of greeting others'
misfortune with a shrug or a grin is neither mature nor admirable.
I am sure these people are not as bad as all that, just as I am sure
that they are not in touch with the 'pure sources of feeling' and the
'real flavours' of life, whatever these entities may be; Coleridge put
Wordsworth right on peasants a long time ago. Perhaps too many
people in England do watch television, or do they watch it too much
of the time? Anyway, *nostalgie de la boue* is not the answer; it is silly
to sleep on straw in the inn yard if you can get hold of a bed; and
while it is no doubt better to be gay and have sores than to be un-
gay and not have sores, it is better still to be fairly gay and not have
sores.

Amis's piece was entitled 'Is the Travel Book Dead?'; but
despite Laurie Lee's attempts to kill it off, it survives, though
increasingly elbowed aside by guides. Somewhat of a mixed
blessing are the occasional guides written in that twilight
linguistic zone between English and some other language.
Like this, for instance, in the *Guide to Pompeii* which Daniel
George received as a Christmas present:

Always at left there is a third little bedroom, in which one observes a little picture with cocks, and upon a pile, a little love upon a cray-fish . . . In the triclinium are three paintings: Ganimede sleeping, Apollo seated triing on denudating Dafnes, and Paris in the behold of Mercury announcing the arrival of the three Goddesses. The inscription OTIOSIS LOCUS HIC NON EST; DISCEDE MORATOR is translated 'This is not a place for lazies; thou, who stopest, go away.'

Which is reminiscent of Gerald Hoffnung's Parisian hotel brochure claiming 'a French widow in every bedroom'.

Far more ambitious, linguistically speaking, was a phrase-book discovered by Richard Boston where the English had been added by someone whose acquaintance with the language was limited, apparently, to a not very reliable dictionary:

AS SHE IS SPOKE

A French–Portuguese phrase-book, *O Novo Guia da Conversacão em frances e portuguez* by José da Fonseca, was published in Paris in 1836. It was a thorough and conscientious volume that worked its way systematically from the parts of the body to familiar phrases, dialogues, anecdotes, idioms and proverbs. The text was in two parallel columns, one of French and one of Portuguese. The book did sufficiently well to be reprinted in 1853, and perhaps it was this success that gave someone the idea of adding English to the book. This was accordingly done, and the trilingual edition appeared in 1855. This is where the odd bit starts.

The man responsible for adding the columns of English was called Pedro Carolino. I have been unable to discover any external evidence that might point to the nature of his character or circumstances: these can only be guessed at from the published work. He must have had considerable nerve, or else a quite remarkable opinion of his own abilities, to have talked Fonseca into taking him on as his collaborator, for it is at once apparent that he knew not a word of English.

The flavour of Pedro Carolino's approach to the language of Shakespeare may be indicated by his Dialogue 17, called 'To inform oneself of a person':

How is that gentleman who you did speak by and by?
Is a German.
I did not think him Englishman.
He is of the Saxony side.

He speaks the french very well.
Tough he is German, he speaks so much well italyan, french,
spanish and english, that among the Italyans, they believe him
Italyan, he speak the frenche as the Frenches himselves. The
Spanishmen believe him Spanishing, and the Englishes, English-
man. It is difficult to enjoy well so much several languages.

Not with Pedro in charge, it isn't. The book starts out fairly well,
and things start to look peculiar only when we come to the parts of
the body (including 'The inferior lip', 'The superior lip', 'Tha
marrow' and 'The reins'). They come seriously unstuck with 'De-
fects of the Body': 'A blind, A lame, One eyed, A hump, A rheum,
A bald, A ring worm, A scratch, A sprain, A left handed, An ugly,
One handed, A squint-eyed, A wen, A flat-nose, A deaf, The scurf,
A wart.'

The section on 'Degrees of Kindred' demonstrates Carolino's
most inspired linguistic discovery. For there, along with such zany
members of the family as 'The gossip', 'The gossip mistress', 'The
quater-grandfather' and 'The quater-grandmother', are 'A relation'
and 'An relation', 'A guardian' and 'An guardian', 'A widower' and
'An widow'. It is incredible to think that until Pedro Carolino came
along, no one, not even the Englishes themselves, had realized that
just like French and Portuguese and Spanish and Italyan, *English
is a language with genders.*

Once he's pointed it out to you it's obvious, isn't it, that 'A
relation' is masculine and 'An relation' feminine. A further step in
turning English into a Romance language is taken by making pos-
sessive pronouns agree with their accompanying nouns both in gender and number. Thus the word 'nails', being plural and feminine
(obviously), must be accompanied by a plural feminine pronoun –
the result being, for example, 'He has scratch the face with her
nails.'

The world of Pedro Carolino is one of endless fascination. In his
kitchen you find 'The skimming-dish', 'The potlid', 'The spunge',
'The spark' and 'The clout'. At night Pedro sleeps in a bed which
contains 'The bed wood', 'The bed battom', 'The feet's bed', 'The
pillar's bed' and 'The head's bed'. His dinner table would be set
with 'Some knifes', 'Some groceries' and 'Some crumb', and Pedro
would sit down there to eat 'Some black pudding, Some sugar-
plum, Some wigs, A chitterling sausages, A dainty dishes, A mutton
shoulder, a little mine, Hog fat, Some marchpanes, An amelet, A

slice steak' and (a true understanding here of the Englishes' taste in food) 'Vegetables boiled to a pap'.

This exotic fare would be washed down with 'Drinkings' – 'Some orgeat', perhaps, or some 'sirup' *or* 'sirop', or even 'Some paltry wine'.

Every time that it seems as though Pedro has exhausted all possibilities he comes up with a fresh insanity. Here are a few gems plucked from the treasure-chest of his 'Familiar Phrases':

> *Apply you at the study during that you are young.*
> *The room is filled with bugs.*
> *This wood is fill of thief's.*
> *Dry this wine.*
> *He has spit in my coat.*
> *He is valuable his weight's gold.*

Finally – one of Carolino's best inventions – a section called 'Idiotisms and Proverbs'. This includes such idiotisms from everyday English as:

> *In the country of blinds, the one-eyed men are kings.*
> *To do a wink to some body.*
> *He is not so devil as he is black.*
> *The stone as roll not, heap up not foam.*
> *After the paunch comes the dance.*
> *To craunch the marmoset.*
> *To come back at their muttons.*

The first edition of *O Novo Guia da Conversacão* with Carolino's contribution was published in Paris in 1865. Fonseca died in 1866, killed off, for all I know, by the discovery of what his co-author had perpetrated. Be that as it may, Carolino was undeterred and brought out another edition in 1869, omitting Fonseca' name (thereby revealing an ungrateful side to his character). Exactly when the book came to the attention of native English speakers (as opposed to those who learned their English from Pedro) is not known, but in 1883 Field and Tuer in London published a selection from the work with an introduction by James Millington. This was *English as she is Spoke*, a phrase taken from one of the 'Familiar Dialogues' which has since passed into the language on which Carolino committed such mayhem. Also in 1883 the complete work was published in the United States with an introduction by Mark Twain. *English as she is Spoke* went through ten editions in its first year, and has since been republished from time to time on both sides of the Atlantic.

Millington's helpful introduction points out the route by which Carolino arrived at some at least of his idiocies and idiotisms. It is clear that his raw materials consisted of Fonseca's Portuguese–French phrase-book and a French–English dictionary. Hence the abundance of gallicisms. Carolino's 'He laughs at my nose, he jest by me' makes better sense in French as 'Il me rit au nez, il se moque de moi', and of course idiotisms are French *idiotismes*, Portuguese *idioismos*. Since *mousse* in French means both moss and foam, Pedro inevitably picks the wrong one and comes up with 'The stone as roll heap up not foam', just as he confuses *pécher* and *pêcher* to produce 'He sin in trouble water' (perhaps his French wasn't so hot either).

These French origins make all the more remarkable the claims that Pedro makes for his work in the preface: 'A choice of familiar dialogues,' he says, 'clean of gallicisms and despoiled phrases, it was missing yet to studious Portuguese and Brazilian Youth.' Clean indeed! But suspicions that Carolino was a mountebank are settled by the words with which he ends his preface. They are curiously moving:

> *We expect then, who the little book (for the care what we wrote him, and for her typographical correction) that may be worth the acceptation of the studious persons, and especially of the Youth, at which we dedicate him particularly.*

'For the care what we wrote him . . .' as Mark Twain says, these are not the words of a fraud but of a good man, 'an honest man, a man whose conscience is at rest, a man who believes he has done a high and worthy work for his nation and his generation, and is well pleased with his performance'.

Royal Academy Lambasted

Attacking the Royal Academy has been a popular pastime for many years ever since Oscar Wilde observed that 'Varnishing is the only artistic process with which the Royal Academicians are thoroughly familiar!' In 1887 he reviewed an exhibition of parodies of RA art by Harry Furniss:

The annual attacks upon the Royal Academy, with which we are all so familiar, and of which most of us are so tired, have, as a rule, been both futile and depressing. The dull have cried out upon dullness, and the mediocre have denounced mediocrity, and each side has taken itself very seriously indeed. It is always a sorry spectacle when the Philistines of Gath go out against the Philistines of Gaza; so we are delighted to find that there has risen up, at last, a young and ruddy David to slay this lumbering Goliath of middle-class art. Punch has sent forth this Paladin of the Beautiful, the Gainsborough Gallery in Bond Street has given him his vantage ground of attack, and before Mr Harry Furniss' brilliant wit and clever satire the Royal Academicians are now in full retreat, and the opinion of the best military and artistic experts is, that they are rapidly retiring in the direction of Bayswater, a desolate tract of country lying to the north of the Park, where it would be almost impossible to find them, owing to the difficulty of obtaining guides. The final encounter, however, will not take place till the end of this week, when Goliath, who is now occupied in varnishing, the only artistic process with which he is thoroughly familiar, will display his forces in Burlington House, under the patronage of the British public, and under the protection of the British policeman.

Perhaps, however, it is somewhat fanciful to treat Mr Furniss' Exhibition as an attack on the Royal Academy at all. It would be more just to regard it as an attempt on Mr Furniss' part to show the Academician the possibilities of real beauty, and wonder, and pleasure that lie hidden in his work.

Take, for instance, the Tadema (No. 31). Here is all the archae-

ological detail so dear to this industrious painter; all the cups of
polished metal, the strangely embroidered robes and the richly
veined marbles, that exemplify so clearly the 'rights of properties'
in art; and the one thing that was wanting in Mr Tadema's work
has been added, the passionate interest in human life, and the power
to portray it. The two central figures are absolutely fascinating, and
where we yawned before, we now cannot help laughing. Charming,
too, in its delicate feeling for purity is Mr Horsley's 'Lady Godiva'
(No. 27). Nothing could possibly be more chaste than this draped
lay-figure, that rides through the empty streets of Coventry on a
blindfolded horse. The legs of the quadruped are carefully encased
in canvas bags, lest the modest should be offended; the heroine
carries a large umbrella, for fear of accidents; while the introduction
of Mr Horsley himself in the character of Peeping Tom is a masterpiece of autobiographical art. As for Sir Frederick Leighton, he
has rarely been seen to more advantage than in the specimen of his
work that Mr Furniss has so kindly provided for him. His 'Pygmalion and Galatea in the Lowther Arcadia' (No. 49) has all that
wax-doll grace of treatment that is so characteristic of his best work,
and is eminently suggestive of the President's earnest and continual
struggles to discover the difference between chalk and colour. Indeed, every Academician is thoroughly well represented. Mr Frith,
who has done so much to elevate painting to the dignity of photography, sends a series of five pictures, exemplifying that difference
between Virtue and Vice which moralists have never been able to
discover, but which is the real basis of the great Drury Lane school
of melodrama. Owing to the exigencies of space, only one of these
pictures has been hung, but the other four appear in the delightfully
illustrated catalogue, and never has the contrast between life, when
it is 'penny plain', and life, when it is 'twopence coloured', been so
forcibly put forward. The whole series is like the very finest platitude from the pulpit, and shows clearly the true value of didactic
art.

The passing of time has not softened the hearts of the
Academicians' detractors. In 1950 Graham Sutherland was
still describing the Academy as an 'out of date mammoth'.
His wife asked him when he was twenty-one and newly married, to show another picture there. This he did to humour
her, but the 'soirée', as he called it, was too much for him:

I got out the old car and put on a chauffeur's cap and drove my wife to the entrance. Then I hung about swapping stories with the other chauffeurs until they called 'Mrs Sutherland's car!'

In 1961 Burlington House had an exhibition of Sir Edwin Landseer; Geoffrey Grigson laid into it with a verbal bicycle chain:

. . . it would be hard to find a nastier painting than the one the exhibition begins with – 'Young Roebuck and Rough Hounds'. The head of the shot animal lolls down. A hound with a sob-look or love-look in its soft eyes licks the bleeding wound in the neck as if it were licking the hand of the Prince Consort. Other hounds in love (what with?) surround this tableau of having it both ways.

All is now set for concocting 'Dignity and Impudence' (which with a singular and I think quite disgusting cynicism or toadyism or ideological appeasement was sent in last year's exhibition of British art to Moscow and Leningrad). All is now set for the major pop pictures. Also for the slime of 'finish' which hardened on the soft subjects. Also for more than a century of pet dog droppings (the real memorial to Landseer's vision) fouling the pavements of London and New York.

Labelling Landseer a purveyor of 'blood and soft soap', he finished his piece by reminding readers of the artist's own comment on himself: 'If people only knew as much about painting as I do, they would never buy my pictures.'

An anonymous contributor to *Punch* endorsed Grigson's dogophobia: 'Would it not have been more appropriate during the present exhibition of Landseer's paintings to have styled the handbook a dogalogue instead of a catalogue?' Undaunted the Academy has proceeded on its way.

By 1979 things were not much better. Possibly worse. Alex Hamilton of the *Guardian* entitled a piece about the Summer Exhibition 'A Brush With The Art-Loving Public':

Over in the corner the mood was more ruffled, where dense mobs praised 'The 17th Wedding Anniversary: Our Bedroom at Mole End', a seven-sided *tour de force* by Anthony Green RA. It's the kind of picture that induces people to describe it to their companions beside them as if they were blind.

'Shes in the nude, yes, mother, except she's got shoes on.'

'I tell you, Herb, forty-nine people can't be wrong!'

'Three nudes, in fact.'
'They're all his wife, mother. One's looking at TV.'
'And two men.'
'They're either twins or the same man. One's bringing her coffee, the other one's in pyjamas flying in through the window with a present.'

Then Hamilton unwisely set about accosting likely looking people to inquire if they were exhibitors:

A young man with matted hair, and paint-bespattered trousers and canvas shoes. 'Exhibitor? Nah,' he growled. He strode off along the wall like a medieval swordsman, bouncing his comments off the canvases: 'Bad, bad, bad, bad, bad, bad.'

And:

An old bearded man in a wheelchair. No response except to point at his ears. Deaf too.

But it was all very English and sociologically informative. As for business:

Fruit sold well, and chickens, and items like corks and shoes, though nudes were slow.

'Dammit! Matilda, that's not the fish you were wearing yesterday!'

Bewitched, Bothered or Bewildered?

'Be impressionist by all means,' wrote W. P. Frith RA in 1888, 'but let your impressions be as complete and as true to nature as those received by the old masters. Let it not be possible for anyone to say of your impressions, as was said of some impressionist work now popular, "If nature made that impression upon the man, how much wiser he would have been if he had kept it to himself." '

Since this mild and cautious observation the invective against new trends in art has multiplied in volume at the same rate as art has thrown up new forms. The high tide of innovation on the one hand, and of abuse on the other, was reached in the late sixties and early seventies; these were the decades of 'Abstract Expressionism', 'Pop Art', 'Op Art', 'Minimal Art', 'Performance Art' and other forms.

But as far back as 1908 Epstein's nude statues erected for the BMA in the Strand had caused a scandal; one newspaper solemnly warned that they were 'a form of statuary which no careful father would wish his daughter, or no discriminating young man his fiancée, to see'. So did his 'Rima' in Hyde Park (1925). John Galsworthy didn't like it:

Since hearing from you I've seen the Epstein. My dear fellow! How can you use the word aesthetic in its connection? It's nothing but a piece of unrealized affectation. I confess it made me feel physically a little sick. The wretched woman has two sets of breasts and a hip joint like a merry thought.

(Epstein had a short way with uninformed critics. When the Soviet leaders visited Britain in the 1950s and Nikita Kruschev made a vigorous observation about the Epstein statue in New College Chapel, the sculptor sent him a telegram. It read: 'I stick to my business, which is art. Suggest you stick to yours, which is butchery.')

Another literary man, A. C. Benson, was puzzled by the latest art on show in 1917 and wrote this account of a visit to a gallery:

Then to an exhibition in Bond Street and saw Nicholson's 'Smuts', together with many other pictures – odd and pleasant, ugly and strange, bright and dull. A very odd one by Sims – three girls in white supporting an evidently intoxicated elderly lady in black; they are in a meadow laid with green linoleum; from a bush hard by projects a stiff human image, as if carved in camphor – and the whole is called 'Remembrance' . . .

The fashion now is for bright pictures. I begged Nicholson to explain things to me, but he laughed mockingly. 'What are we to

'I think it was along about here that he slipped a disc.'

'It says "Air Conditioning by Ajax".'

do with these?' I said in a room of pictures with colours like strong stenches. 'Well, not look at them,' says Nicholson.

Really opaque art criticism, however, goes into orbit post-Second World War, although Picasso, Braque and Gris were painting before the First World War, under the watchful and discerning eye of Gertrude Stein. Tom Wolfe in his vitriolic survey of modern art hype, *The Painted Word*, stresses this time lag:

Now we can begin to understand how it happened that the Modernists, Braque & Bros., completed almost all their stylistic innovations before the First World War, and yet Modern Art seems to belong to the post-war period. It is simply because the Boho Dance took place before the war and the Consummation took place afterward. This is not what is so often described as the lag between 'the artist's discoveries' and 'public acceptance'. Public? The public plays no part in the process whatsoever. The public is not invited (it gets a printed announcement later) . . .

It was American critics like Clement Greenberg and Harold Rosenberg, says Wolfe, who promoted the idea of a few embattled artistic geniuses, unloved and uncomprehended, under constant threat. And it was Greenberg who pointed the way painting had to go:

In Greenberg's eyes, the Freight Train of Art History had a specific destination. He called for 'self-criticism' and 'self-definition' – 'Self-definition with a vengeance,' he said. It was time to clear the tracks at last of all the remaining rubble of the pre-Modern way of painting. And just what was this destination? On this point Greenberg couldn't have been clearer: *Flatness* . . . He used Pollock's certified success to put over Flatness as *the* theory – the theoretical breakthrough of Einstein-scale authority – of the entire new wave of the Tenth Street *cénacle des cénacles*.

'Pollock's strength,' he would say, 'lies in the emphatic surfaces of his pictures, which it is his concern to maintain and intensify in

all that thick, fuliginous flatness which began – but only began – to be the strong point of late Cubism.' And all through bohemia the melody played . . . *That thick, fuliginous flatness got me in its spell* . . . 'It is the tension inherent in the constructed, re-created flatness of the surface,' Greenberg would say, 'that produces the strength of his art' . . . *That constructed, re-created flatness that you weave so well* . . . 'his concentration on surface texture and tactile qualities' . . . *Those famous paint-flings on that picture plane* . . .

Ah, the music was playing! And Clement Greenberg was the composer! Other artists were picking up on his theories and Rosenberg's, sometimes by reading them in the journals – *Partisan Review, The Nation, Horizon* – but more often in conversation. With The Club going down on Eighth Street the artists of bohemia were now meeting all the time, every day, and talking up a storm. They outtalked any ten canasta clubs from Oceanside and Cedarhurst.

Greenberg was no slouch at conversation himself, despite his jerky windups and his not very elegant deliveries. Somehow the rough edges went perfectly with the *moral conviction* that seemed to radiate from his eyeballs. A forty-one-year-old Washington DC artist named Morris Louis came to New York in 1953 to try to get a line on what was going on in this new wave, and he had some long talks with Greenberg, and the whole experience changed his life. He went back to Washington and began thinking. *Flatness*, the man had said . . . (You bet he had) . . . The spark flew, and Louis saw the future with great clarity. The very use of thick oil paint itself had been a crime against flatness, a violation of the integrity of the picture plane, all these years . . . But of course! Even in the hands of Picasso, ordinary paint was likely to build up as much as a millimeter or two above mean canvas level! And as for the new Picasso – i.e., Pollock – my God, get out a ruler!

So Louis used unprimed canvas and thinned out his paint until it *soaked right into* the canvas when he brushed it on. He could put a painting on the floor and lie on top of the canvas and cock his eye sideways like a robin and look along the surface of the canvas – and he had done it! Nothing existed above or below the picture plane, except for a few ultramicroscopic wisps of cotton fray, and what reasonable person could count that against him . . . No, everything now existed precisely *in* the picture plane and nowhere else. The paint was the picture plane, and the picture plane was the paint. Did I hear the word *flat*? – well, try to out-flat this, you young Gotham rascals! Thus was born an offshoot of Abstract Expressionism known as the Washington School. A man from Mars or Chester, Pa, incidentally, would have looked at a Morris Louis painting and seen rows of rather watery-looking stripes.

Meanwhile back in England where flatness was not so big, the concept of space filled, as it were, the vacuum. Robert Wraight had some pungent things to say about it in his book *The Art Game*:

Paradoxically, the simpler and emptier the work to be described, the more involved the language became. The impossibility for even the best-intentioned critics to find anything new to say about successive exhibitions of banal hard-edge abstractions and abstract-expressionist paintings, produced by British artists under the influence of the Tate Gallery's American show in 1956, made one suspect that certain critics in the art reviews had a standard form of notice which they re-jigged to suit different artists. Everyone was writing about 'space' as if he had created it. Let there be space, the critics said, and there was space – thousands of huge, idiotic canvases full of it. Even the artists became convinced that their empty pictures were filled with some exciting new quality called space. No one ever explained coherently what the term meant. It was not the illusion of aerial space created by the use of perspective and tone values. That, one gathered, was out of date and beneath contempt. It had something to do with the way in which a painting directed the spectator's attention away from itself and to the space around it. One way of doing this was by leaving the canvas completely blank except for a few strokes of paint placed as if they were about to fall off the edge of the canvas. Artist Roger Hilton, one of the leading British exponents and a pioneer of this genre, explained his own ideas thus:

> *I have moved away from the sort of so-called non-figurative painting where lines and colours are flying about in an illusory space; from pictures which still had depth, or from pictures which had space in them; from spatial pictures in short, to space-creating pictures. The effect is to be felt outside rather than inside the picture: the picture is to be not primarily an image, but a space-creating mechanism . . . a kind of catalyst for the activization of the surrounding space.*

Ultimately this quest for a sort of painting that would direct the viewer's attention away from itself was crowned with complete

THE NEW SPIRIT OF PAINTING

de Loonig
Trembling
Arsebandit
Heineken
Space-Invaders
Ealing
Balonsky
Hostage
Grapefruit-Segments
Keesing
Kellogg
Hatchback
Wolly
Anchovy
Hatton
Tampon
Ruislip

Wolly

ROYAL ACADEMY OF ARTS

BURLINGTON HOUSE
Jan 10 - July 25

success, when thousands of 'space' paintings to which no one paid any attention were produced.

Just as some of the paintings could be taken to mean a lot of things or nothing, so the criticism that trailed along in their wake could be marvellously oblique and ambiguous. (An exhibition of British art sent to America in 1965 described itself as emphasizing 'the growing accent on rich ambiguity'.) Wraight quoted some examples of the riper art critical prose of which this is the most striking:

. . . In the end they are reabsorbed into the incommensurability and into the indefinite opening of the void of the cycle of external relations which ordain among themselves in the expanse of the surroundings.

Whether this helps us to comprehend works like Rauschenberg's 'Monogram' (a long-haired goat, stuffed, its face battered and a car-tyre placed round its middle) is doubtful.

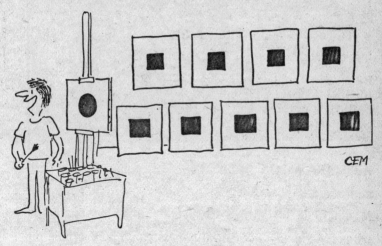

'Nancy!'

The Tate Bricks

In 1975 the Tate exhibited its celebrated heap of bricks. When the story of their purchase got out, there were cries of outrage, but the public flocked to see them. For a while the gallery was consumed in a bush fire of ridicule and recrimination. Headline writers gleefully exploited the story's potential and Carl Andre's Minimalist sculpture of 120 fire bricks (arranged in a rectangle, two bricks deep and measuring 5 by 90 by 27¼ inches) was subjected to every available variant of the pun:

TATE DROPS A COSTLY BRICK
TATE BRICKBATS
TATE GALLERY STONEWALLING
BRICKS BUY DOESN'T CEMENT FEELINGS
BRICK-A-BRAC ART
THE HOT BRICKS FROM THE TATE
CROWDS WARM TO TATE FIREBRICKS

The US newspapers offered:

ART LIKE A TON OF BRICKS

and

MORTAR IS THE MESSAGE

while the English provincial papers could be excruciating:

FIREBRICKS THAT GRATE
                            (*Northern Echo*)

MORTAR-FIED
                            (*Belfast News Letter*)

The most obscure was:

A BRICK IS A ROSE, IS A PRIMROSE
                            (*The Times*)

Colin Simpson in the *Sunday Times* Business News opened the barrage:

The Tate Gallery receives an annual grant of £500,000 from public funds. This is five times as much as the Victoria and Albert Museum, and £100,000 more than all provincial museums and galleries put together. The money is spent by the trustees, who account for their stewardship every two years.

Their latest report is raising eyebrows at the Treasury and in academic – as opposed to artistic – circles. The underlying message of the sumptuously illustrated 275-page catalogue is that modern art is alive and well, and some of its practitioners are laughing their way to the bank. Some forms of public expenditure, it seems, are still sacred.

'The function of the Tate,' write the trustees in the sumptuous 275-page catalogue, 'is to reflect the art of our time.' The Tate, they claim, is the national collection and has a responsibility to show the greatest achievements . . . such collections set standards and are the focal points in the cultural life of the nation. They provide an incentive and a yardstick for those who are responsible . . . for promoting the idea that art is worthwhile.

Carl Andre, a sculptor, and the John Weber Gallery of New York would agree with this dignified and admirable sentiment. In the summer of 1965, while on a canoeing holiday, Andre suddenly decided that it was time to create low sculptures. He bought 120 bricks from a brickyard, arranged them in a low pile on the floor of an art gallery, put a price-tag of $12,000 on them and waited for customers. None came. Being short of money, he took the bricks back to the brickyard and got his money back.

The tale thereafter has an inevitability worthy of the late Gerald Hoffnung. In 1972 the Tate saw a photograph of Andre's bricks and offered to buy them. Andre went back to the brickyard only to find it had closed. However, nothing daunted, he found some other bricks, which in due course were crated and sent to London together with careful instructions on their assembly.

The Tate is understandably coy about how much it paid for this insouciant masterpiece. One trustee explained: 'If we published one price, every artist in the country would come and ask for more. It would ruin the market.'

Andre's bricks can be assembled fairly quickly, but Victor Burgin's work of art took a twelve-month to create. It consists of eighteen sheets of foolscap, each with a few words typed on it. It is called 'Room 1970' and the idea is that the sheets are to be pinned up around any room. 'Mr Burgin,' write the trustees, 'values economy of expression and will avoid twelve-page solutions when he can get away with half a page.'

Nevertheless, the catalogue entry explaining Burgin's economy of expression runs to more than a thousand words.

Once again the Tate declines to reveal how much it paid Burgin for his year's work, but Sir Norman Reid, director of the gallery, does concede the possibility that in one or two of the purchases, the Tate is 'skating on rather thin ice'.

. . . The *clou* of the conceptual collection is undoubtedly Claes Oldenburg's 'Lipsticks in Piccadilly Circus, London 1966'. Oldenburg has been even more economical than Burgin, as his offering consists of a magazine cutting stuck on a postcard measuring 4 by 5½ inches. He explains his creative process in the catalogue:

> *My first grasp of London was the tide of the Thames, and the constant rising and falling . . . So I devised a giant copper ball which could be placed in the river and which would rise and fall with the tide like the plumbing in a toilet.*

The idea did not meet with the wholehearted cooperation of either the GLC or the Department of the Environment, and the project foundered when the file was sent to the Port of London Authority. However, Oldenburg kindly offered to design a new monument to replace Eros in Piccadilly Circus. His first project was a giant retractable lipstick made to rise and fall according to the state of the tide, but the Tate settled for an alternative design using a cluster of lipsticks instead – possibly in an effort to be different from Yale University, which commissioned from Oldenburg a rectractable lipstick monument mounted on caterpillar tracks.

The City of London is well represented by no fewer than four works by a gently ribald artistic partnership called Gilbert and George who operate a modest company called Art for All of Fournier Street, E1. The catalogue tells that Gilbert and George 'were almost teetotal until they tried to communicate their art to the public. They started to drink because they found that drink was a catalyst of communication, a way of presenting their work to the public. They consider drinking to be a duty rather than a pleasure and told the trustees that for some time, drinking has been a part of their work.'

Their favourite medium is the videotape, and the Tate has a splendid one called 'Gordons makes us drunk', which lasts for twelve minutes. It shows the two artists sitting in the front room of 12 Fournier Street drinking gin, while George murmurs several times, 'Gordons makes us drunk . . . very drunk.'

Gilbert and George are sculptors, but the Tate has no examples of their work in that field. They have managed, however, to acquire a collection of photographs taken by the two sculptors in their local pub. These are all framed together in *passe-partout* and the assemblage is entitled 'Balls'.

That article opened Pandora's box. Bernard Levin opined in *The Times*:

. . . a pile of bricks is a pile of bricks, or, as Thurber put it: 'You might as well fall flat on your face as lean over too far backwards.' The terrible truth of this kind of situation is that a view is not necessarily wrong merely because it is espoused by the *Daily Mirror* (which believes that the director of the Tate is called Sir William Reid), the *Daily Mail* (ever in the forefront of those who think their five-year-old child can paint as well as Picasso), and the Daily Another Newspaper (whose reporter got the point without realizing it, when she said: 'Looking at the modern art exhibits . . . everything began to look like an exhibit, including the attendant's chair and the out-of-order stamp box').

The director of the Tate, Sir Norman Reid, replied to Levin's article with a dignified letter challenging the view that 'a brick is a brick for ever' and quoting Wordsworth's condemnation of a similar attitude in his support:

A primrose by a river's brim
A yellow primrose was to him
And it was nothing more.

This, he obviously felt, was a clincher. His view was not widely shared: a *Sunday Times* reader wondered sarcastically 'what would count as a forgery of the firebrick sculpture masterpiece'. Terence Mullaly in the *Daily Telegraph* made a helpful suggestion: Why didn't the Tate just photograph such objects and display the photographs? 'In this way they would fulfil their obligation of recording all trends without using the taxpayer's money to confer on trivia the status of art.' The *Daily Mail* gleefully ran a series of its own 'modern sculptures'

featuring people like John Bratby, the artist, and comedian
Charlie Drake. Their sculptures had titles like 'Nude Wall
with a View' and 'The Drain', the latter, it was suggested,
being possibly attractive to a purchaser who wished to pour
money down it.

The bricks began to attract competition. A Benfleet artist,
described as a self-taught amateur whose usual place of exhibition was on the Thames Embankment, placed a protest
pile of bricks in his front garden with a price tag of £10,000
on them. Sculptress Anne Lindsay, of Lambeth, exhibited
sixteen bricks collected from a friend's rubbish dump spread
out on a piece of newspaper. She was reported as saying:
'Someone has offered to buy half of mine, but I thought it a
shame to break up the composition.'

Not everyone was against the bricks, or the trustees for
having bought them. Norman St John Stevas said: 'They were
absolutely right. They have a judgement to exercise and they
exercised it.' The Minister for the Arts, Hugh Jenkins, at
first displayed some inclination to hunt with the hounds; but
if there was one thing *everyone* could agree on, it was that
their contempt for Mr Jenkins exceeded their dislike of bricks.
After a tremendous right hook from Bernard Levin, who
described him as the biggest Philistine since Goliath, Mr
Jenkins decided to run with the hare and declared that he
'did not question the trustees' judgement' and was 'happy
with the situation'. Richard Morphet, the deputy keeper of
the Tate's Modern Collection wrote a long article which the
general public would unfortunately have missed, as it was in
the *Burlington Magazine*. He was replying to an editorial in
the magazine criticizing the purchase of the bricks. He placed
the sculpture in its historical context, compared it with other
Andre's in the gallery and even tackled the delicate matter of
the individual's reaction to it; the bricks make the spectator
'immediately aware, from any angle, of the whole shape and
structure of the work, and also of the precise relationship
between the parts and the whole. While the whole is boldly
and unambiguously stated, almost as if it had been punched
out from a matrix, it is simultaneously apparent that it is

composed of individual "particles" (the bricks) of a specific size and in a specific orientation. The fact that anyone can see this does not mean it is unworthy of comment, for it is part of the content of the work.'

Morphet then went on to explain why not very much had been *done* to these bricks by the artist: 'Each brick occupies its position by straightforward placing and gravity alone. Nor, of course, is it painted or its appearance altered in any way. Moreover, Andre did not even commission its manufacture; the bricks existed already. The sculpture thus exemplifies Andre's concern with greatly reducing the degree of art's traditional interference with things as they are, and with revealing aspects of the world as it is.'

The public have a way of misunderstanding artistic theory. Their attitude to the reduction of 'art's traditional interference with things as they are' was exemplified by the *Sunday Times* article on the bricks entitled 'A Pile of Words' which began by facetiously suggesting that the page on which the article was to be written should really have been left blank, relieved perhaps 'by a light hand-drawn border and the words *A Present from Joe* stencilled roughly in the middle'. The author had fastened on to the idea of Minimal Art as the kind in which 'most of the burden of interpretation can be unloaded on to the viewer'.

This bluntly expressed a widely held suspicion that the artistic input of Minimal Art was, well, minimal.

Since money, and the supposed misuse of it by the trustees, was what most of the fuss was about, it is appropriate that a report in the *Daily Telegraph* City Pages should have the last word on the affair. On 18 February 1976, it stated that 'market men watched London Brick with more than usual interest but the price shaded to 59½p on the absence of orders from the Tate Gallery'.

'The repose and calm of this work of art reflects the simplicity and restraint of my earlier period, the symbolism remains personal and eludes exact interpretation.'

Fall-out from the Tate Bricks

Following the Tate bricks affair the press chased off after other startling examples of modern art. They found some in a New York gallery that had just put on a 'retrospective' of Neke Carson's Performance Art. The performance included, *inter alia*: a man who knelt down and scratched his head, collecting the resultant fall of dandruff on a black cloth; another man who pushed a long carrot along the frames of paintings hung in the gallery; a man who placed little red dots beside each picture; and a girl in a dinner-jacket who sang 'Life is Just a Bowl of Cherries'.

In Britain, Jeff Nuttall kept the lamp of Performance Art aloft and by 1980 had become a sufficiently GOM of the genre to write a volume of memoirs which was issued with collected scripts. They attracted an acid review from Paul Bailey in the *Observer*:

. . . In Volume Two of *Performance Art* we are granted some glimpses of Jeff in the act of aspiring:

Milk first and sugar and lemon
And blood with a creaming of semen

Those lines come from 'Sunday Blood', which is 'a statement of dense, numb pessimism, as austere a piece of art as ever saw the light of whatever bulb the skilled Nick Hepple lit it by'.

Jeff hasn't always been dense and numb, though. In 1968, he informs us – in one of those phrases that only he is capable of making – he, Jeff, was 'into balls'. In a sense, I would venture to suggest, he has never been out of them. All of Jeff's friends are 'into' something or other. Diz, for example, is 'into' sardine tins – there's a picture of him 'desporting his famous collection'. Carole is 'into' boats, and one 'malodorous' boat in particular: 'It smells like the domicile of a contented tramp – sweat, groin, cooking fat, strong tobacco.' Carole lives there 'to celebrate the mystery, or maybe the simple fact, of her menstrual functioning'.

And then there's Rose McGuire, Jeff's ex-partner in the 'Jack Shows'. Rose is 'into' vegetables. Hand Rose a pound of onions and the occasional turnip and she will come up with a work of art so mind-stretching in its simplicity and power that even Jeff is lost for the *mot juste* to describe it. There's a picture of Rose bearing her 'caged vegetables'.

It was Rose who inspired Jeff to his most daring performance. She drew for him (the drawing is on page 51) two ejaculating penes surrounded by the words 'piddly piddly boo'. Never one to resist such a charge to the creative juices, Jeff stepped out into a Cardiff street with milk in his mouth, which he then proceeded to let fall in dribbles – just like the objects Rose had drawn. An old lady, not understanding that Jeff was perpetrating Performance Art, took offence and slapped his face.

My bourgeois sympathies are with that old lady. She saw through Jeff in an instant. She didn't have to endure his colossal conceit, his semi-literacy, his tedious accounts of pints consumed and women laid, his easy, and distasteful, references to the First World War and the concentration camps. She didn't have to read 'Your blood is the signature of the last man in,' or hear Jeff lecture on the impure arsehole. She would sympathize with a bright four-year-old of my acquaintance who is going through what I intend calling his 'Jeff phase', a phase we all delight in in childhood. She saw Jeff coming, as it were, and she *knew*.

Performance Art had never been very big in Britain but there had been a number of rows in the sixties about public money being dished out for 'happenings'. Over £500 of Arts Council grant, for instance, was given to a three-man living sculpture. They walked around with a ten-foot pole balanced on their heads. And a Labour MP protested about another Arts Council beneficiary who operated in Nottingham. His project involved sweeping dust into artistic piles. The artist, Raymond Richards, talked about his brushes in a newspaper interview.

A little hand comes out of the top of one and points at things, then pops in again. I have also got my long-distance brush on elastic so it springs back and I can use that for brushing up objects at a distance.

A frequent source of bewilderment, and often derision, was the exhibition of ordinary objects with startlingly inappropriate labels. Art critic Nigel Gosling described a work by Michael Craig-Martin:

It consists simply of an actual glass of water on an actual glass shelf. But if you look at the glass you will find that it is entitled 'Oak Tree'. And this, according to the artist, is what it is – an oak tree which happens to look like a glass of water.

Of this the *Sunday Times* commented sourly:

Carl Andre, that outworn classicist from the sixties, merely left his brick piece untitled (instead of calling it say, 'Gumboots' or 'The Fighting Temeraire').

In contrast to things that were not what they seemed, the ICA put on an exhibition of soiled nappies that were definitely soiled nappies. Twenty-two of them were displayed in glass cases marked 'Constipated', 'Normal', 'Not Homogenous', 'Loose', and 'Diarrhoeal'. The exhibition by Mary Kelly was entitled 'Post-Partum Document' and the catalogue explained the exhibits in tones of high seriousness: 'The last stronghold of the heterosexual sexual imperative is infant care. The specificity of this labour is essential to the reproduction of the relations of production insofar as the monolithic mother-child relationship which it welds becomes the basic structure upon which adult socialization is founded.'

The stained nappies were the work of Mary Kelly's son between the ages of five and seven months. They failed to impress the *Daily Mail* reporter whose final paragraph on the exhibition ran as follows:

Last night the reaction of a senior nursing officer was: 'Dirty nappies should either be cleaned or thrown away.' But the artist was at pains to deny that she was doing this as a joke. 'I am doing it because I have been influenced by the women's movement, because I am an artist and a mother,' she said.

The logical conclusion of Minimal Art was Invisible Art. This did in fact make a brief non-appearance. A newspaper reported that police were called to an exhibition of Invisible Art in Tarragona, Spain; a fight had broken out between the artist and a man who tried to pay for a £350 blank canvas with an invisible cheque.

'I think it's been done before.'

Bad Vibes

George Bernard Shaw fulminated continually against what he regarded as third-rate church music; he called it, in an attack on Mendelssohn, 'oratorio mongering'. The affected manner in which these pieces were sung and listened to excited his ridicule; Ernest Newman was similarly irreverent:

For my part, if I had the power I would insist on all oratorios being sung [instead of in evening dress] in the costume of the period – with a possible exception in the case of the *Creation*.

Dr Hubert Parry's oratorio *Job* brought out the worst, or best, in Shaw – who slashed it to ribbons:

As to Job, there is no sort of grit in him: he is abject from first to last, and is only genuinely touching when he longs to lie still and be quiet where the wicked cease from troubling and the weary are at rest. That is the one tolerable moment in the work; and Job passes from it to relapse into dullness, not to rise into greater strength of spirit. He is much distracted by fragments of themes from the best composers coming into his head from time to time, and sometimes cutting off the thread of his discourse altogether. When he talks of mountains being removed, he flourishes on the flute in an absurdly inadequate manner; and his challenge to God, 'Shew me wherefore Thou contendest with me,' is too poor to be described.

Not until he has given in completely, and is saying this last word, does it suddenly occur to him to make a hit; and then, in announcing that he repents in dust and ashes, he explodes in the most unlooked-for way on the final word 'ashes', which produces the effect of a sneeze. The expostulation of God with Job is given to the chorus: the voice that sometimes speaks through the mouths of babes and sucklings here speaks through the mouths of Brixton and Bayswater, and the effect is precisely what might have been expected.

'Some of the most frivolous, the most inane and even the most wicked music in the world is to be found in such forms as the oratorio, the Mass, and anthem, or the like . . .' grumbled Shaw, whose love of music was in inverse proportion to his hostility to conventional religion. He hated the anaemic respectability of it all, summing up his contempt in a characteristically lacerating aside about the Brahms Requiem:

I do not deny that the Requiem is a solid piece of music manufacture. You feel at once that it could only have come from the establishment of a first-class undertaker.

'Heard Melodies are Sweet,
but Those Unheard are Sweeter'

Shaw was the least impressionable of men when it came to singers. In his early days in London he was the music critic on a magazine called the *Hornet* (a job which, as he candidly admitted, he gained through deception, the official critic of the magazine being a socialite with no pretensions to musical knowledge who deputed the actual writing of the pieces to Shaw; the editor was unaware of this).

Shaw never missed an opportunity of puncturing over-inflated reputations. Here is his comment on the 1877 Rossini *Otello* in which Enrico Tamberlik achieved great success:

In order to represent the operatic Othello respectably, a voice and some faculty for acting are indispensable. Signor Tamberlik possesses neither of these qualifications. He sings in a doubtful falsetto and his movements are unmeaning, and frequently absurd. For the C sharp in the celebrated duet 'L'ira d'avverso fato', he substituted a strange description of shriek at about that pitch. The audience, ever appreciative of vocal curiosities, eagerly redemanded it. Signor Garrion, as Roderigo, seemed laudably anxious to make as much of his part as possible, and succeeded – more, probably, to his own satisfaction than to that of the audience. He sang his music correctly, but the quality of his voice is not pleasant. Monsieur Faure's Iago was generally understood to be a deeply studied conception. Possibly it was, for there was no indication of it on the surface. His vocalization lacked the crispness necessary for Rossini's florid music, and his acting consisted merely of shaking hands warmly with his colleagues for no apparent reason.

Elsewhere Shaw lamented the absence of any tenor of quality to sing a decent Manrico in Verdi's *Il Trovatore*:

. . . The thought of that dynasty of execrable imposters in tights and tunics, interpolating their loathsome B flats into the beautiful melodies they could not sing, and swelling with conceit when they

were able to finish 'Di quella pira' with a high C capable of making
a stranded man-of-war recoil off a reef into mid-ocean . . .

(The exhibitionistic high C that Shaw complains of is not in
Verdi's score.)

Another applecart Shaw unceremoniously overturned was
the idea that the Italians were a nation of born musicians. He
quotes with approval the remarks of Ruskin concerning the
singing he encountered south of the Alps:

Of bestial howling, and entirely frantic vomiting up of damned souls
through their still carnal throats, I have heard more than, please
God, I will ever endure the hearing of again, in one of His summers.

A good corrective to romantic notions about Italy, where, said
Shaw:

The chance of being picked off the streets and brought out as *primo
tenore* at the opera occupies the same space in the imagination of the
men as the chance of selecting a Derby winner does in England.

Although plenty of rude things are said about singers who fall
below the mark, composers have to taken even more casti-
gation. Operas that have suffered the rough side of the critical
tongue include Saint-Saens' *Samson and Dalila* of which Shaw
wrote:

I did not wait for the third act of *Samson*, but I assume that the
hero attempted to bring the house down by a drinking song before
resorting to the pillars.

This was a complaint at the inappropriate excesses of Grand
Opera in the Meyerbeer style. A recent production of Meyerbeer's *L'Africaine* at Covent Garden showed that to some, at
least, his work was as dire as ever:

People who know about these things maintain that *L'Africaine* is
Meyerbeer's masterpiece, in which case heaven preserve us from all
his minor works . . .

wrote the *Spectator*'s critic, and expanded on the opera's
shortcomings:

Meyerbeer's greatest fault was his earnest desire to give people what he thought they wanted – the Sid Yobbo-Dirty Digger syndrome. Not for nothing has the Paris opera house been known as *la grande boutique*. One can imagine the planning meetings with Scribe: 'Right, we're going to have a Portuguese council meeting with an Anathema thrown in somehow, a prison scene, a shipwreck and an exotic wedding – on the banks of the Niger, in the Malay peninsula, India, Madagascar, take your pick – now write a libretto.' Thus, too, did Hollywood work, and the plot of *L'Africaine* is as preposterous and the characters as cardboard as anything Maria Montez ever appeared in.

But at least the singing was OK:

The production is confined to getting the characters in roughly the right place (near the footlights). Meyerbeer only wrote for the best singers, and the management has used its chequebook profitably. Placido Domingo was in excellent voice and his rousing delivery of 'O paradis' (a poor aria) was unfairly rewarded with half the population of the Indian sub-continent falling upon him armed to the teeth (he gets away).

More persistent themes in attacking music have been those of ideology and decency; Richard Strauss's *Salome*, for instance, attracted obloquy; a physician wrote to the *New York Times* a letter beginning: 'I am a man of middle life who has devoted upwards of twenty years to the practice of a profession that necessitates a daily intimacy with degenerates.' Based on this experience he was able to declare that *Salome* was a 'detailed and explicit exposition of the most horrible, disgusting, revolting and unmentionable features of degeneracy that I have ever heard, read of, or imagined'. Clearly the good doctor was not a close reader of the Bible.

'Disgusted of New York' has always had his counterpart in Russia. After the revolution *Pravda* tended to fulfill this role, attacking Shostakovitch's *Lady Macbeth of Mtsensk* in 1936 on the grounds of aesthetics and of pornographic intent:

. . . The music quacks, grunts, growls, strangles itself in order to represent the amatory scenes as naturalistically as possible. 'Love' is smeared all over the opera in the most vulgar manner. The merchant's bed occupies the central place on the stage. On it all 'problems' are solved. *Lady Macbeth* enjoys great success with the bourgeois audiences abroad . . . It tickles the perverted tastes of the bourgeois audiences with its fidgeting, screaming, neurasthenic music.

Western critics have frequently objected to music on ideological grounds too. The *Figaro* critic, for instance, in 1932, described Darius Milhaud's *Maximilian* as 'the work of a Communist travelling salesman'. And more recently the productions of Eastern European operatic directors reinterpreting well-known operas in the light of Marxist-Leninism have induced the occasional fit of critical apoplexy: 'The Welsh, predictably adept at keeping up with the Joneses, have asked Harry Kupfer to come from Dresden and dismember *Elektra*,' wrote Rodney Milnes in his *Spectator* review of the Welsh National Opera's 1978 production:

. . . Mr Kupfer's programme note for *Elektra* is the purest, most highly refined horse manure, and should be required reading for those who want a foretaste of what opera will be like after the fall. Some examples: 'Chrysothemis . . . is the type who makes dictatorship possible because she does not question the ways through which they [*sic*] may be made possible. Chrysothemis must learn [note the 'must'] during the opera that she cannot live in the world just as a private individual but that she must take a stand on certain issues.' God help us all. And I rather liked 'Hofmannsthal knew Freud, whereas the Greeks did not.' My goodness, I never thought of that. But of course the Greeks didn't need to. What makes this all the more distressing is that Hofmannsthal had clear and practical ideas on the relationship between the individual and society.

Thus Mr Kupfer's fatuous production has nothing whatever to do with Hofmannsthal. It is played at a sustained level of hysteria that precludes any kind of intellectual response, with most of the de-individualized cast rolling around on the floor, masturbating, or having each other regardless of gender or blood-tie. Understatement is not a weapon in Mr Kupfer's armoury. The set, which might have looked quite chic five years ago, is a slaughterhouse with clingwrap walls, buckets of blood, and a huge crumbling statue of Agamemnon, between the legs of which the principals chase each other before indulging in the above-mentioned practices. It makes nonsense of sight-lines: those on the other side of the auditorium couldn't see Clytemnestra's entrance, and I missed a naked black girl having her throat cut. Whether she was there because Mr Kupfer happens to like naked black girls, or to make an interesting point about colonialism, I have no idea. I wouldn't expect Hofmannsthal to know the answer either. A few members of the audience managed a gentle 'boo' at the end of this mindless travesty. I do hope they haven't been rounded up and are not, even now, being persuaded in some Cardiff mental institution 'to take a stand on certain issues'.

'So Much Noise to Make an Omelette'

Janet Flanner covered the Venice Festival of Contemporary Music for the *New Yorker* in 1950; there she overheard a French visitor's acid comment on Ernst Křenek's new atonal symphony:

Tant de bruit pour faire une omelette.

('What the Venetians liked best,' she added, 'were the free tickets and the opportunity to dress up.')

Modern composers have encountered violent antagonism, but hostility to anything new in music is traditional. Emperor Joseph's kapellmeister attacked Mozart's music which, he complained, had 'too many notes'. But the passions aroused in the twentieth century seem to be greater, perhaps because the departures from musical convention have been more marked. Debussy's impressionist *La Mer* got terrible notices in 1907:

One thing only was obvious, and that was that Debussy's ocean was a frog pond, and that some of its denizens had got into the throat of everyone of the brass instruments and stayed there from beginning to end, with woeful results.

This was the *New York Daily Tribune*'s view, while the *Boston Daily Advertiser* had a subtle interpretation to offer:

It is possible that Debussy did not intend to call it *La Mer* but, *Le Mal de Mer*, which would at once make the tone-picture as clear as day. It is a series of symphonic pictures of sea-sickness. The first movement is 'Headache'. The second is 'Doubt', picturing moments of dread suspense, whether or no! The third movement, with its explosions and rumblings, has now a self-evident purpose. The hero is endeavouring to throw up his boot-heels!'

Of Debussy's *Iberia* a wit suggested that there was a typographical error in the programme:

I have it! The first letter of the title fell off, and one must read *Siberia*. Then everything becomes clear.

The *Boston Daily Advertiser*'s critic Louis Elson, who seems to have been an uninhibited writer to say the least, also had some fun at the expense of Rimsky-Korsakov's *Scheherazade*:

The Russians have captured Boston! . . . The *Scheherazade* engagement began with a bombardment of full orchestra, under cover of which the woodwinds advanced on the right. The violins now made a brilliant sortie on the left flank of the main body. It was a magnificent charge; at one time the concertmaster was quite alone, but his cavalry soon rallied around him. A furious volley of kettle-drums followed, while Gen. Gericke brought up the trombone reserves and the remaining brasses. At this the entire audience – including some very big guns – surrendered.

American critics were also prepared to knock their own country's composers. It seems hard now to understand how a much-fêted composer like Aaron Copland had to see his music subjected to undignified comparisons:

Let us not forget that the leading English reviewers characterized Schumann's Symphony in B flat when they first heard it as belonging to the 'Broken Crockery School'. Our objection to Mr Copland's broken crockery is that it is not of the first quality.

This was nothing to the treatment meted out to Edgard Varèse's work *Intégrales*, the finale of which sounded to Ernest Newman's ears like:

A combination of early morning in the Mott Haven freight yards, feeding time at the zoo and a Sixth Avenue trolley rounding a curve, with an intoxicated woodpecker thrown in for good measure.

Probably the most resisted development in music, however, has been Schoenberg's twelve-tone system. An artist and writer on musical theory, Schoenberg couldn't be dismissed as an ignoramus by his detractors. But they recorded their distaste with the maximum possible animus, nonetheless:

Schoenberg states, 'I write what I feel in my heart.' If this is really so, we can only assume that from 1908 or so, Schoenberg has been suffering from some unclassifiable and peculiarly virulent form of cardiac disease

said *Musical Opinion*.

If Schoenberg has had difficulty gaining public acceptance ('Forty-five years have passed since he wrote his Chamber Symphony, and it will certainly be another forty-five before it is programmed by popular demand,' wrote a critic in 1950), John Cage has had even more. He is, however, well known if only for his celebrated composition of 1952, 'Silent Work 4' 33" ', which consists of a pianist sitting immobile in front of a closed piano for that period of time. Extraneous sounds in the concert hall – coughs, sneezes, rustling programmes, etc. – are, Cage explained, part of the music too. His quirky off-beat humour was an ideal foil for anxious critical inquiry. In a letter to the *New York Herald Tribune* critic (who had attacked his work) he said:

Life goes on very well without me, and that will explain to you my silent piece '4' 33" ' . . .

He became something of a celebrity and an expert on mushrooms, winning $6,000 by answering questions about them on an Italian TV quiz show.

Following Cage there have been a series of musical happenings which have left the public bemused and not noticeably enthusiastic for new ideas. There was a concert in the sixties that featured musicians standing round a tank of tropical fish on the sides of which unscored sheets of music paper had been stuck. As the fish swam about, their positions would now and then coincide with one of the lines of the stave, so that they bore a fleeting resemblance to a note. When this happened, the musicians would play the note. And Peter Heyworth described the work of an Italian composer, Chiari, at the Palermo Festival of Contemporary Music in 1963. In his *Per Arco* 'a cellist sits slumped, like a spastic moron, over his instrument, and during some fifteen minutes does nothing but make an occasional unsuccessful attempt to draw his bow across the strings of his instrument. This work was described by an admirer as "tragic".'

All of which puts one in mind of American composer Virgil Thomson's summing up of Cage's musical compositions:

They do not seem to have been designed for holding attention, and generally speaking they do not hold it.

Grandes Dames

Ruth Gordon once described to George S. Kaufman a new play in which she was appearing: 'In the first scene I'm on the left side of the stage, and the audience has to imagine I'm eating dinner in a crowded restaurant. Then in scene two I run over to the right side of the stage and the audience imagines I'm in my own drawing-room.'

Kaufman listened, then mused, 'And the second night you have to imagine there's an audience out front.'

Some actresses paper over a thin part just by being their own lovable selves. Or they camp it up sufficiently to please their fans. Dorothy Parker famously remarked of a Katherine Hepburn performance that 'she ran the whole gamut of emotions from A to B'.

Mannerism can take over from acting all too easily, and great ladies like Sarah Bernhardt ended up reproducing their most popular effects like conjurers at a children's tea party. Sometimes the play was chosen with an eye for its potential in this respect. Bernard Shaw grumbled about a Sardou play for which Bernhardt had a special affection:

Sardou's latest edition of the Kiralfian entertainment which Madame Bernhardt has for years past dragged from sea to sea in her Armada of transports, is called *Gismonda*, and is surpassingly dreary, although it is happily relieved four times by very long waits between the acts. The scene being laid in the Middle Ages, there are no newspapers, letters, or telegrams; but this is far from being an advantage, as the characters tell each other the news all through except when a child is dropped into a tiger's cage as a cue for Madam Bernhardt's popular scream.

The ingredients of this sort of thing were all miserably predictable, whatever the title:

What does it matter whether such an entertainment is called *Gismonda*, or *Theodora*, or *Venice*, or *Constantinople*, or *The Orient*, or *Captain Boyton's Water Show*? Personally, I prefer the water show, because the sixty-foot header interested me, which Madame Bernhardt has long ceased to do . . .

Sometimes even professionalism deserted the *grandes dames* as their triumphs became a series of self-fulfilling prophecies. In 1903 Eleanora Duse presented *Hedda Gabler* at the Adelphi – in Italian. Max Beerbohm was amongst the somewhat bemused audience:

Signora Duse suggested the weary calm of one who has climbed to a summit high above the gross world. She was as one who sighs, but can afford to smile, being at rest with herself. She was spiritual, statuesque, somnambulistic, what you will, always in direct opposition to eager, snappy, fascinating, nasty little Hedda Gabler. Resignedly she shot the pistol from the window. Resignedly she bent over the book of photographs with the lover who had returned. Resignedly she lured him to drunkenness. Resignedly she committed his MS. to the flames. Resignation, as always, was the keynote of her performance. And here, as often elsewhere, it rang false.

However, it was not the only performance of *Hedda Gabler*. There was another, and, in some ways, a better. While Signora Duse walked through her part, the prompter threw himself into it with a will. A more raucous whisper I never heard than that which preceded the Signora's every sentence. It was like the continuous tearing of very thick silk. I think it worried everyone in the theatre, except the Signora herself, who listened placidly to the prompter's every reading, and, as soon as he had finished, reproduced it in her own way. This process made the matinée a rather long one. By a very simple expedient the extra time might have been turned to good account. How much pleasure would have been gained, and how much hypocrisy saved, if there had been an interpreter on the OP side, to shout in English what the prompter was whispering in Italian!

But all this doesn't really matter with a *grande dame*. 'You will tell me no doubt,' wrote Shaw in *Saturday Review*, 'that Mrs Patrick Campbell cannot act. Who said she could? – and who wants her to act? – who cares tuppence whether she possesses that or any other second-rate accomplishment? On the highest plane one does not act, one *is*.' Quite so.

Plays with a Message

Bernard Shaw disliked being subjected to pretentious, empty plays. One that attracted his scorn was *The Manxman* that played at the Shaftesbury Theatre in 1895:

In the bill *The Manxman* is described as 'adapted from Hall Caine's celebrated novel'. Who is Hall Caine? How did he become celebrated? At what period did he flourish? Are there any other Manx authors of his calibre? If there are, the matter will soon become serious; for if that gift of intolerably copious and intolerably common imagination is a national characteristic in the Isle of Man, it will swamp the stage with Manx melodramas the moment the islanders pick up the trick of writing for the stage.

Whether the speeches in *The Manxman* are interpolated Wilson Barrett or aboriginal Hall Caine I cannot say, as I have not read the celebrated novel, and am prepared to go to the stake rather than face the least chapter of it. But if they correctly represent the colloquial habits of the island, the Manx race are without a vernacular, and only communicate with one another by extracts from Cassell's National Library, the Chandos Classics, and the like. In the Isle of Man you do not use the word 'always': you say, 'Come weal come woe, come life come death'. The most useful phrases for the tourist are 'Dust and ashes, dust and ashes', 'Dead sea fruit', 'The lone watches of the night', 'What a hell is conscience!' 'The storm clouds are descending and the tempest is at hand,' and so on. The Manx do not speak of a little baby, but of a baby 'fresh from God'. Their philosophy is that 'love is best – is everything – is the cream of life – better than worldly success'; and they conceive woman – or, as they probably call her, 'the fair sex' – as a creature 'giving herself body and soul, and never thinking what she gets by it. That's the glory of Woman!' And the Manx woman rather deserves this. Her idea of pleasantry is to sit on a plank over a stream dangling her legs; to call her young swain's attention to her reflection in the water; and then, lest he should miss the coquetry of the exhibition, to cut off the reflected view of her knees by wrapping her skirt round her ankles in a paroxysm of affected bashfulness.

Shaw was rather peeved to discover that on visiting the Lyric a year later *The Manxman* was still extant – 'For did I not slay him at the Shaftesbury and remonstrate vehemently with Mr Hall Caine for letting him loose?'

Ethnic drama like this could be painful. A really awful example of it was provided by Ian Maclaren, *non de plume* of John Watson, a Scottish writer of portentous pulp novels. H. G. Wells caught the flavour of them: 'the babblings of green fields and "mithers" on deathbeds, the impossible self-sacrifices, the nose-blowings and spectacle-wipings, the faithful beast business and the sentimental addresses to the unknown reader . . .' Translated to the stage, they became what Max Beerbohm called 'A Load of Weeds from the Kailyard'. One such play entitled *Beside the Bonnie Brier Bush* was ferociously biblical. Lachlan Campbell's daughter, Flora, has secretly married. When he finds out the father flies into a stage rage; later he is filled with, of course, remorse. As Max Beerbohm relates:

The father catches sight of Flora's sun-bonnet, and into that receptacle he pours the tears on which the curtain was bound to fall. Already, I think, he has had something to say about 'the Laird's will'; but it is (so far as I know) in the next act, when his hair has turned white through grief, and when 'the Laird has laid his name i' the dust', that he is at his strongest in biblical references. He meets two children in a wood, and beckons to them. Rather reluctantly, they come; and he, folding them in his arms, and turning up his eyes, quotes a text which I will leave you to guess: if I wrote it down here, I should feel as uncomfortable as I felt in hearing the actor mouth it. He then proceeds to repeat the story of the ewe-lamb. I have said that it is 'so far as I know' in this act that he is most biblical. But I dare say he is even more biblical in the last act, for which, partly because I was bored, and partly because I was disgusted, I did not stay. What becomes of him finally I do not know. I conjecture that he dies in sight of the audience. Ian Maclaren, as I well remember from that book of stories, had a large and varied assortment of death-beds, with moonbeam or sunbeam fittings as required.

From time to time openly propagandist drama is staged. For instance, after Dr Buchman's Moral Rearmament Group got going in the twenties and thirties, it was one means used for making known their philosophy. Beverley Baxter went to the first production:

The first presentation by the Group is *The Forgotten Factor*. The Group were good enough to invite me to the opening night, but I resisted the temptation until this week, when, having been in bed with a cold for three days, I felt that a little moral rearmament would not do any harm.

Everyone in the theatre was smiling as we took our seats – even the box-office staff handing out the tickets which are free, the ushers with their no-charge programmes, and the two pianists who linked themselves in melody.

I saw three MPs there, and they were smiling. As an unregenerate snob, I succeeded in catching the eye of a peer of the realm, and his face lit up too.

We were obviously going to be one cheerful family enjoying a moral charade by happy boys and girls on the stage.

I agree that few things are more depressing than organized cheerfulness, and nothing more crushing to the human vanity than to find people who are already in such a condition of congenital happiness that you cannot possibly add to it.

On the other hand, I could not help comparing the atmosphere of the morally rearmed Westminster Theatre with the refreshment room of a London railway station, where last week I was reactionary enough to interrupt the private conversation of four waitresses and ask for a cup of tea. The icy, impersonal contempt with which a saucerless cup was handed to me, without the young person even glancing in my directon, was undoubtedly the chill which caused my cold.

Eventually the smiling pianists at the Westminster came to a harmonious end and up went the curtain on a choir of smiling boys and girls (all without make-up) who sang very well indeed.

Mr Ivan Menzies was then announced as a D'Oyly Carte star, together with his own explanation that the Prime Minister of Australia adjourned both Houses of Parliament to hear him sing about Moral Rearmament.

Mr Menzies sang a song about the Third Way. You know the idea . . . not your way, not my way, but a third way. Husbands and wives, Tories and Socialists, employers and employees. Instead of taking the high road or the low road, we all travel in the centre. Having reached this point of philosophy, Mr Menzies then did a jolly dance while all the boys and girls in the choir smiled.

I must confess that I found the dance slightly disconcerting, but then, as far as Moral Rearmament is concerned, I am obviously at the bow-and-arrow stage.

Mr Cecil Broadhurst, a cowboy from them thar Canadian prairies, then sang a pleasing self-written number about seeing the King ride by at the Victory Celebrations. (My own impression is that I saw the King drive by, but we can let that pass.)

After the cowboy had gone a group of four miners appeared and told us in a homely, well-timed eloquence how Moral Rearmament had made them realize that nothing could be accomplished without national unity, personal unity and industrial unity.

They were first class and deserved the applause we gave them.

Mr Peter Howard, author – former political columnist, former farmer, former rugger captain of England and a big shot in the Moral Rearmament World – then appeared and told us in dynamic language that from this country must go out the message of unity, one for all and all for one, without which Europe and civilization could not be saved.

He called for a colossal renaissance in human values, then he explained that the American play we were about to see was written by an Oxford don, and had so impressed audiences at Washington that . . . I thought he was going to say 'that they voted Republican', but he did not. The play also stopped trouble in the Nova Scotia mines during the war, and was received with profound interest by the Yorkshire miners. A great many people had been 'changed' by the mere witnessing of the drama.

I looked around in the hope that Mr Agate was present, but all that I saw was the peer still smiling.

The Forgotten Factor starts as an American Junior Miss, domestic comedy, and develops into a struggle between a stubborn American employer and an equally stubborn union leader. There are tough guys who say, 'Knock him for a loop,' and in every way the play is a credit to the don who wrote it, clearly demonstrating the advantages of Oxford over the other place.

The worthless son of the employer sees the light and thus brings the dispute as well as the play to an end.

The acting and production are professional in standard, the whole thing being rattling good entertainment and on the side of the angels. Afterwards the enthusiastic audience, which had not paid for its seats, was invited to stay behind and have some free refreshments.

As a dramatic critic I have no quarrel with *The Forgotten Factor*. It is good fun, and funny even when it is good. The message of universal brotherhood ignores the subtleties and the problems of economics, but I suppose there is nothing the world needs so much as the conception of the human family.

The only objection I see is that it makes people smile all the time, which gives a suggestion of harmless idiocy. But remembering the four waitresses at the railway restaurant I am ready to admit that a few more smiles wouldn't do us any harm.

'The People Who Come for their Hats Like it'

James Agate went to see the first night of a P. G. Wodehouse musical, unpromisingly titled *Oh, Kay!* The plot was difficult to describe:

In so far as I can make anything of the imbroglio of this piece, it concerns a cretinous earl so harassed by the super-tax that he is reduced to rum-running in his last remaining possession, his yacht. With him is his sister, who is apparently called Kay. Kay, clothed in a macintosh, makes a burglarious midnight entry into the house of one Jimmy Winter, whom she had previously saved from drowning. Jimmy, who is arranging to marry a second wife before completely divorcing the first, now falls in love with Kay. It also happens that another rum-runner, one 'Shorty' McGee, has also chosen Winter's house in which to store without permission his stock of illicit liquor. The establishment possesses forty unexplained housemaids and a baker's dozen of inexplicable footmen, who from time to time interrupt such action as there is. This is the entire story, and I can frankly say that I have known nothing in the musical-comedy line of greater melancholy.

'Listening with maximum intentness and a desperate anxiety to be amused', Agate was unable to find in the entire work:

. . . one single spark of wit or even humour with which to credit either of the authors. 'What is a poltergeist? A ghost that palters,' and 'He's a topping bishop. What's that? A bishop who plays golf' – these represent fairly the best of the writing. But 'What sort of flowers does your fiancée fancy?' and 'I shall act accordion, I mean according', represent, I think also fairly, the general level of this libretto. I am not to be persuaded that Mr Wodehouse, whose stories notoriously banish melancholy from our universities, cannot do better than this.

One of the miseries of drama criticism has always been the extent to which plays have a length of run in inverse proportion to the critic's enjoyment of them. Agate and Beverley Baxter had a conversation about this one night:

We recalled the beautiful production of *The Moon is Down*, the gripping play, *The Russians*, the moving revival of *Abraham Lincoln* and others of that ilk. The theatre public ignored them all. Even the costly attempt at a new technique in Tolstoy's *War and Peace* drew a blank.

'You must not despair,' said James. 'You must go on hoping.'

At this point we adjourned to hear the last act of Ivor Novello's *Arc de Triomphe*. On the way I asked a young lady who keeps the gentlemen's hats in pawn if she liked this new Novello show.

'Very much,' said the young lady.

'Have you seen it?' I asked.

'No,' she answered, 'but the people who come for their hats all like it.'

'The people who come for their hats' like quite a lot of things that critics cast aside. Sometimes, though, musicals can leave the audience, let alone the singers and dancers, gasping, and ethnic musicals are often particularly dire. Sheridan Morley sat glumly through an Italian import in 1978:

The current shambles at the Adelphi, *Beyond The Rainbow*, is an Italian musical which has already run more than four years in Rome (where it outsold both *My Fair Lady* and *Superstar*) and also in Austria, Germany, Spain and Mexico where theatrical-musical tastes seem to be, to say the least, a little undemanding. Apparently choreographed by a marine gym instructor on a bad morning, *Beyond The Rainbow* has been converted into English, of a kind, by way of some Leslie Bricusse lyrics: 'It may be they are dreary, But we shall make them cheery' is one couplet I'm going to find it hard to forget, though 'She's the best, Let's get undressed' will also take some beating, as does the audience. Italian musicals, to risk a generalization on this evidence, have many of the qualities of a school play and not the better ones: very simple, very slow and very loud.

The plot, such as it is, concerns God's arrangements for a second flood and a local priest's uneasy love for one of his communicants: in Rome, it would appear, the sight of a priest being kissed on stage by a girl, in however sisterly a fashion, was of itself enough to guarantee box-office queues. Adelphi audiences may require something more. What they get, for their £5 a stall, is a highly and

understandably embarrassed performance from Roy Kinnear as the
local mayor, and a star turn of cautious charm from the original
Italian actor, Johnny Dorelli, who may well be remembered (by
those who share my passion for useless information) as the man who
once sang 'Volare' in a Eurovision Song Contest.

Sadly he hasn't got a song like it here, though it would be churlish
not to note a couple of splendid revolving stages and an immacu-
lately trained dove who appears for the curtain calls, and not before
time. Earlier, when a bell rings the entire cast feel obliged to go
'Ding Dong Ding Dong' and then, afraid we'd missed the point,
imitate rope-pullers. It's that kind of evening, but if you have very
small children, preferably under about three, this will do nicely for
Christmas.

There is another form of musical evening potentially more
torturing than a bad musical; a bad pop-concert. Fortunately
the noise of the fans often drowns out most of the noise from
the stage. But not if the singer has a very powerful voice.
Sheridan Morley went to see Tom Jones in action – the man
of whom the Duke of Edinburgh inquired after a Royal Variety Show: 'Do you gargle with pebbles?'

Having been recently reprimanded by a reader for not reviewing the
Palladium frequently enough in these pages, and having nothing
better to do one October night, I took myself to see Tom Jones,
modestly billed there as 'A Man and a Half . . . the World's Most
Exciting Performer'. Hopes that he might turn out to have three
eyes or even fifteen toes were later dashed by his 'in person' (or 'in
1½ person'?) appearance, but before even that took place there was
the first half of the bill to get through. Those of us who were settled
down in time for it (not in fact very many; Palladium audiences are
a breed unto themselves, apparently incapable of sorting out correct
ticket numbers until near the interval and even then in serious
doubt about what a stall could possibly be) were treated to a series
of turns which would have looked somewhat shoddy even if seen at
the end of the pier in Bridlington, let alone at the leading variety
theatre in the land.

Following the interval, and a stern announcement to the effect
that 'This is Tom Jones' just in case there were any of us who had
slipped in hoping for Joyce Grenfell, the singer himself appeared
looking curiously like Eamon Andrews. It was, he assured us, nice

to be back in London, England and the efforts of that sentence more or less used up his chat for the following hour. Throwing a scarf into the audience with the cautious ecstasy that is Mr Jones's stock in trade, he proceeded to work his way through twenty or so numbers, shaking himself the while like an actor auditioning for St Vitus.

. . . Mr Jones is, in the words of his own hit, not unusual . . . at least not as a singer; as a sex symbol is he nothing short of inexplicable.

'I Made an Excuse and Left'

Unfortunately filth doesn't get reviewed much. It is assumed that the potential audience know what they want and where to get it; thoughtful critiques of individual shows are therefore inappropriate. Nonetheless, journalists do go on sociological fishing expeditions from time to time, and end up writing *I made an excuse and left* type articles about their experiences. Stuart Wavell did a piece entitled 'Fannies By Gaslight' for the *Guardian* in 1975. In it he explored the world of strip clubs, and their clientele. He found himself seated next to a loquacious middle-aged man who was 'a sort of trouble-shooter in the wall cavity business':

The band stopped playing, and both of them became comperes announcing the lovely and very delectable Sandra, or Za-Za. Or with it Sonya? All eyes swivelled. Festooned in fluorescent ruffles and a boa, the person to whom I shall hereafter refer as Sonya appeared from behind a mirror to the accompaniment of a scratchy recording of 'Desert Island Discs', or something similar, interspersed with the authentic South Sea sound of a parrot being strangled. My memory of Sonya was somewhat obliterated by what was to follow, rather in the same way that the pain of childbirth is said to be quickly forgotten. She had, I recollect, a delightful smile, which is all she was wearing as the parrot gave its last squawk.

. . . I endeavoured to clap in the right places and generally keep her spirits up during this humiliating trial. I fear my efforts were not appreciated; the English like to remain quiet on these occasions.

My companion was lost in thought for several minutes after Sonya tripped off. 'That television programme really did the business a lot of harm,' he said finally. I asked him what he meant. 'They picked on a couple of cowboys and made out that the whole wall cavity trade was rotten.'

In the sixties satire was able to enlist filth in the fight against hypocrisy. Kenneth Tynan described Lenny Bruce in the *Observer* as 'the most original, free-speaking, wild-thinking gymnast of language this inhibited island has ever engaged to amuse its citizens'. But an anonymous reporter on another page of the paper seemed to have been stunned by the performance, which he described incredulously:

Arrived in good time, expecting full-scale turn-out. Expectations justified. Bar jammed. First man inside was wearing Vincents tie; beyond him, two brawny fellows in Old Wellingtonian ties. Atmosphere like tail-end of Knightsbridge wedding reception.

Wedged in by waiters behind long table against wall. During good dinner, continue survey of fellow-diners, who appear solid middle class. Spotted political correspondent of *New Statesman*, and Vicky, the cartoonist. Not a rebel in sight.

Entertainment starts, three-piece band, girl singer, small stage. Fill glass, open notebook, settle back for Lenny Bruce, feeling definitely in swim.

Bruce comes on, about thirty-five, red-rimmed eyes, dark trousers and usual upper garment, resembling black version of tunic worn by Chinese Communists – an unfrock coat that gives him air of man on run.

Quiet start, on religion, Jews and death of Christ. Hard to follow. First word of which meaning is absolutely plain is four-lettered, shouted at audience. Audience braces: sound of seat-belts being pulled tight. Lose count of incidence of four-letter word. Wonder whether am present at some kind of breakthrough. Put away notebook, lest gets into wrong hands.

B. tells story about his arrest in San Francisco for use obscene language. Backward town. Makes point that everyone in court enjoyed using his word. Become aware that not everyone in club enjoying it as much.

Heckling from rear, which B. resents, telling one fellow he should be lynched, and another that he (B.) will get a pair of pliers and do him an inprintable injury. Pro-Bruce faction, estimated at one-sixth of total audience, delighted by this riposte. Reflect wouldn't fancy B. as our prison warder.

B. delivers extended homilies about venereal disease, fornication, religion and contraceptives, evidently hammering point that inhibitions root cause world's troubles. Loses sympathy of bulk of audience. B. grows more abandoned, obscenities more frequent.

B. simulates orgasm on drums. Suppress unreporterlike feelings of embarrassment and shock. Fair-haired man in glasses exchanges brave looks with lady companion.

B. concludes by asking for a single spot and reciting poem about Eichmann. End of show; applause in which not all join. On way out, test inhibitions, find them in better order than for some time. Take deep breath nice clean Soho air.

In 1971, the *Dirtiest Show in Town* arrived in London ('also the shortest and arguably the worst' noted Sheridan Morley). It consisted of chants and dialogues which combined comico-lyrical material on sex with heavily committed cerebration on pollution and assorted evils. Morley didn't care for it:

. . . it has to be said that this theatrical gangbang is as tasteless, shapeless and aimless an off-Broadway jamboree as it has ever been my painful duty to endure. The message that like, well, sex is good man and war is kinda bad is not wholly new to me, and the single-minded arrogance with which the author/director belts across his banalities is truly stunning. That alas is the only thing about the evening which is.

The most celebrated sex show of the seventies was the all-nude *Oh Calcutta!* Although it began in a welter of outrage, facetious headlines ('No Nudes is Bad News') and witty asides ('This is the kind of thing to give pornography a bad name'), it drew the crowds. It got prosecuted in Australia and, in a TV version, in the USA. In Stockholm naked couples in the audience were thrown out before the show could begin – which seemed faintly hypocritical. In Paris, crowds arriving at the theatre were obliged by order of the police to leave their binoculars at the door – which seems *very* hypocritical. It settled down to a long run and soon became a favourite for charabancs of OAPs. An *Evening News* reporter spotted two nuns and a Roman Catholic priest in the audience. They *might* have mistaken the show for something else, like the two American ladies who went expecting a musical set in India.

When the cast changed the press had another look at it, but could only report that there now seemed 'more roundheads than cavaliers'. Anyway, the cast and backstage staff seemed to thrive on it. For instance, Margot Martin, fifty-eight, who darned the panties and trousers that got ripped during the show, told one reporter how wholesome she thought it all was. Before that, she had been wardrobe mistress to Anna Neagle.

Saved

It is peopled by characters who, almost without exception, are foul-mouthed and dirty-minded and barely to be judged on any recognizable human level at all. Nobody in his senses will deny that life in South London, or anywhere else for that matter, can be sordid, sleazy and sinister . . .

Thus Herbert Kretzmer, writing about Edward Bond's notorious play *Saved*, produced at the Royal Court in 1965. The slightly apologetic tone of the last sentence was echoed in some of the other notices:

It takes quite a lot to shock or disturb me. But . . .

began the *West London Observer*'s critic, adapting the familiar cliché: 'I'm no prude, but . . .'
   Saved, as if to compensate for 'quite a lot' of things that hadn't affected him, fairly shocked him rigid:

It is nothing short of propaganda for sadism and sexual perversion, and seeing it has left a scar which will remain with me for the rest of my life.

So to 'Disgusted of Tunbridge Wells' is added 'Scarred of Shepherd's Bush' in the ranks of people who know when things 'have gone too far this time'.
   Was it the matter or the manner of the play that gave greater offence? *The Times*' critic seemed to think it was the matter:

Saved, which concerns the liaison between a spaniel-like South London boy and a vixenish good-time girl who spends most of the evening trying to get rid of him, is a blockishly naturalistic piece, full of dead domestic langueurs and slavishly literal bawdy. It contains the ugliest scene I have ever seen on any stage – where a teenage gang daub a baby with excrement and stone it to death.

One can no longer take cover behind the phrase 'bad taste' in the face of such material. But one has a right to demand what purpose it fulfils.

So did the *Sun*'s critic, David Nathan:

Absolute monstrosity is eventually as boring – and as unlikely – as absolute goodness.

Like John Osborne, Edward Bond was prepared to do battle with the critics, landing a good haymaker on J. W. Lambert in the process:

Lambert's initial hysterical reaction to my play *Saved* has hardened into a rather eccentric defensiveness. He writes that *Spring and Port Wine* is a better play than *Saved* because, among other reasons, although it deals with meanness, cowardice, emptiness and cruelty, it is 'wholly enchanting from beginning to end'.
    How comfortable!

'There is no excuse for this sort of piece,' J. C. Trewin, the *Illustrated London News*' critic observed magisterially. One wonders what sort of 'excuses' should usually be advanced by dramatists for their work. A public discussion held at the Royal Court to give both admiring and hostile critics a chance to air their views might perhaps have unearthed some. *The Times*' reporter, however, was a little baffled by the disparity of views:

According to Miss Mary McCarthy, who opened the discussion, the play was concerned with 'limit and decorum'. She thought it showed a 'remarkable delicacy', and praised the infanticide scene for its 'delicate escalation'.
    This was not a view that had occurred to the play's other critics – even its admirers. And other surprises came to light when the author entered the discussion. Mr Bond has already commented publicly on his play, and with every new pronouncement it grows in significance. In the quarterly magazine *Censorship* he has described it as a study of the consequences of violence and 'misdirected sex'. In an open letter to his critics he has said that it is 'about a liberal . . . and about his attempts to pacify his environment' and claimed 'that there are still further qualities of analysis, and vision

in the play . . . If I had written a meretricious, modest little piece
. . . I could have had the critics clapping their hands off.

There didn't seem to be much compromise as a result of the
teach-in.

The odour of a *News of the World* campaign against vice
pervaded many of the attacks made on *Saved*. The outraged
cries of critics like 'Scarred of Shepherd's Bush' were loud
enough to filter through to the bumbling hierarchy of the Arts
Council and its parliamentary patrons. When the Expenditure
Committee of the House of Commons delivered its report in
1971, it wrote a delightful footnote to the controversy:

They find it hard to believe that the plays of Edward Bond, per-
formed under [British] Council sponsorship in three Eastern European countries, could have been fully understood by theatregoers
other than expatriates and a small intellectual élite.

The committee was referring to the loss incurred by the British Council on the English Stage Company's 1969 tour. The
Guardian commented drily:

The Bond plays in question were *Saved* and *Narrow Road to the
Deep North*. The tour came about after invitations from Yugoslavia,
Czechoslovakia, and Venice (the first two particularly requesting
Saved). Press comment was extremely favourable, the British Council says in a note to the committee. Expatriates and intellectuals
evidently regarded the visit as 'the highlight of the Belgrade Festival', and the English Stage Company won joint second prize.

'Oh Godot!'

When B. A. Young used the phrase 'the best of Beckett' in a *Financial Times* article, he triggered one of those anonymous letters that are the less restrained counterparts of those proudly read out on Radio 4's 'Any Answers'. It referred to him as a 'pitiable imbecile' to imagine that there could be a best of Beckett when it was all so contemptible. *Godot*, however, endures, and people were still prepared to wait for him (or it) in 1964 when the play was revived at the Royal Court, nearly ten years after its first production. At that time, wrote Anthony Cooper in the *Daily Express*, it was a fashionable party game to guess what *Waiting for Godot* was about. 'Now it no longer seems to matter.' This perception was the nub of the matter – or non-matter. The play created large, empty and ambiguous spaces, which the audience could fill at leisure. It drew a characteristic snort from Milton Shulman in the *Evening Standard* when he first reviewed it:

Waiting for Godot . . . is another of those plays that tries to lift superficiality to significance through obscurity.

It should please those who prefer to have their clichés masquerading as epigrams. 'We always find something that gives us the impression we exist,' is Mr Beckett's clumsy way of rehashing Descartes' old phrase, 'I think, therefore, I am.'

Similarly his symbols are seldom more demanding than a nursery version of *Pilgrim's Progress* . . .

Shulman's objection was to bogus philosophizing. A more common objection was that nothing whatever happened. That was not the point, said the play's defenders, which is to say, that *was* the point. Indeed its nothingness seemed to be infectious. Nicol Williamson, who played Vladimir in the 1964 revival, gave an extremely Vladimirish interview to the press

in which he said he had spent eighteen months ravenously
wanting to get married, but now just wanted to stay alone in
his flat with four bags of potato peelings which hadn't been
emptied for seven weeks: 'I seem to like being alone. There's
nothing I can do about it. And there's nothing as real as
nothing.'

Is this a profound remark or a stupid one? Or a profoundly
stupid one? It's the sort of conundrum *Godot*'s first audiences
had to break their teeth on. And it was all put over in an
infuriating dialogue which, as Philip Hope-Wallace pointed
out, bore a striking resemblance to those familiar music-hall
exchanges that get nowhere: ' "You know my sister?" "Your
sister?" "Yes, my sister," and so on, ad lib . . .'

Some of the audiences didn't react too well, as Peter Bull
describes in his account of searing experiences at the hands
of disillusioned Godot waiters:

Of course a lot of people were blackmailed into coming to *Godot* by
the quotes in the press plastered outside the theatre and in the
newspaper columns. It was no good expecting to find 'one of the
funniest plays in London' if two tramps wrangling for a couple of
hours on a stage, naked except for a leafless tree, wasn't your idea
of a gay evening out. Then there were those who thought they
wouldn't be asked out ANYWHERE if they hadn't seen it, thanks
to Mr Tynan's pronouncement about it being a 'conversational
necessity'. Sometimes I longed to stop prospective customers
streaming up to the box-office and try and divert them to *Dry Rot*
at the Whitehall Theatre, though I fancy a lot of them thought they
had been seeing the latter anyhow.

But theatrical London did flock to it, and in consequence the
piece did one's reputation a great deal of good, though a lot of
members of the profession were not strong enough to stay the
course. Early in the run my phone rang one morning and it was Mr
R. Morley on the other end.

'Guess who was in front last night?' he asked.

'Boris Karloff,' I replied correctly.

'AND me,' he said, hurt. 'At least, for the first act,' he added.
'But I told the people I was with that there was no point in staying
for the second, as it was exactly the same apart from you being
dumb in it.'

I told him coldly that I was blind in the second act, and that I had troubled Mr Harold Hobson's memory 'like the swansong of humanity', but Mr Morley could not be tempted to return, and indeed his memory was so troubled that he used to ring me up periodically and mutter on the phone:

'I've been brooding in my bath, and it is my considered opinion that the success of *Waiting for Godot* is the end of the theatre as we know it.'

Peter Bull describes what the cast put up with when *Godot* went on tour:

. . . the Monday following we opened at the Arts Theatre, Cambridge, which was to be quite a different pair of tramps. You would have thought by the laughter, bookings and general behaviour that we had brought the great Laughing Success of the Century to their doors and we played to virtual capacity. The running time went up by fifteen minutes in order to give the audience a chance to get over their apoplectic fits, and dons showed us round their collections of precious glass and things. We were patronized by the local theatre groups, who kindly interrupted their activities for a second to tell us what THEY were doing NEXT season, and Peter Woodthorpe (ex-Footlights star) had a great personal triumph on the stage, in the press, and all over the street, which plunged Timothy and me in an orgy of beastliness to him. He took it in fairly good part and we pressed on to Blackpool.

. . . what possessed the management to book us in there must be shrouded for ever in mystery. But even this cardinal error was eclipsed by their invitation to the Blackpool old-age pensioners to view *Waiting for Godot* at one shilling a head on the Monday night. It was soon apparent that this gesture was not far short of insanity. The OAPs were very angry indeed, after the first few minutes, at not only having to witness *Waiting for Godot*, but also having to pay twelve pennies for the privilege. They determined to have their say, which meant that during the second act we couldn't have ours, so there was a bit of an *impasse*. Bedlam reigned, what with the banging of seats, yells of derision and one or two pertinent remarks when the tramps suggested hanging themselves. We started off with 700 persons in the Grand Theatre, and finished up with under 100. We took one quick curtain and there were rumours of the police being called out for 'our special safety' as it says on some fire curtains.

Playwrights should be wary of handing discontented audiences lines with which they can answer back. The OAPs obviously got their pound of flesh out of *Godot*. The most recent play to arouse such antagonism was Howard Brenton's *The Romans in Britain* at the National Theatre. Bryan Robertson in the *Spectator* showed himself worthy of the tradition of *Godot* OAPs:

Michael Bryant as Caesar in Britain has to shout 'What a fucking island!' towards the end of the first act and most of us, I believe, would have liked to yell back 'What a fucking play!'

Criticizing Coward

'Everyone but Somerset Maugham said I was a second Somerset Maugham, with the exception of a few who preferred to describe me as a second Sacha Guitry,' said Noël Coward at a time when he had three plays running at once in the West End. His considerable success at an early age was not unqualified by critical bitchiness. James Agate said that his characters were 'vicious babies, sprawling upon the floor of their unwholesome crèche':

Mr Coward is credited with the capacity to turn out these very highly polished pieces of writing in an incredibly short time. And if rumour and the illustrated weeklies are to be believed, he writes his plays in a flowered dressing-gown before breakfast. But what I want to know is what kind of work he intends to do after breakfast, when he is clothed in his right mind.

Close Shave . . .

Attacking Shaw is not easy: he had so often said it all himself. He once described the creature that was G.B.S. as 'hopelessly unnatural and void of real passion . . . I have never pretended that G.B.S. was real: I have over and over again taken him to pieces before the audience to show the trick of him.'

A few people landed some good jabs on him, despite his agility:

God help us if he would ever eat a beef-steak. (Mrs Patrick Campbell)
His brain is a half-inch layer of champagne poured over a bucket of Methodist near-beer. (Benjamin de Casseres)
. . . the first man to have cut a swathe through the theatre and left it strewn with virgins. (Frank Harris)
He started from points of view which no one else was clever enough to discover, and he is at last discovering points of view which no one else was stupid enough to ignore. (G. K. Chesterton)

In 1977 Shaw received a real battering from a first-class batterer. After reading an article by Michael Billington in the *Guardian*, in praise of Shaw, John Osborne exploded into its letter columns:

LOOKING BACK AT SUPERMAN

Sir, Michael Billington cannot have read the plays of George Bernard Shaw since his Oxford days. To call him 'the greatest British dramatist since Shakespeare' is close to having a critical brainstorm, as well as perpetuating an exam-crazy classroom myth. Having recently seen *Saint Joan* in London and *Caesar and Cleopatra* in Sydney, it is clearer to me than ever that Shaw is the most fraudulent, inept writer of Victorian melodramas ever to gull a timid critic or fool a dull public.

He writes like a Pakistani who had learned English when he was twelve years old in order to become a chartered accountant.

From childhood I have read these plays, watched them, indeed toured as an actor and stage manager in them on one-night stands. Apart from this experience, any fair-decent writer I know could put his finger on the crass, vulgar drivel in any of them.

Simply read the stage directions of *Candida* (opening this week). I had the misery of once playing Marchbanks in this ineffably feeble piece. This is Shaw's idea of a 'poet' (having no poetry in him at all). The poet, a ghastly little cissy, is bullied interminably by an idiot, Muscular Christian Socialist, who, in turn, is mothered by an insufferably patronizing bully of a woman. As a ten-minute sketch on BBC2 in 1898 from South Shields it would do. But as a full-length stage play it is hard to think of anything more silly, apart from the rest of the so-called *oeuvre*.

The one possible exception is *Pygmalion*, in which I toured the Welsh valleys in 1954 for the Arts Council. But the miners were still better than the play. I, however, was very funny as Freddy Eynesford Hill, which does go to prove that you can't make bricks entirely without straw – something play reviewers can never grasp about plays or actors.

But the 'greatest British dramatist since Shakespeare (?)'. Ben Travers could have had G.B.S. before breakfast in Australia watching the Test . . .

By the time I was twenty-five I had been in (admittedly bad, but no matter) productions of: *Arms and the Man, Candida, You Never Can Tell, Devil's Disciple, Caesar and Cleopatra, Saint Joan, Major Barbara* and, perhaps worst of all, Chekhov-for-philistines, *Heartbreak House*.

Try learning them, Mr Billington; they are posturing wind and rubbish. In fact, just the sort of play you would expect a critic to write. The difference is simply: he did it. Yours faithfully,

John
Osborne

It is delightful to speculate how Shaw might have handled this old-fashioned mortar attack. As it was, Professor Hornback wrote in to observe mildly that had Shaw created Mr Osborne he would have 'relieved his heavy dullness with something lovable'.

Authors Answer Back

Playwright Clifford Bax, in the 1940s, got tired of receiving critical notices. He was not the first dramatist to decide that critics couldn't recognize genius when it was staring them in the face. By way of retaliation, he published a *Letter to a Young Playwright* which listed the shortcomings of his adversaries:

Among play critics I have known only two who were not publicly ludicrous on account of an immeasurable self-esteem. The self-esteem is so embarrassing to any normal person that I, for example, hardly know where to look when I have converse with one of them because it is precisely as though I had to speak with an air of inferiority to a ridiculous and bedizened tart.

Beverely Baxter who had just been to see *The Golden Eagle*, Bax's latest offering at the Westminster Theatre, praised the rhetorical vigour of Bax's pamphlet.

That, of course, is excellent. It has gusto, it has style, and it has popular appeal. If only Mr Bax would write dialogue with one half that fervour he would become the darling of the box-office.

Nor is he content to liken us to a woman of the streets. We are also 'vampires and morbid parasites who exist upon the blood of the creative men and women' (there is an element of truth in this), and we are both 'pompously brainless and stupendously vain'.

The Golden Eagle is not about a steamer plying to Brighton, but concerns that unfortunate, pretty lady Mary, Queen of Scots. The play opened charmingly with Rizzio doing his stuff, the arrival of the worthless Darnley, the music- and dance-loving Mary having sprightly jokes in a French accent with her ladies, and Scottish nobles plotting in all directions.

The costumes were delightful and probably authentic, the cast was a distinguished one, and the weather (for Scotland) was perfect throughout the play. The first act was thoroughly enjoyable, and I began to think harsh things about my critic colleagues.

But in the second act Mr Bax showed that he was in a dilemma. As a student of history he has a deep respect for accuracy, but as a playwright he should know that accuracy is the very death of self-expression. He also realized that the audience would have to be kept historically informed, which resulted in lines like this: 'Madam, I remember your father, King James V of Scotland.' 'When you married the Dauphin as a young girl.' 'You must listen to Stuart because he is your illegitimate brother.'

These are important facts, but didn't Mary know about her father, her husband and her illegitimate brother?

Shakespeare had a much better idea. He never allowed history to get in the way of theatrical effect. *The Golden Eagle* is laboriously exact.

I am sorry to say that I must award the verdict to the critics on points. This play is not good theatre. It is not good Bax. Every now and then it has absurdities, such as when the rough and honest Bothwell assures Mary that there is no time to reach Darnley's house and prevent the explosion which was to kill her miserable husband.

How far away was the house? Two miles, according to Bothwell. There were saddled horses in the courtyard, and the explosion was timed to take place in about ten minutes. It seems to me that even a Scottish horse ought to be able to get that distance under ten minutes.

There is much fine acting in this play, and Mr Robert Atkins proves, if it needs proving, that he can direct a costume play to the satisfaction of the senses.

Miss Claire Luce is delightful in the first act, but later becomes marooned on the Island of All For Love. Arthur Wontner can make music out of words, and Torin Thatcher as a mighty Scot not only acted well but looked like a rugby international.

I am sorry the play was not better. Bax *vobiscum*.

Additional opinion by Mr Culbertson: The Queen had a tough hand to play.

As the elder Dumas said, 'Why write plays at all? It is so easy not to write them.'

Actors and actresses often have an even tougher time getting their due than the playwrights, and sometimes critical notices

have a personal flavour. Diana Rigg appeared briefly nude in
Abelard and Heloïse. An American critic uncharitably described her as: 'built like a brick mausoleum with insufficient
flying buttresses'. But references to insufficiency of acting
ability are probably more wounding, like Oscar Wilde's summing up of a performance of *The Three Musketeers*: 'Athos,
Pathos and Bathos'.

Playwrights, film directors and actors have been known to
strike back at their critics – sometimes literally. Agnes Bernelle's husband punched Bernard Levin before an audience
of millions on 'That Was The Week That Was' because of his
rude review of Bernelle's 'horribly arch' show. (Not as nasty,
however, as a critic of Helen Hayes' performance in *Caesar
and Cleopatra*; she 'suffered', he wrote, 'from fallen ar-
chness.') Alexander Walker was attacked by Ken Russell on
television. Walker had described Russell's film *The Devils* as
a product of the 'Torquemada School of Film Direction'.
Wolf Mankowitz was so outraged by critical reception of his
musical *Belle*, about Dr Crippen's murders, that he had a
coffin carried down Fleet Street borne by chorus girls in
fish-net tights and accompanied by loud-speaker vans dis-
pensing counter-propaganda for the show. It closed after six
weeks.

Probably the most alarming ploy was adopted by Ryan
O'Neal. After Hollywood journalist Rona Barrett was unkind
about one of his films he sent her a beautifully gift-wrapped
present through the post. Inside the layers of pretty paper
and coloured ribbon was a tarantula.

But audiences too can give critics something to think about,
as Max Beerbohm found on a visit to *Romeo and Juliet*:

A strange thing happened at the Lyceum Theatre some nights ago
(and happens, I suppose, nightly). The twilight of dawn had crept
into Juliet's bed-chamber, and envious streaks had laced the sev-
ering clouds in yonder east, and the nurse had announced the
approach of Lady Capulet, and all was as it should be, till Romeo,
claiming the one more kiss before his flight, clasped Juliet in his
arms and kissed her; whereat the audience howled with laughter for
several seconds.

(Beerbohm was puzzled by this, wondering if there was some comic aspect of *Romeo and Juliet* he had previously missed.)

Bernard Shaw took a swipe at fashionable women in audiences. In a letter to *The Times* in 1905 he explained the sort of thing he had to put up with:

Every argument that applies to the regulation of the man's dress applies equally to the regulation of the woman's. Now let me describe what actually happened to me at the Opera. Not only was I in evening dress by compulsion, but I voluntarily added many graces of conduct as to which the management made no stipulation whatever. I was in my seat in time for the first chord of the overture. I did not chatter during the music nor raise my voice when the Opera was too loud for normal conversation. I did not get up and go out when the statue music began. My language was fairly moderate considering the number and nature of the improvements on Mozart volunteered by Signor Caruso, and the respectful ignorance of the dramatic points of the score exhibited by the conductor and the stage manager – if there is such a functionary at Covent Garden. In short, my behaviour was exemplary.

At nine o'clock (the Opera began at eight) a lady came in and sat down very conspicuously in my line of sight. She remained there until the beginning of the last act. I do not complain of her coming late and going early; on the contrary, I wish she had come later and gone earlier. For this lady, who had very black hair, had stuck over her right ear the pitiable corpse of a large white bird, which looked exactly as if someone had killed it by stamping on its breast, and then nailed it to the lady's temple, which was presumably of sufficient solidity to bear the operation. I am not, I hope, a morbidly squeamish person, but the spectacle sickened me. I presume that if I had presented myself at the doors with a dead snake round my neck, a collection of black beetles pinned to my shirtfront, and a grouse in my hair, I should have been refused admission. Why, then, is a woman to be allowed to commit such a public outrage? Had the lady been refused admission, as she should have been, she would have soundly rated the tradesman who imposed the disgusting headdress on her under the false pretence that 'the best people' wear such things, and withdrawn her custom from him; and thus the root of the evil would be struck at; for your fashionable woman generally allows herself to be dressed according to the taste of a person whom she would not let sit down in her presence. I once, in Drury Lane

Theatre, sat behind a *matinée* hat decorated with the two wings of a seagull, artificially reddened at the joints so as to produce an illusion of being freshly plucked from a live bird. But even that lady stopped short of the whole seagull. Both ladies were evidently regarded by their neighbours as ridiculous and vulgar; but that is hardly enough when the offence is one which produces a sensation of physical sickness in persons of normal humane sensibility.

I suggest to the Covent Garden authorities that, if they feel bound to protect their subscribers against the danger of my shocking them with a blue tie, they are at least equally bound to protect me against the danger of a woman shocking me with a dead bird.

Yours truly,

G. Bernard Shaw

Being an audience is certainly hard work. If it isn't the rest of the audience, the play, and the acting, it is the whole grisly hassle of queuing to purchase a seat; being treated like a leper because you have an agency ticket (which costs more; the agency have double-booked you and the small print is that the management accepts no responsibility); selling your house to raise sufficient money to buy a drink in the bar, which has anyway been designed for teetotal sardines; and generally being harried from pillar to post. Alan Brien described the dubious pleasures of theatre-going in his article 'So You Want To Be An Audience' published in *Punch*:

The theatre, you soon discover, has been designed for some vanished race of dwarfs with bat ears and hawk eyes. The original audience could see round pillars, catch a mumbled aside bounced off the prompter, and divine which of three blurred pink young men in identical sports jackets is actually moving his lips at any moment. You arrange your enormous legs at right-angles to your torso, vainly attempt to claim one of the seat-arms for one elbow (one of them must be yours whichever end of the row you count from) and try to breathe in without producing a wheeze which groans along the woodwork, ricochets back through the iron supports and ends by twanging the broken springs in your upholstery. Soon you actually begin to hear words, even scraps of sentences and snatches of sound effects. None of them, however, seems to have anything to do with the play. 'If Ethel thinks I am going to carry her trays she can just go and . . .' 'I've taken the order from the bald head with the dyed hair in Row C, thank you very much.' 'How many tonics do you want with these whiskies, Ada?' Occasionally even this contemporary dialogue is drowned by the sound of some sporty employee tobogganing down the stone steps from the gallery on a tin tray while her supporters rattle their spoons in chipped mugs as encouragement. Really luxurious theatres even have synchronized lavatories which all flush juicily and refill at the same moment – usually when the hero is saying, 'My God, Bettina – we might be in the middle of the desert.'

Inventing Shakespeare . . .

Since Shakespeare is probably more acted than any other playwright in Britain and suffers from the additional handicap of being a national institution, it is not surprising that his works have suffered such abuse at the hands of bowdlerizers, vain, incompetent, and sometimes drunken actors, and an army of self-appointed script editors who put in things the Bard unaccountably left out or deleted material he had unaccountably left in. In his survey of this dismal history of take-over bids for Shakespeare Kenneth McClellan describes some of the more startling attempts to get the Bard to move over in favour of a more expansive ego:

. . . Turning to *King John*, (Beerbohm) Tree noticed that the careless Bard had forgotten to include the signing of Magna Carta, and obligingly interpolated a tableau depicting that event. (Victor Lucas pointed out to the present writer that Shakespeare may well never have heard of Magna Carta.)

It must be said that the surviving 'still' of Tree's Battle of Angiers is beautiful, an Uccello battle-piece come to life.

Tree's *Midsummer Night's Dream* (1900) provided live rabbits, and what joyless creature would rather have had poetry? In *Twelfth Night* (1901) a sextet of sub-Malvolii mimicked Tree's walk and gesture. Olivia's garden extended terrace by terrace to the very back of the stage. It was impossible to shift, so that apart from small 'front scenes' the entire play had to take place in Olivia's garden, whether this was dramatically feasible or not.

As Shylock (1908) Tree outdid Irving by rushing through the empty house, the light from his lantern being seen in every room, and then out again over the bridge. In court he had the whole population of the Guidecca ghetto to support him, though surely it is much more effective for Shylock not to have a friend in sight.

His Hamlet (1891) rivalled Irving's in deep unspoken passion for Ophelia (he later endowed Professor Higgins with a similar passion for Eliza). Laertes, almost as dangerous to the star as Claudius, was relieved of many of his lines; Osric was excused attendance altogether; the First Gravedigger was bowdlerized; and the play ended with an off-stage 'heavenly choir', forerunner of so many in Hollywood.

In *Richard II* (1903) Tree copied Charles Kean's episode of the entry into London, his hunted look being unforgettable, but completely at variance with York's description of his demeanour. These innovations, said Shaw, 'could only have occurred to one whose mind was completely free from all preoccupation with Shakespeare'.

'It is difficult to live up to one's posters,' observed Tree. 'When I pass my name in such large letters I blush, but at the same time instinctively raise my hat.' It was doubly difficult to live up to Tree's performances if you weren't even Tree. 'With the constant supervision you so thoroughly exercise,' complained a stage manager, 'you have no use for a stage manager. What you really require are a couple of *tame trained echoes!*'

Another hazard that the Bard might reasonably have been spared were geriatric actors with no idea of when to stop. Tyrone Guthrie recalls seeing actor manager Sir Frank Benson at the age of about seventy in his 'rouged and ruined masculine beauty':

In the part of Caliban he turned a few creaky handsprings, and at one part of the play a pair of parallel bars appeared on the Magic Island, and Caliban, gravely and to the embarrassment of a respectful audience, hung upside down.

Benson had a rival in Sir Philip Ben Greet, who was, says McClellan:

. . . without doubt the worst actor who ever lived, though this may not have been the reason for his knighthood. The drawling whine of his delivery was one of the least agreeable sounds ever heard in the theatre. The best that can be said for him is that, as against most other actor-managers, he inflicted comparatively little of his own acting on his audiences.

The lack, not only of illumination, but of normal comprehension in Greet's performances and productions must surely be unparalleled. As Touchstone, for instance (Metropole, Camberwell, May 1896), he failed to realize that the burlesque verses with which the jester caps those of Orlando are improvized, and actually plucked them from a tree. 'This was a new reading with a vengeance,' commented Shaw in the *Saturday Review* of 2 May 1896, and went on: 'He completely missed the piled-up climax of the speech to William, and was, in short, as bad a Touchstone as a critic could desire to see. It is no disgrace to an actor to be unable to play Touchstone; but why, under these circumstances, and being a manager, he should cast himself for it, passes my understanding.

Greet's stolidity of mind was reinforced by a rabid Puritanism. He refused to produce 'that dirty play' *Measure for Measure*, and vetoed inter-sexual friendships among the younger members of his company, with what effect on their ability to act together can be imagined. No more than Tree or Benson did he ever bother to learn his lines, and on one occasion when he was playing First Gravedigger, his altercation with Second Gravedigger (Wilson Featherston) as to which of them was due to speak the next line was audible at the back of the gallery.

In view of all this it is refreshing to read Shaw's delighted reaction to a *Hamlet* at the Lyceum in 1897:

The Forbes Robertson *Hamlet* at the Lyceum is very unexpectedly at that address, really not at all unlike Shakespeare's play of the same name . . . The story of the play was perfectly intelligible and quite took the attention of the audience off the principal actor at moments.

Unfortunately the production overran the stamina of the cast by a number of performances. Shaw first saw it in October 1897, and by the time he revisited it in December the strain was beginning to tell:

Public feeling has been much harrowed this week by the accounts from America of the 144 hours' bicycle race; but what are the horrors of such an exhibition compared to those of the hundred nights' run of *Hamlet*! On Monday last I went, in my private capacity, to witness the last lap but five of the Lyceum trial of endurance. The performers had passed through the stage of acute mania, and were for the most part sleep-walking in a sort of dazed blank-verse dream. Mr Barnes raved of some New England maiden named Affection Poo; the subtle distinctions made by Mrs Patrick Campbell between madness and sanity had blurred off into a placid idiocy turned to favour and to prettiness; Mr Forbes Robertson, his lightness of heart all gone, wandered into another play at the words 'Sleep? No more!' which he delivered as, 'Sleep no more.' Fortunately, before he could add 'Macbeth does murder sleep,' he relapsed into Hamlet and saved the situation. And yet some of the company seemed all the better for their unnatural exercise. The King was in uproarious spirits; and the Ghost, always comfortable, was now positively pampered, his indifference to the inconvenience of purgatory having developed into a bean-fed enjoyment of it.

Strain had other adverse effects on performers, however, and Shaw is particularly eloquent on the tradition of preparing for melodrama by getting oneself into the mood for it:

We all know the melodramatic style which grew up in the days when actors who played 'emotional' parts habitually got themselves into the requisite maudlin condition by making themselves half drunk. This was the true origin of the detestable veiled voice and muzzy utterance which no longer produce any illusion except that of the odour of spirits. The actor of the past did not walk across the stage to open the door: he plunged headlong at the handle, and, when he had safely grasped it, rolled his eye round to give some pretence of dramatic significance to an action which really expressed nothing but his doubts as to his ability to walk straight . . .

These excesses produced a whole style of drunken acting which lingered even when the reason for it had disappeared. Or almost disappeared; McClellan recalls unfortunate experiences at Stratford in more recent times:

Some years ago an actor went on drunk as Thersites, interpolated the 'horse' speech from *The Taming of the Shrew*, and then fell asleep on the stage. Another actor who had not bothered to learn the part of Macbeth broke off in the middle of a speech and told the audience, 'You know all this better than I do.'

Spectators' tolerance has been extended to some curious experiments in sets and the 1962 *Tempest* directed by Peter Brook and Clifford Williams had some appealing novelties viewed by Kenneth McClellan with a rather jaundiced eye:

. . . the perspex scenery was a complete entertainment in itself and Shakespeare's text was utterly superfluous. Caliban brought on an enormous bone and held it in such a way as to suggest that he was rather sex-conscious, something already hinted at in the lines. The goddesses were represented by gigantic corn-dollies, from the skirts of which three men in drag emerged to speak the lines.

If sets could be peculiar, actors are sometimes just as inappropriate. Extraordinarily badly miscast was a production of *Hamlet* in 1951 reviewed by Beverley Baxter under the headline: 'The Worst *Hamlet* I Have Ever Seen', where the miscasting, it appeared, extended even to the minor roles:

When the curtain descended on the usual array of corpses last night at the New Theatre, even a stage detective would have known that Henry Sherek's production of *Hamlet* had gone wrong. The fact that no one cheered when the company took its first bow should have been a further warning.

Unfortunately the curtain kept going up and coming down to polite applause until there was one curtain too many – and the gallery gave the whole thing a hearty Boo. Like Hitler their patience had become exhausted.

Never before have I seen such a reception given to a Shakespearean play. At last the impossible had happened.

Mr Alec Guinness is a brilliant actor whose career will not be halted by this failure. But what in the world decided him to play Hamlet with a moustache and a goatee? Certainly Shakespeare makes Hamlet refer to his beard but one need not be so scrupulous about a mere figure of speech.

. . . the puzzlement did not end with the principal role. That excellent actor Walter Fitzgerald decided to play the king as if he were Captain Bligh of the *Bounty*. His voice reeked of the sea and he only made a pass at the queen when there was nothing else to keep him occupied. Then there was the ghost of Hamlet's father. Never has anyone deteriorated so little in dying. He instructed Hamlet with all the heartiness of a coach urging his team to go in and win.

As for that innocent child Ophelia, she appeared before us dressed like good Queen Bess and might have been a woman of fifty until she had a chance to speak.

But the climax came when the strolling players arrived. I am a man of a kindly nature who takes no joy in hurting those who are without defence, but Mr Ken Tynan, who did the First Player last night, would not get a chance in a village hall unless he were related to the vicar. His performance is quite dreadful . . .

This provoked a reply to the *Express* from the aggrieved actor which ended '. . . my performance in *Hamlet* was not "quite dreadful"; it is, in fact, only slightly less than mediocre. I do not actually exit through the scenery or wave at friends in the audience.'

There had, actually, been worse *Hamlet*s. Max Beerbohm witnessed the most improbable production ever when Sarah Bernhardt imposed upon the loyalty of her public sufficiently to play Hamlet, not previously considered an ideal feminine role, and to play it in French:

HAMLET, PRINCESS OF DENMARK
17 June 1899

I cannot, on my heart, take Sarah's Hamlet seriously. I cannot even imagine anyone capable of more than a hollow pretence at taking it seriously. However, the truly great are apt, in matters concerning themselves, to lose that sense of fitness which is usually called sense of humour, and I did not notice that Sarah was once hindered in her performance by any irresistible desire to burst out laughing. Her solemnity was politely fostered by the Adelphi audience. From first to last no one smiled. If anyone had so far relaxed himself as to smile, he would have been bound to laugh. One laugh in that dangerous atmosphere, and the whole structure of polite solemnity would have toppled down, burying beneath its ruins the national reputation for good manners. I, therefore, like everyone else, kept an iron control upon the corners of my lips. It was not until I was half-way home and well out of earshot of the Adelphi, that I unsealed the accumulations of my merriment.

'Her friends ought to have restrained her,' added Beerbohm. 'The custom-house officials at Charing Cross ought to have confiscated her sable doublet and hose.' Alas they did not, which allowed her to betray 'nothing but herself, and reveal nothing but the unreasoning vanity which had impelled her to so preposterous an undertaking'.

Even now the most hazardous productions are still those

which are by implication star vehicles. *Hamlet, King Lear, Othello* are too often irresistible to the actor who wishes to crown his achievements with a performance that will make the history books. Sometimes the circumstances are unpropitious. Gielgud's *Othello* at Stratford in 1961 was left permanently grounded by 'an Iago whose movements were incessant and unpredictable ("Bannen to right of him, Bannen to left of him")' – as one critic put it. This was a production with toppling scenery and operatic effects; Gielgud was therefore struggling along as best he could. But in 1980, heralded weeks in advance by blasts of publicity, some of which may later have appeared unwise, a star vehicle was trundled on to the stage of the Old Vic. It was the beginning of the great:

'O'BETH AFFAIR'

In September 1980 Peter O'Toole opened in Bryan Forbes's production of *Macbeth* at the Old Vic. The fall-out from the first night was spectacular. Critics joyfully abandoned cliché and caution; they *all* hated this one:

Macbeth staggers from the murder chamber drenched in enough gore to service a transfusion unit at a twenty-car pile-up on the M1.

O'Toole 'staggers' round the stage sounding as if he were spitting out a list of words he'd inadvertently swallowed.

Wolfit on a bad night.

He delivers every line with a monotonous tenor bark as if addressing an audience of Eskimos who have never heard of Shakespeare.

The *Guardian*'s expertise in Eskimo language was superior to the *Pravda* correspondent's understanding of English. He reported the symphony of abuse thus: O'Toole had 'surged up with new facets of talent. The British press has noted this event *Macbeth* as a milestone in theatrical history.'

Time Out summed up the carnage, critical and theatrical:

The press has taken an appropriately Jacobean revenge on the perpetrators of *Macbeth* (Old Vic), the critical sound and fury following the first awful performances almost matching the scope of the PR job that the newspapers did on Peter O'Toole and Bryan Forbes before the opening. Notwithstanding this gleeful but deserving demolition job on a show of monumental ignorance and ineptitude the audiences are coming in droves, so it may end up being played for laughs and become the kitsch hit of the decade. As if in farcical harmony with the imagery of the state in decay, the benighted cast vainly grapple with a fusillade of wilful props, unravelling costumes and a set designed for mountain goats. Meanwhile O'Toole concentrates on missing the furniture, and thereby reduces Macbeth's accelerating corruption to a series of languid, colourless ruminations in which key lines simply blow away like ashes. A crippling lack of vision about either the play's themes (ambition, sexual blackmail, the legitimacy of power), Shakespeare's poetry, or contemporary presentations of Elizabethan drama clearly renders the performers virtually catatonic with indecision. No rotten vegetable stalls have yet opened for business outside however, despite our leader's appeal to the entrepreneurial spirit. (Ros Asquith)

Almost no aspect of the production escaped censure, but since it had evidently been conceived as a star vehicle, O'Toole himself took most of the flak. People objected to his manner of speaking the lines:

It was P. G. Wodehouse who memorably said that that 'tomorrow and tomorrow' speech has got a lot of spin on it but, as delivered by Mr O'Toole, it is hit for six like a full toss.

Eccentric rhythms reminiscent of Ralph Richardson are relayed to us in the fretful tones of Malcolm Muggeridge.

O'Toole himself remarked disarmingly at a press conference that when he began the project he 'just opened his mouth and a lot of rust poured out'. His replies to the critics were spirited:

What's all the fuss about anyway? It's only a bloody play! They [the audience] didn't laugh enough. They didn't get the jokes.

This engaging dismissiveness was unfortunately little use as a morale booster when Timothy West, the Old Vic director, disowned the production. The plot, as it were, thickened. Here are Benedict Nightingale's comments on the second night:

The second night was at least interesting at its curtain call. A vocal gentleman slithered at the last moment into the seat behind me to bawl 'bravo' and howl 'fuck 'em' when Bryan Forbes, the director, came onstage to defend his cast against its enemies. Actually, the label 'Judas' was directed, not at the critics, but at the Vic's top management, which had tried and failed to change the production and had presumed to admit so to the public prints. What was less clear, however, was which of the unprepossessing candidates onstage was supposed to be the betrayed Christ. Perhaps Mr Forbes meant himself. He had attempted several miracles, such as passing off three Tennysonian lovelies as the witches, asking us to take seriously a ghostly Banquo who hadn't so much daubed himself in red paint as swum five lengths in it, and getting a good performance out of O'Toole; and none of them had been much appreciated.

More likely, he meant O'Toole himself, of whom the most charitable thing to say is that his interpretation is eccentric. He appears to see Macbeth as a surly brutalized oaf who alters not one jot from Duncan's inexplicable description of him as a 'worthy gentleman' to his own overdue death. At any rate, he lolls and swaggers across the stage, his mouth sometimes agape, sometimes not, and part-barks, part-bellows, part-chants out hoarse iambs in an actorish staccato, so that 'no one' becomes 'no wan', 'but here' 'bat hair' and 'Duncan' 'Dunken'. And everything and everyone is similarly hectored, whether it's his wife, Macduff, Dunken, Banquo's ghost, the cream-faced loon, the dagger, hell, or his own soliloquizing conscience. The assumption seems to be that the rest of the world, including us in the audience, are stone-deaf and very, very stupid. Was this the Monty Python loudmouth with the handkerchief knotted over his ears, or the actor I admired not long ago as Uncle Vanya and Vladimir in *Godot*? Unbelievably, the latter; and his performance should be suppressed before it irreparably damages a whole generation of British schoolchildren and causes diplomatic incidents abroad. It is a sustained disaster.

Nightingale was tough on the show. James Fenton in the *Sunday Times* was tougher:

Don't trust those reviews. The spectacle is far worse than has hitherto been made out, a milestone in the history of coarse acting. It moved the *Daily Mail* to giggles, and I was in such difficulties that I often wondered whether it would be better to leave the theatre and explode outside. But something froze the laughter on the lips.

It was the premeditated awfulness of O'Toole's performance. There was no question of risks taken, or brave attempts which had simply failed. This was the kind of awfulness which could have been seen a mile off.

Brian Grimwood's poster, with its sweet little owl and its dear little bat with knitting needles, was awful in a way which promised a children's picturebook version of the play. On the other hand, Keith Wilson's set appeared to have been loaned by a minor public school, with a special vote of thanks to the masters' wives, who did such sterling work in cobbling together the costumes from a heap of old drawing-room curtains, and who slaved away behind the scenes to produce such authentic effects as, for instance, the cloud of dust which billowed from Macbeth's tunic when Banquo clapped him on the shoulder. (A stock joke in coarse acting shows.)

The production was notable for the incomprehension with which lines were delivered and for the most wild moments of 'interpretation'. In Scene II, the King pointed to an apparently half-dead figure on the floor and said, 'What bloody man is that? He can report,/as seemeth by his plight, of the revolt/The newest state.' But the poor Captain seemed in no state to do any such thing. The second witch went into a paroxysm of agony before delivering the lines, 'By the pricking of my thumbs/Something wicked this way comes.' Brian Blessed, as Banquo, said, 'Look to the lady,' and actually threw Lady Macbeth (Frances Tomelty) to the nearest bystander. You could see what had been going through his mind. He was thinking, 'That Lady Macbeth, she's a rum sort, I wouldn't trust her as far as I could throw her . . . come to think of it, how far can I throw her?'

My colleagues have commented on the Knightsbridge witches, the sword that bent in the duel, the classic gaffe when Macduff announced that 'Macbeth was from his mother's womb untimely ripped', the laughter of the audience when Mr O'Toole arrived drenched in gore and announced after an age-long pause that he had done the deed (had he not told us, we might have supposed that some discontented members of the cast had placed a bucket of blood over his dressing-room door), the moment when the Macbeths walked straight into the scenery, and a hundred or so other minor points which a little time (a century, for instance) might straighten out.

As to Mr O'Toole's performance, it was deranged. 'I have,' says Macbeth, 'a strange infirmity which is nothing/To those that know me.' At first, I thought that this must be a portrayal of drunkenness. It had a slurred slowness, like that of the drunken driver who imagines he will go undetected if he sticks to the kerb and never exceeds ten miles an hour. Later, I began to wonder whether the boorishness and imperception of the delivery might not be better explained if one thought of a Macbeth who was in the habit of getting stoned out of his mind, so that his brain over the years had turned to Gruyère cheese. Finally, I was forced to reject both theories in favour of a worse explanation, that this Macbeth stemmed from an utterly private conception of personal glory, a conception so private and so intense that it rejected any offer of help or advice in its realization, a conception that spurned the play, spurned the company, and spurned the audience.

After a short London run, the production went on tour playing everywhere, it should be said, to packed houses. In Bristol the University Newsletter remarked that it had the 'largest advance sale for a straight play in the sixty-eight year history of the Hippodrome'. This seemed to vindicate O'Toole's comment that the reviews will be 'fish and chips' paper tomorrow'.

When the dust had settled and 'O'Beth' slipped back into London, Milton Shulman of the *Evening Standard* did a thoughtful corrective article in which he pointed out that the main reason the production was given such a pasting was that O'Toole was being judged 'by the most demanding standards of Shakespearian acting . . . The truth is that, if O'Toole were an unknown repertory actor, no one would much complain about his performance and no one much would come to see it.' He might have added that brilliantly executed pre-publicity was also a factor which ensured that, if the production sank, it would sink like the *Titanic*, though in this case it was with the loss of all hands; (notwithstanding, as Bernard Levin acidly put it, 'Timothy West's vigorous attempt to precede the women and children into the lifeboat').

The reverberations of the O'Beth affair rumbled on into the winter. Peter O'Toole resigned as associate director of the Old Vic in December. There was a bomb scare at one of the performances prompting the headline 'Macbomb' in the *Sun*. Then the theatre announced it was closing down altogether after its grant was withdrawn. But the best valediction for O'Beth appeared just after the first night in the *In Memoriam* column of *The Times*:

Macbeth – wise and good king of Scotland for seventeen years 1040–57.

Shakespeare emerges bloody but unbowed from his periodic mangling at the hands of producers and actors. It is more difficult for him to survive a total rewrite. Kenneth McClellan discusses a well-meaning example of this, John Bowen's attempt to provide a television text that would 'help students find a way into Shakespeare's *Julius Caesar*':

A ten-year old of normal intelligence needs no help to 'find a way into' *Julius Caesar*. Bowen quotes the opening of the quarrel scene, and imagines the reader or auditor asking: 'Who is Lucius Pella, who hasn't appeared in the play so far, and won't again? What does "noted" mean in this context, and "meet" and "comment"? Can "nice" mean "pleasant" – if so, it doesn't make sense.'
   The answer is that only an impenetrable dullard would ask such questions when experiencing so exciting a play. What does it matter who Lucius Pella is? In a modern play, say one of those boardroom epics, one character may tell another that he has messed up the Parkinson contract. No one wants to know what the Parkinson contract is – the script writer himself wouldn't know. It is only a straw in the gale of dramatic conflict.
   John Wain said in a broadcast that as a schoolboy he was strangely stirred and moved by lines totally unrelated to his own experience, such as:

   In the most high and palmy state of Rome,
   A little ere the mightiest Julius fell . . .

Anyone who cannot be so stirred and moved will never get anything from Shakespeare. And who will appreciate the original any the better for hearing, for instance, John Bowen's reduction of the lovely scene between Brutus and Portia to the following:

Brutus: *Were you listening?*
Portia: *No. Except for them to go. I didn't take a pill, though.*
Brutus: *I suppose I should have offered them a drink. I didn't think of it.*
Portia: *What did they want?*

Brutus: *They wanted me to kill Caesar.*
Portia: *Oh.* [Pause] *And are you going to?* [Pause]
Brutus: *We'd better send the children to your mother.*

So much for 'Shakespeare for Schools'.

Books written about Shakespeare are legion; indeed he is
the focus of a small publishing industry; all sorts of critical
theories about the plays have been peddled, some more, some
less lunatic than others. There is also a worthy tradition of
unilluminating stodge in Shakespeare criticism, an example
of which attracted James Joyce's withering scorn:

It will be seen that the substance of this book is after the manner
of ancient playbills. Here is no psychological complexity, no cross-
purpose, no interweaving of motives such as might perplex the base
multitude. Such a one is a 'noble character', such a one a 'villain',
such a passage is 'grand', 'eloquent', or 'poetic'. One page in the
account of *Richard the Third* is made up of single lines or couplets
and such non-committal remarks as 'York says then', 'Gloucester,
apparently surprised, answers', 'and York replies', 'and Gloucester
replies', 'and York retorts'. There is something very naïve about
this book, but (alas!) the general public will hardly pay sixteen
shillings for such naïvety. And the same Philistine public will
hardly read five hundred pages of 'replies' and 'retorts' illustrated
with misquotations. And even the pages are wrongly numbered.

Another favoured product of the Shakespeare publishing industry used to be the literature designed to prove beyond a
peradventure that whoever wrote Shakespeare, it wasn't
Shakespeare. Solomon Eagle, alias Sir John Squire, had a
little innocent fun at the expense of one of the 'Baconians'
who had devoted his life to adducing arbitrary and improbable
evidence that Sir Francis Bacon wrote Shakespeare's works:

Most people who read his pamphlet, *The Shakespeare Myth*, must
have been astounded by the naïvety of some of the 'proofs' there
contained. The fact that Bacon was called Bacon – a name so easily
interchangeable with pig, hog, and rasher – was a great help; for
where the application of ciphers did not obtain one word it might
obtain another. Bacon, according to Sir Edwin Durning-Lawrence,
must have been at least as preoccupied with ensuring his identifi-

cation by posterity as with the writing of good verse, for he would take great pains to work in such a word as 'hang-hog', or to make three consecutive lines begin with words – such as Pompey, In, and Got – out of the initials of which could be constructed the appellation 'pig'. Everything was pork that came to Sir Edwin's net, and he would by tortuous ratiocination get evidence from the most seemingly innocent contemporary English and foreign engravings. For there was a secret brotherhood at work carrying on the Baconian tradition, and the artist who gave the portrait of Shakespeare two left sleeves (the confirmation of this was, I think, obtained from the editor of the *Tailor and Cutter*) had a subtle and profound intention. Sir Edwin collected a very large library in connection with his work, and the study of it was his passion; but, save industry, he had none of the qualifications for his task.

I myself obtained in a strange way an amusing insight into his looseness of procedure. He had been writing letters maintaining his thesis in a contemporary weekly. Wondering whether he could be hoaxed, I sent to the paper a letter over what might have seemed, to a man with any real detective faculty, the suspicious signature 'P.O.R. Ker'. In this letter I called Sir Edwin's attention to a quotation (which I had myself invented and written in Elizabethanese) which I ascribed to one of the best-known works of Greene. My 'quotation' (I forget its wording, but it contained phrases about 'Shakescene' and 'the semblance of a hogg') made it perfectly clear that Shakespeare was merely Bacon's dummy. Any man with the slightest qualifications for his work would have looked up Greene for reference – and would not have found it. Not so Sir Edwin. He wrote in at once (the editor, in order to spare his feelings, did not print the communication) to say that the fact that Mr Ker's important and convincing reference had been ignored by the Shakespeareans showed their utter incompetence.

But the most striking thing about him was his detestation of Shakespeare. There are people who hate Napoleon; there are people who object to Torquemada; there are even people who feel a pronounced distaste for Nero. But never has anyone loathed and despised a dead man as the really mild and amiable Sir Edwin despised and loathed Shakespeare. No epithets were, he felt, too opprobrious for this rascal, who for three hundred years had cheated another man out of his due fame. He denied Shakespeare any virtue at all; he pointed out that there existed no proof that Shakespeare could even read; and he habitually referred to him as the 'drunken, illit-

erate clown of Stratford', 'the sordid moneylender of Stratford', and
'the mean, drunken, ignorant, and absolutely unlettered rustic of
Stratford'. So strong, indeed, were his feelings that when *The Times*
says that 'One cannot but feel that he was happy in not living to see
the celebrations which the British Academy and other friends of
literature are to hold in 1916, the third centenary of Shakespeare's
– not Bacon's – death,' it is not making a weak and untimely jest,
but stating the sober truth.

When Sir Edwin died, who was there to take up the mantle
of Baconian scholarship? Squire discovered an indefatigable
propagandist in the shape of a Mr Harman who not only
attributed all of Shakespeare to Bacon, but all of almost everybody else. 'The Baconian authorship [of *The Faerie Queene*],'
says Squire, 'forces Mr Harman to the conclusion that some
of Spenser's sonnets were written by Bacon when he was eight
or nine years old. But Mr Harman is a strong man. After all,
Mozart was a precocious child, so why not Bacon?' It is
delightful, says Squire, to yield oneself to the pleasure of
following the Harmanian trail:

I have noted the works which in the course of his narrative or in
footnotes he ascribes to Bacon. The Authorized Version of the Bible
is not mentioned. But, apart from his voluminous acknowledged
writings, Bacon wrote the works of Spenser (including *The Faerie
Queene*, the longest poem in the world, which Bacon published
before he was out of his twenties); the works of Shakespeare; practically the whole body of Elizabethan poetical criticism (including
Webbe's *Discourse of Poesie*, Puttenham's *Art of Poesie*, Sidney's
Apologie, Daniel's *A Defence of Ryme*, and Mere's *Palladis Tamia*);
many of the poems of Gascoigne (written by Bacon before he was
twelve); certain works imputed to Nashe, Greene, and Gabriel
Harvey; the poems of Sir Walter Raleigh and the *Last Fight of the
'Revenge'*; the works of Essex; Sidney's *Arcadia* and *Astrophel and
Stella* (with this key Bacon unlocked his heart); Lyly's *Euphues* (a
long book); Bryskett's *Discourse of Civil Life*; Sir Humphrey Gilbert's *Discourses* and the account of his last voyage; *Leicester's Com-
monwealth* and *Leicester's Ghost*; and other minor scraps. If this be
all correct, we shall have to revise our opinion of the Elizabethan
time as a time replete with various genius. All we shall be able to
refer to now will be 'the spacious Bacon of great Elizabeth'.

An enormous number of people – including supposed writers and their relations – must have been in the secret. Sometimes they must have marvelled at Bacon's extraordinary behaviour, as for instance when he wrote for Raleigh a laudatory poem on the Queen:

> *Bacon (who, in my opinion, is the author of the poem) makes use of the opportunity in taking up the personality of Ralegh to express his own feelings. He was undoubtedly most unhappy at his exclusion from access and the waning of all his hopes of advancement. This is what is reflected under the disguise of Ralegh's loss of favour in the poem.*

They must have wondered how on earth Bacon expected his grievances to be remedied if his complaints were published over another man's name, and why, if Raleigh could address poems to the Queen *in propria persona* without loss of caste, Bacon could not do the same. But no doubt most of them, for many were impecunious, did not allow such questions to bother them much. They were content to take Bacon's bribes for the use of their names. What he must have spent in subsidies to sham authors one gasps to contemplate. No wonder that for years he was in such financial straits, and that at one point things came to such a pass with him that he was arrested for debt.

There is, sadly, little of this eccentricity left in Shakespearian/ Baconian scholarship. But it has had a late flowering in Dr Rowse's final, categorical, incontrovertible and non-debateable discovery of Shakespeare's 'Dark Lady'. Bernard Levin reviewed the book that spilled the beans:

WHO WAS THAT LADY?
Shakespeare the Man by A. L. Rowse

What ant has got into Dr Rowse's trousers and bites him so that he leaps and capers and yells and makes such an egregious ass of himself with his ridiculous boasting, his absurd claims that his speculations are proofs, that he has settled all outstanding questions for ever?

> *. . . puts out of court all the existing editions of the Sonnets . . . all the biographies of Shakespeare . . . impossible to impugn the historian's account of the matter . . . definitive answers . . . nonsense written about William Shakespeare . . . comes from ignorance of the Elizabethan age . . . my new finds . . . impossible to impugn because borne out by historical fact . . . we now know,*

> *after centuries . . . complete and absolute corroboration . . . im-*
> *perceptive generations have missed . . . complete vindication of*
> *fact and argument . . . there can be no mistake about it . . . vague*
> *conjectures, for generations, have told us nothing . . . now all quite*
> *clear . . . commentators with no historical sense have totally lost*
> *themselves . . . disregard mountains of otiose commentary . . . see*
> *my* The Elizabethan Renaissance *. . . see my* The Elizabethan
> Renaissance *. . . see my* The Elizabethan Renaissance *. . . see*
> *my* The Elizabethan Renaissance *. . .*

Cucullus non facit monachum; Dr Rowse is entitled to reply that his
buffoonish behaviour does not itself invalidate his claims. True: so
let us now ignore the conduct of the accused and proceed to the
evidence. It is no secret (at least if it is a secret it is a bloody miracle,
in view of the author's pre-publication trumpetings) that Dr Rowse,
in this book, claims to have established beyond any further doubt
the identity of the Dark Lady of the Sonnets, and to have done so
by the use of 'strict attention to chronology, the correlation of what
Shakespeare tells us, the topical references with historical circumstances at every point, the minute and precise corroboration of
internal with external information'.

Let us take a few examples of his rigorous method. His candidate
for the role of Dark Lady is one Emilia Lanier, née Bassano, and
she appears in the manuscripts of a shady Elizabethan astrologer
named Simon Forman, whom she consulted, and with whom she
(according to Forman's account) had an affair. Now Shakespeare's
love was, as he repeatedly insists, dark; brows, eyes, hair were all
black. We cannot be so sure about her skin, for Sonnet 130 (ignored
here by Rowse) says, *If snow be white, why then her breasts are dun*
– only, it seems, by comparison with snow; still, if she existed at all
(Rowse does not even consider here the 'anti-personalist' view of
the Sonnets as flights of pure poetic imagination), she was dark. So
Rowse takes us to Forman for confirmation of the fact that Emilia
was dark. And all Forman says on the subject is 'She was very
brown in youth.' This, for Rowse, is enough; 'Evidently,' he says,
'she was exceptionally dark.' Why he imagines Forman added 'in
youth' if Emilia was still dark, and how Forman's 'brown' becomes
the repeated 'black' of the Sonnets – on all this the man of 'minute
and precise corroboration' is silent.

That's nothing. Shakespeare's Dark Lady was musical; indeed,
played a musical intrument (Sonnet 128), which seems to be the
virginals. It is therefore necessary for Rowse to find that Emilia

played the virginals, too. Watch now how the Doctor does it. Forman says that her husband was 'a minstrel'; on page 100 Rowse embellishes this, saying that she was 'musical . . . married off to another musician'; on page 111, discussing Emilia's prospects on the death of her mother, he says that she 'no doubt had been taught to play on the virginals'; and finally on page 156 we read of Shakespeare that 'we know that Emilia's playing on the virginals was one of the arts by which he had been ensnared'. Such is Dr Rowse's method; from a total lack of any evidence whatever that Emilia played any musical instrument to 'we know that Emilia's playing on the virginals' helped to ensnare Shakespeare. This is not scholarship; it is pyramid selling.

A Cast of Thousands

As providers of unintentional humour the movies are an unrivalled art form. The best bad films have an irresistible quality not to be found in unwatchable plays or unreadable books. A sense of the ridiculous is utterly and delightfully absent.

One of the most distinguished purveyors of expensive Philistinism and implausible melodrama in movies was Cecil B. De Mille. An early effort, *Feet of Clay*, was reviewed in the *New York Times* with some puzzlement:

The acting and the direction of this very strange affair are in keeping with the exaggerations of the narrative, the incidents of which are both improbable and implausible. Some of the scenes depicting aquamarine sports are interesting so long as one does not bother about the subtitles or the story. But after Kerry Harlan (Rod La Rocque) is bitten by a shark and his consequent lameness is seen in his Harlem flat and also at a glaring garden party, one is apt to presume that Mr De Mille was indulging himself in making this production. He is not content with the ordinary triangle muddle, as he makes this a quintet affair.

. . . The story is built around the shark's bite. Harlan manages to keep his lameness a secret from his bride, but she will dance, and finally in a jealous fit he decides that he is going to cut in and be her partner. He stumbles several times and eventually falls, bringing down a string of coloured lanterns.

. . . There is a wide difference between some of the subtitles. One reads: 'When the air is charged with tempest, trifles can breed tragedy.' A spoken title reads: 'Snap into it, Sapho! This is no refuge for society dames with broken arches.' And another says: 'I must beat it, as Benedick will dock me again if I'm late.'

One of the ridiculous scenes, and there are not a few of them, shows Dr Fergus Lansell (Robert Edeson) entering Harlan's flat. After a perfunctory glance at Harlan's foot – which it is said must be kept off the ground for a year or gangrene will set in – Dr Lansell sniffs the air, having obviously detected the perfume used by his wife. She is hiding in one of the rooms, the last to be opened.

It is not necessary to go into the individual acting of the principals in this production, as none of them excels in any particular scene nor seems especially fitted to the role allotted to him or her.

Biblical and religious subjects represented an irresistible challenge to De Mille's powers of vulgarization. The treatment could be a little wild; as the famous clerihew has it:

Cecil B. De Mille
Much against his will
Was persuaded to keep Moses
Out of the Wars of the Roses

But De Mille was splendidly confident in the face of his detractors. 'Give me any couple of pages of the Bible and I'll give you a picture,' he remarked. Also he was quite indifferent to the wails of the critics, whose objections may be summed up in Pauline Kael's judgement of his work: 'He made small-minded pictures on a big scale.'

Graham Greene appreciated more than most the characteristic De Mille brew of absurdity and lavish production values. Of *The Crusades* he wrote:

Mr Cecil De Mille's evangelical films are the nearest equivalent today to the glossy German colour prints which sometimes decorated mid-Victorian Bibles. There is the same complete lack of a period sense, the same stuffy horsehair atmosphere of beards and whiskers, and, their best quality, a childlike eye for details which enabled one to spend so many happy minutes spying a new lamb among the rocks, an unobtrusive dove or a mislaid shepherd. As the great drawbridge falls from the besieger's tower on to the walls of Acre, you cannot help counting the little cluster of spent arrows quivering under the falling block; when Richard of England takes the Cross from the hairy hermit, the camera, moving its eye down the castle walls, stays on a couple of pigeons nesting in a coign of masonry. But one chiefly enjoys in Mr De Mille's films their great set-pieces; he handles, as no other director can, an army of extras. It is not a mere matter of spending money. The cavalry charge outside Jerusalem, the storming of Acre: these are scenes of real executive genius. No clanking of tin swords here, but a quite horrifying sense of reality, as the huge vats tip the burning oil down on to the agonized faces of the men on the storming-ladders, or when the riders meet at full gallop in the plain with a shock which jars you in the stalls.

. . . Neither of the two principal players, Miss Loretta Young and Mr Henry Wilcoxon, really gets a chance in this film. The programme says all there is to be said about them. Mr Wilcoxon is 'six feet two inches tall, weighs 190 pounds. He was nicknamed "Biff" as a child.' Miss Young 'is five feet three and weighs 105 pounds'. The information is not as irrelevant as it sounds, for the acting can roughly be judged in terms of weight. Mr Wilcoxon leads over the hairy hermit, played by Mr C. Aubrey Smith, by six pounds, and Miss Katherine De Mille, who has an agreeably med-ieval face, as Alice of France beats Miss Young by ten pounds. (To quote the programme again: 'She avoids starches, sugars and fats; eats all greens and only enough meat to get the necessary proteins.')

As for the others there was a delicious moment when I thought the Earl of Leicester said 'Aye, Colonel,' to Richard when he was told to attack, but I think the din before Acre may have confused my ears. The Earl was made up distractingly to resemble Mr George Moore. He had one of the few English names in a finely orchestrated cast which included Sven-Hugo Borg, Fred Malatesta, Vallejo Gant-ner, Paul Sotoff, Hans von Twardowski, and the name I liked best, Pedro de Cordoba. One had to judge these actors by their names as their weights were not given.

De Mille was not the only director of historical extravaganza who came unstuck. Bosley Crowther was less than kind to the great Sergei Eisenstein's *Ivan the Terrible, Part II*, when he reviewed it in the *New York Times* in 1959:

The first part of *Ivan the Terrible* proved a monumental sort of film, conveying the dark magnificence of Russian medievalism, when it was shown here twelve years ago. This second part, which went on last evening at the Murray Hill Theatre, is but a pale extension of that great tableau, appearing to have been made from pieces of it picked up from the cutting-room floor.

Of the action he said:

Who is chasing whom and who gets butchered are matters of some doubt and less dramatic concern.

And of the acting:

Nikolai Cherkassov's performance – or, rather, his appearance – in the Ivan role is mainly a matter of his posing in grotesque get-ups and attitudes. The indication is that he is supposed to represent a lonely and angry man. He appears to be more of a mad one, with a peculiarly pointed head.

Static acting could sometimes be forced upon the players, as was the case in Sarah Bernhardt's performance in *Jeanne Dore*. The *New York Times* critic reported the result:

The film (itself) was so arranged before it was sent to this country that all evidences of the actress' lameness because of her artificial leg have been deleted. So the film, as it reached America, never shows the actress walking. In every scene in which she appears she is shown either seated or standing, and whenever she starts to walk the scene is immediately changed through the devices of the switch-back, the cut-in, or the printed legend. Thus, if Madame rises from a chair and starts to walk across the room to a window, she is seen to rise, the picture is snuffed out for an instant, and when it again covers the screen the actress is shown at her destination.

The effect is no more confusing that in the average picture, which often baffles and irritates all but the incorrigible movie fan. The picture is so focused that the feet of the actress do not show, or if they do, only for short intervals, so there is nothing in the many scenes of the protodrama, which is melodramatic in the extreme, that would apprise the uninformed of her misfortune.

They don't make actresses like that any more.

A Note on Period English

Since the advent of Michael Caine on the screen, audiences have got used to the idea that even heroes in movies don't necessarily speak the Queen's English. In the thirties and forties, apart from comics, who of course spoke funny, a very odd-sounding form of speech was in operation – as Richard Boston pointed out in an article in the *Guardian*, 1976:

The Emeric Pressburger–Michael Powell film of Nigel Balchin's novel *The Small Back Room* was on the box at some incredibly late hour on Friday night and Saturday morning last week, and what a good film it proved to be. The central situation is as immediate as ever, but time has given a period charm to this 1948 film.

What had dated more than anything else, though, was the language. This was partly a matter of the words – the Jerry planes, the hush-hush project, and the 'I know it's all a lot of rot, old chap, but . . .' Even more it was a matter of the extraordinary accents people apparently used less than thirty years ago. Bat was pronounced bet in those days. The Small Beck Room's hero is called Semmy Rice, and a lot of the ection takes place in his flet. There's another character called Ceptain Stuart. A terrible eccident heppens. Thenk you.

This eccent is still not quite extinct. The other day Posy gave me a definition of the word crèche. It's a collision of two cars in Knightsbridge. That's the only repeatable joke I've ever heard from Posy.

A different, but no less entertaining use of language was highlighted by Robert Herring when he reviewed *Koenigsmark*:

This . . . is a consistently feminine film. The second of the two Elissian Landi-scapes to grace our screens within a week, it has a villain who snarls, 'There are some things stronger than a woman's caprice,' and a heroine who delights us with 'Not good-bye but *au revoir*'. The events of August 1914 are described in these terms: 'War's been declared' – 'Reallah?' – 'Yahss.' And then the heroine appears as colonel-in-chief of whatever regiment she is colonel-in-chief of, and we realize that had Jeanette MacDonald played, as she should have, the title role, this story of love, life and loyalty in the grand duchy of Lautenburg would have been just as amusing and far more convincing. The sets, it should be mentioned, are of that elaborate French kind which look as if the cameraman had photographed the property room while the art director was having his lunch. They represent ducal libraries, lounges, boudoirs, armouries, and ballrooms as long but also as narrow as corridors. One of the nicest things that happens in the film is the fire which overtakes them.

Rib Ticklers that Don't

Penelope Gilliat in her article on 'The English Joke' explored the nature of that dubious commodity with the expertise of one who has struggled through blizzards of them in places where the English are supposed to be enjoying themselves:

The ocean around the island must be alive with gags. Every few miles along the coastline an old pier barnacled with double entendres sticks into the sea, a long, silvery arm of jokes encrusted with lights like the sequins of drag queens in pantomines, with bright little booths selling unimaginably censorable beach postcards and at the end of it a theatre that is a shrine of the most terrible jokes in the world ('Paris, city of madness, where only the river is Seine . . .).

I'm afraid perhaps you have to have been an English child to stomach it, reared on riddles in Christmas crackers and double-meanings in *Puss in Boots*. I don't know how else to explain the success of the *Carry On* pictures, which are made like old socks, or the Whitehall farces, which might be directed by traffic-meter wardens, or the Palladium, where one waits for the funny man as people in sane countries wait for the nudes; we must have a very great passion for jokes to do it.

An inexplicably enduring embodiment of the English joke was Norman Wisdom who made dozens of unbearable films in the fifties and early sixties:

The latest Norman Wisdom film, [1963] *A Stitch in Time*, is the second comedy in a fortnight that ends up in a hospital ward with the leading characters encased in plaster. (The other is *Mad, Mad, World*.)

In this new department of dread holiday humour, the joke is to see the patients falling about with merriment at someone else's pain – either at the sight of yet another bone going, or at the sight of a leg in plaster being agonizingly jacked up to the ceiling and then dropped crash onto someone's precious watch. 'When their ribs break, you'll laugh till your ribs ache!' (*Sunday Sadist*); 'Warner Bros., the greatest name is family entertainment, has done it again! Take the kiddies!' (the *New Brutalist*).

I can just see, squinting, the humour to be wrung out of bedpans – the Rank Organization has been wringing it ever since I can remember – but broken bones really aren't the biggest laugh in the world. Nor are the perfectly healthy teeth that Norman Wisdom jerks out by mistake in a glum riot in a dentist's clinic, nor the spastic gait that he puts on as a disguise, nor the patient on crutches who is knocled down by our hero while he is driving a motorized stretcher like a maniac around the hospital corridors. Nor indeed are the brutal swallowing mishaps that seem to be a running theme in *A Stitch in Time*. A head butcher swallows a presentation watch, a dental patient swallows a whole roll of cotton wool that he has shoved down his throat by Norman Idiocy, and then a St John Ambulance man in a brass band swallows his flute.

After watching the film for a while you begin to think that the thing that should have been swallowed is the star's pride. Norman Wisdom's films usually include a character who is planted to tell us how lovable he is, but I've never known the line to be advertised quite so hard before. In between knocking ill people down and driving his best friend's unconscious head like a battering ram into an ambulance, he keeps getting told about his lovability by a soppy nurse. He is the only man in the film who cares enough about a little orphan in hospital to give her back the will to live, and he is also the only man at a charity ball who understands what real charity is. What spinach.

Miss Gilliat was no less unkind about a Wisdom film entitled *Press for Time*, 'a pun that must mean he plays either a dry cleaner or, as it turns out, a reporter'. The actor specializes, she continued, 'in a bashfulness verging on mental deficiency'. All this, however, was not as relentlessly unfunny as the breed of 'middle-class' coy sex comedy that succeeded the 'working-class' idiom of big bottoms, boobs labelled 'United Dairies' and Nazi mother-in-laws.

Prudence and the Pill was one such, taking advantage of the sixties climate of supposedly liberated pill-popping women, but remaining trapped in the traditional nudge, nudge ethos of funny sex. Penelope Gilliat dealt with it succinctly:

I remember at least two awful stage comedies in the last couple of years that had the same central deadening comic ideas, about birth-control slip-ups among the privileged and middle aged. Leaving aside their sentiments, their lack of humour can be concussing. The experience of *Prudence and the Pill* is like being kicked in the forehead by a cart-horse.

Glossy Vacuums

Selling tranquillity and reassurance in glossy packages is usually profitable. Alexander Walker gives us a taste of the Italian way of handling this sort of material, which depends chiefly on amnesia, sentimental peasantry, untruthful ethnic stereotypes, cigarette ad. scenarios – and, of course, a happy ending. The film was called *Sunflower*, which an irreverent headline writer changed to 'Cornflower':

Welcome back, amnesia. And give a big hand also to the husband everyone thinks is dead – everyone but his wife, that is. How *Sunflower* takes me back! You'd think nothing had happened in the world since 1945 when this was the cinema's most fashionable malady and also its most cliché-ridden plot. Actually we all know what the big event is that has happened since then. Carlo Ponti has opened up Russia so that his wife, Sophia Loren, can make a film there.

. . . Sophia mingles with the crowds under Lenin's dome, outside Stalin's tomb, as she seeks Marcello Mastroianni, the husband who went missing on the Russian front, and now and then accuses stray Muscovites of looking like an Italian 'because of your hair, your walk, the colour of your eyes'. All she keeps getting in reply is 'Nyet'. Heartbreaking? Not exactly. Sophia does her one-note best to look woebegone, but the camera keeps making it all look like a Big Occasion, as if she was really on her way not to find a husband, but to seek an audience with the Pope. Perhaps it is hard to shake the dust of Italy off your clogs. 'They remind me of Neapolitans,' Miss Loren told the hand-out writer about the Russians. 'They wear their friendliness where you can see it – on their faces.'

. . . *Sunflower* has a story that an illiterate chambermaid might consider a bit beneath her customary standards. It moves along with the pace of scene-shifters at La Scala. Every so often someone announces, 'The war's over,' or 'Stalin's dead,' or, plainly at a loss what exactly to report, 'Oh, so many years have passed.'

Dubbed American floats in the air in the general vicinity of the Italian characters while their lips babble on fiercely in the rush to catch up with it. For all the help Russia is to the story, everyone might have stayed at home and made the movie more comfortably in the Tuscan hills or on the back lot of Cinecitta.

Costume is always a vital ingredient in such movies. The last word in fashion was provided for Faye Dunaway in an abysmal film called *A Place for Lovers*. Alexander Walker inspected the outfits:

You know all's not well with Faye Dunaway when she turns up at this uninhabited palace outside Venice and flops down on the best four-poster after simply dropping her valises on the front doorstep, where they remain for the next forty-eight hours. Dying, that's what she is – so why unpack? What seems like half an hour of screen-time later, just when you're wondering if the makers have forgotten the credit titles, she revives slightly to send for Marcello Mastroianni to come and keep her company. After that, the only thing left to wonder at is, have the people also forgotten the movie?

A Place for Lovers is one of those costly, empty films that look as if they've been made with someone's blank chic. It's filled with Beautiful People. People like Miss Dunaway, who may be on her way to death's door from some nameless cinema disease that doesn't interfere with her looks but *en route* has scooped the wardrobe empty of Theodora Van Runkle's jet-set creations. Each crisis she passes through, on goes a new gown. Mastroianni can only look at her in that quizzical Italian way which may denote love, amazement or just envy. The luxury of how the rich die! And, oh, the lethargy of it, too! Five scriptwriters have laboured – collectively or consecutively, it's not stated – to do as little as possible in the way of providing a story, and after eighty-eight minutes have merely managed to move things from the marchese's Venetian palace to a millionaire's Alpine chalet. There Miss Dunaway, who's taken to posing to show how her spirits are sinking, decides at least to die generously and gives away all her pretty things to the local pig-keeper's daughter and then, when she changes her mind about dying, is caught above the snow-line in an above-the-knee-line number while every other sensible person is in woollies.

Women's Realm

Sandy Dennis, the hapless heroine of *Sweet November*, is wasting away. Queried about the nameless disease, her friend Theodore Bikel explains, 'It's quite rare, but it's incurable.' The movie is also afflicted with an incurable disease. *Sweet November* is the kind of squishy whimsey that is always referred to as 'a woman's picture'. This means not that it was written or directed by a woman but that, as the trade press says, it will 'undoubtedly appeal to *femme* audiences'. Doubt might give us hope. It's a story about a kook who is also a "doomed" girl – (a synthesis of the "smart", Broadway-style repartee of *Barefoot in the Park* and *Any Wednesday* and *A Thousand Clowns*, with the worst of Robert Nathan and Margaret (*The Constant Nymph*) Kennedy. Each month, our gallant, forlorn heroine takes into her life and her bed a different man with a problem, for therapeutic purposes – his, not hers. Impotents presumably need not apply. The nature of the therapy is not disclosed, but the man seems to be considered cured when he falls in love with her. Jennifer Jones was the forties specialist in this kind of swill . . .

Taste, never a conspicuous commodity in Hollywood, appeared to have sunk to an all-time low with this film, expertly filleted above by Pauline Kael. It contained a centre-piece song which charmingly encapsulated the film's insulting view of ideal feminine attractions – apparently a 50/50 mixture of lunacy and infantilism:

A girl I know,
she is partly mad,
Yet beyond that smile,
she is partly sad.
She is partly calm,
she is partly wild.
But she is mostly woman –
No,
She is mostly child.

The attractions of this sort of this thing are not immediately obvious, and clearly Pauline Kael was mystified:

There still seems to be an attraction for movie audiences in a kind of subnormal philosophizing issuing from the smiling mouths of unfortunates – Irene Dunne, paralyzed in a wheelchair, singing 'Wishing will make it so', or Sidney Poitier, in *To Sir, with Love*, hiding his sorrow at the racial discrimination he suffers while encouraging the young to go out and conquer the world with good manners. This is the miserable tradition in which dying Sandy Dennis spews out such wisdom as 'People must be remembered, Charlie. Otherwise, they were never here at all. All we are are the people who remember us.' She's an icky little rabbit Babbit. If you're wondering why *Sweet November* opened in February, the answer is that it's Radio City Music Hall's valentine to the public. I'm sure pictures like this give people pimples.

In 1970 one of the worst ever examples of the genre came out, *A Walk in the Spring Rain* starring Ingrid Bergman. Alexander Walker was unkind in an almost loving manner having experienced, as he put it, a 'kind of compensatory enjoyment of the film's very badness, which is not uncommon with film critics'. His alternative script, a beautifully judged parody of the film's mixture of sententiousness and fake rustic, took the form of 'The Country Diary of Ingrid Bergman':

3 September: We are going to be so happy here in our cabin in the Great Smoky Mountains. The way my husband Roger put his pipe in his mouth tonight, I know he is going to write a good book. And what do you think! A neighbour called Will Cade had already put hot bricks in our bed to air it. 'Do you want me, too?' I asked Roger. 'A brick only goes so far, Libby,' he said. Back home Roger may be a Harvard professor, but he is still the man I married.

4 September: My moss-green up-country suit today. It seemed the only thing. Will Cade came round before breakfast – everyone in these parts calls him 'Weeel'. Can't get out of my mind how much he looks like Anthony Quinn. He brought us an armful of sweet-gum wood and told us he calls it 'tradin' wood' – the wood you cut in the spring to trade for the widow's favours in winter. My, this Will is quite a man!

5 September: The gum wood made the smoke go out of our chimney all twisty. Will soon put it straight.

6 September: Roger was just a little bit annoyed when Will dragged him away from his book on constitutional law to take us frog-hunting. I can never bear to see any wild thing killed, so I pretended that what interested me was the jug of moonshiner's hooch Will had brought along. If the Bridge Club could have seen me trying to swing that jug over my shoulder! Looked in the mirror tonight. You know, I know I am a grandmother, but I still have that radiant quality.

10 October: Snow, snow, snow . . .! 'What do you do for green vegetables this time of year?' I asked Will. 'There's cress in the branch stream, Mrs Roger,' he said. He even carried me out to it. Told Roger I would love some animals in the house, but he is deep in his book.

11 October: Will came round with two beautiful little baby goats! the 'billy' kind – not the 'nanny', which smells.

11 December: I have just *got* to set this down. This Will Cade and his world of animals and plants and seasons makes me tremble strangely in my tweeds. 'I can love a woman so the roof jumps clean off the house with the happiness inside,' he told me the other day. I believe he could, too! Roger read me a bit out of his book tonight, but somehow I kept seeing pictures in the fire and couldn't concentrate on constitutional amendments.

23 February: I am afraid Roger is becoming just a little bit of a pedant.

24 February: I was in the barn. Will came in. It happened. We did not do anything as vulgar as roll in the hay, but we pressed each other's hands together the way Roger and I were taught to do when we took that course at the Essalin Institute last summer so we could *experience* our marriage more truthfully. My white hands in Will's baked-clay ones, my bosom against his rough denim shirt . . . I looked at myself in the drinking trough afterwards. I was radiant!

25 February: The most terrible day of my life. I hardly know how to set down what happened. First, I was planting seeds when our daughter Ellen arrived from Boston. I immediately thought: 'Her marriage has broken up!' But it was worse! She is going to college! 'It's not every day that Harvard accepts a *female* law student,' she said. This means she wants me to come home and act as baby-sitter

while she works for her Master's. In other words, leave my Will
. . .! Well, I refused there and then. Are only the young free to
choose, to get taken by rapture, to find joy . . .? But this isn't the
worst that has happened. I was walking down the country road in
my simple pink frock with the tie belt that matches the dogwood
when Will's son – the one he called 'Boy' – laid hands on me. I
resisted. God knows what might not have happened had his father
not appeared and knocked him down. It appears that in falling Boy
sustained a brain lesion.

28 February: Boy was buried today. Will turned the sod himself.

1 March: Roger and I are returning to Harvard. His book has not
turned out well and he will be glad to get back on to full pay. Will
wanted me to stay. Well, I am genuinely sad for him, but these
country people recover quickly. 'It passes as quickly as marshmallow
in a cup of cocoa,' he used to say. It is a fine philosophy. Meanwhile
Ellen has begun her law classes and I can look forward to a life of
collecting our little grandson Bucky at the school gates – and to all
this talk of Women's Liberation, I say 'Shute!'

Love Means . . .

In 1970 a new word entered the lexicon of four-letter ones. Love. This astonishing achievement was chiefly brought about by a thirty-two-year-old American classics professor who wrote a screenplay called *Love Story* and then novelized his own film script. ('Those who have read the movie . . . can finally watch the book,' commented *Newsweek*.)

Segal was modest about his discovery of love. 'I didn't create [the] message,' he said, 'I just happened to hear it before anyone else.' According to his postbag 'brawny athletic boys' cried for Oliver and Jenny, his hero and heroine; moreover the *Sun* added enthusiastically, 'Mums, dads, grandmothers, teenagers, hooligans and college graduates openly wept over the final chapter.' It must have been the hooligans who alerted President Nixon to the author's political potential. He appointed him to the Advisory Body of the Peace Corps. When Segal met him at the White House the President said: 'What the Peace Corps needs, Professor Segal, is love.' Segal replied quick-wittedly: 'What the love corps needs, Mr Nixon, is peace.' To which the President is reported to have said: 'H'm.'

Pauline Kael wrote of a screen version of *Romeo and Juliet* that it presented an unpleasant spectacle of movie-makers 'drilling into the "generation gap" as if it were an oil well'. Nor did she like this new story of young love that ended with a welcome disease that carried off the heroine. It was, she wrote, 'one of the most ineptly made of all the lump-and-phlegm hits . . . Those who are susceptible to this sort of movie may not even notice that Ali McGraw is horribly smug and smirky, though if you share my impulses, whenever she gets facetious you'll probably want to wham her one.'

Millions did not share her impulses however, and flocked

to see this film that 'bypassed the brain and assaulted the tear-ducts' (*Newsweek*), a 'lying, thoughtless and evasive piece of nonsense' (James Fenton in the *New Statesman*). Fenton then nailed one of the more vivid examples of the film's purposeful untruthfulness:

Cutting himself off from family and fortune on graduation and marriage to an Italian baker's daughter, [Oliver] suffers the privation of being kept on his wife's earnings; privation means about $3,000 p.a. and vacation jobs, but as he has only a year to go at Harvard Law School before taking a cushy job, this doesn't break his spirit . . .

A slum, for the film, is a nice flat you rent at $82.50 a month. Poverty is when you both have to work. A tragedy is a painless disease.

Attempts were made to drum up an image of *Love Story* as the harbinger of decency and good clean values backlashing against the tidal wave of filth in which cinema audiences were supposedly engulfed. As Alexander Walker put it: 'Every element of reality that might grate against the mood has been screened out of the finished commercial for love – every one, that is, except the solid bourgeois necessity of money.' The film served 'both Hymen and Mammon'. A characteristic Ali McGraw aphorism in the movie was the remark that 'Love means never having to say you're sorry' – a startling reversal of most people's experience (except perhaps that of the *Sun*'s lachrymose hooligans). 'However, the message that I took away, dry eyed, from *Love Story*,' wrote Walker, 'is that *wealth* means never having to say you're sorry.' Or then again, as Christopher Hudson opined in the *Spectator*: 'Happiness is a warm bed pan . . .'

'Mary Poppins in Schmalzberg'

A lady from Cardiff had been to see *The Sound of Music* (a money-spinning film version of the stage musical) over three hundred times by the end of 1965. 'There is only one love scene,' she said, explaining some of the reasons for her fascination, 'and that is quite restrained. When Christopher Plummer and Julie Andrews kiss, I've heard teenage couples around me shout, "Go on mate," but it's not that sort of scene. She is a girl from a convent.'

It emphatically was not 'that sort of scene' or that sort of film. After the film was made, Christopher Plummer was reported as saying, 'Working with Julie Andrews was like being hit over the head with a Valentine's card.' For some, watching *The Sound of Music* was like being caught in a storm of Valentine cards. But with her 'dutch-doll face and gym-mistress zip' Julie Andrews 'spanked a flabby and lumbering vehicle into some sort of life'. Philip Oakes then continued on the subject of the music:

. . . nuns sing in cloisters. Miss Andrews (who plays Maria) sings in her bedroom. Christopher Plummer sings in self-defence. Most of what they sing is pretty awful. Charmain Carr – agreeably ardent as Plummer's eldest daughter – has a good song about young love in 'Sixteen, Going on Seventeen'. But the remainder come stodgily from the Rogers and Hammerstein hymnal with lots of those lines about whiskers on kittens and larks learning how to pray, which fairly reek of high sentiments and tired minds.

Ken Tynan wondered at the description in the opening caption of the film's period as 'the last Golden days of the thirties' (golden for whom? Hitler? Ivor Novello?).

However, as Alexander Walker pointed out in the *Evening*

Standard, it nevertheless had every ingredient needed for success:

It has a convent of singing nuns who warble in their wimples, 'Sister Mary is not an asset to the abbey.'

It has a family of seven children, all of different sizes and cuteness and guaranteed to come out with endearing remarks like, 'I'm incorrigible – what's incorrigible mean?'

It has views of Salzburg that are a pastrycook's fantasy and panoramas of the Austrian Alps that are a mountaineer's paradise. It has lakes with swans on them, and bunches of edelweiss, and lederhosen, and shaving brushes in hat trims and a Tyrolean folk festival.

Of those seven endearing children Dilys Powell commented acidly:

When the great W. C. Fields (or was it Ned Sparks?) was asked how he liked children, he replied: 'Toasted.' I feel the same about child-choirs, at any rate unless they are invisible; and here the spectator is suffocated by assorted child-singers.

'Wet'

This notice recently appeared of a film called *Last Feelings* in *Time Out*, and may have dampened the ardour of some potential film-goers:

Slim, dark, good-looking teenage boy, misunderstood but eager to please, speaks dubbed English, seeks substitute family, wants sincere girlfriend and wishes to become swimming champion. Only months to live, however. Is this why my eyes swim as much as I do and why I am wetter than any swimming pool you care to think of? Write soonest with s.a.e.

They Got Burnt . . . or Stung

'Looked at from an accountant's point of view – the only sensible one for pictures of this sort,' the extra expense in burning up imitation skyscrapers for *The Towering Inferno* was only marginally worth it 'considering the crowded disaster market'. This was Richard Schickel's view in *Time*, as he detailed the budgetary profile of the movie. 'Based on not one but two bad novels, featuring four stars above the title instead of just one and having scarcely less important figures among the supporting players . . . Merely to turn out a single skyscraper they consumed twice the amount that Universal spent to destroy Los Angeles in *Earthquake* . . .'

As most people know, the film was about people burning to death in a skyscraper which burned so well because a jerry-builder skimped on honest architect Paul Newman's safety specifications. There were sub-plots. 'Bad marriages and love affairs naturally come apart, good ones grow better as the flames leap higher.' And there were a lot of hot ladies, as Kenneth Robinson pointed out in the *Spectator*:

This film features one of the hottest girls in town, Jennifer Jones, whose body is set on fire as she falls down the side of a blazing San Francisco hotel. No, wait a moment: Miss Jones is the one who falls to death without catching fire which is something of a novelty. I lost count of the women who jumped through windows, their clothes alight, each performing a graceful arc like a corpse de ballet.

Not every performer in this huge burnsnight is so elegant. There is a lift full of people who catch fire unexpectedly and with dreadfully unreserved comments. One man even lurches into the lobby like someone from the Ministry of Funny Walks and then for a terrible moment it really seems that two naughty lovers are intending to burn to death in bed.

People burning to death was popular with audiences. Getting stung to death – no less unpleasant one would have thought – was unaccountably less so. Philip Bergson reviewed *The Swarm* in *The Times Educational Supplement*:

The eponymous swarm are killer bees from North Africa which attack a USAF early warning missile centre without any warning at all and then proceed to ravage middle America. Their periodic manifestations, peppering the skies with darkness, look as convincing as if the projectionist had dropped iron filings into his machine. Their human opponents – well, the synopsis says they are human – seem to have been picked by a pin out of *Spotlight* or some out-of-date casting album. The longest surviving is Dr Michael Caine as a world-famous entomologist and tax exile who just happens to be passing; Henry Fonda spends all his not inconsiderable time on-screen in a wheelchair (obviously suffering from total collapse after reading his parts of the screenplay); and there is a fetching little romantic sub-plot involving glum schoolmam Olivia de Havilland (who sounds as if she's just stumbled off the set of *Gone with the Wind*) and two aging hicks vying for her attention; if you go after a hearty meal, it's likely to fetch your dinner up.

The film was not a success though it cost twelve million dollars. As Ted Whitehead observed in the *Spectator*: 'An appalling waste of both currency and bees.'

Many Hands Make Heavy Going

Barry Took writing in *Punch* in 1978 wondered aloud about what lay behind the incredibly complicated credits of a film called *The Greek Tycoon*:

During the past few months I've become increasingly fascinated by the number and variety of screen credits that appear at the beginning and, at seemingly interminable length, at the end of a film.

Often the jobs described sound exotic or strange, and frequently downright peculiar. What, for instance, is 'a gaffer'? Who or what is 'best boy'? What does he do? How does he justify his description? Who is he better than? I can see that there would be no credit for 'worst boy', but you must admit that it's a bit puzzling.

And why is it that some films, good films, too, can have less than two dozen technical credits (*Driver* with twenty-three is a good example) while other films can have over eighty?

The Greek Tycoon has eighty-three technical credits ranging from Producer to the enigmatic title 'Controller'. That doesn't mean that only eight-three people were involved either, that's just categories. *The Greek Tycoon* is credited with two producers, two co-producers, three executive producers, an associate producer (notable perhaps because he's one of the few people who can be persuaded to associate with producers) *and* a production consultant. There are, in addition, credits for four production managers and one production associate. Hardly surprisingly, under the heading 'Producers' Secretaries' are six names. If there are fourteen people concerned in producing one film, clearly they are going to generate a lot of paperwork, particularly if they're not speaking to each other.

The Greek Tycoon also excels in its music credits. They include Executive in charge of Music: David Platz. Very good too. David Platz is an experienced and successful man in the world of music and a very good choice. Then there's 'Music composed and orchestrated by' Stanley Myers – another top-notch name. Then there's the 'Main Title Theme' by John Kongos, arranged and conducted by Ron Frangipane, and the credit 'Music supervised and conducted by' Harry Rabinowitz, yet another excellent musician and among the top ten MDs in the world. But then there's a song, 'Funny Kind of Love Affair', sung by the delectable Madeline Bell, words and music by Mike Moran, arranged and conducted by Mike Moran. There's more. 'Taverna music arranged by George Theodosiadis.' The music editor is Michael Clifford.

So, with music as with production, there's plenty of help around. Eight people, excluding the singer, have a hand or hands in the film's music, including, if my arithmetic is kosher, three conductors. Now the ramifications of the music business have long since left me totally baffled, but that does seem rather a lot of musicians to be involved in a film that has almost no visual music content with the exception of one scene in a taverna. Oh, and I forgot – there's another credit which reads 'Music Recording co-ordinated by Allen Steckler'. I wouldn't have liked his job. All those composers to placate and having to work out who was conducting what, seeing to it that Frangipane wasn't incommoded, if that's the word, when Rabinowitz had the baton, and making sure that Myers and Kongos, not to mention Moran and Theodosiadis, weren't getting involved in demarcation disputes.

Making films like *The Greek Tycoon* is tough, and if you don't believe me ask the unit publicist, or if he's on the other line the assistant unit publicist, or if she's out the assistant to the assistant unit publicist; all three are credited, as are the 'Location Production Runner' ('Here's your cheese and taramasalata on rye'), the Producers' Driver ('You can't all ride in the front'), and (and I bet he had a busy time) the Production Physician, Dr A. Chutorian.

Incidentally, Took added, the film stank.

New Vague and Vaguely New

Healthy Hollywood humbug has not influenced the more pretentious French film-makers, who stick to a well-fried formula of sex and despair. J. B. Priestley wrote a sceptical piece about this after seeing an advance notice for a film:

A film notice reads, 'In one basic sense, it is an existential film, dealing with man's inability to know others or be known by them as anything more than an object . . .' Would I have spotted this if I had been there? Do I know how an existential film differs from a non-existential film? In my youth I read, purely for pleasure, a great deal of philosophy, but that was before existentialism came out. Determined to catch up at last, I have just been poking around in a dictionary of philosophy, looking up the various existentialists. But I would still not risk using existential as a description of a novel, play or film. And I am so thick, so insensitive, that I never seem to have shared Heidegger's angst or Sartre's nausea, except when I have been suffering from food poisoning. And now I can't help feeling, in a fusty-musty way, that all too often existential is just slipped in to add a bit of tone, an extra flavour, another guinea's worth of communication in depth.

That's another thing I've been left out of – this new angst and nausea and desperation about communicating, out of which a few chaps seem to be doing very nicely. When I was learning how to write, I didn't even realize I was trying to get into the communicating business, and so I was spared much anxiety and grief. A few years ago, at a crowded party, I met for the first time one of our most energetic younger playwrights, who had told my wife he was a fan of mine. But after regarding me sombrely for a few moments, he said, 'I can't communicate with you.' Could this have been an existentialist moment?

Alexander Walker provided his reader with a handy recipe so that Do-It-Yourself enthusiasts could make their own New Wave film:

After seeing a beauty of the species, *Il Mare*, I offer the following instructions.

Begin at the beginning with THE TITLE. Do not go overboard. Stick to simple words like *L'Avventura (The Affair)*, or *La Notte (The Night)*, or *L'Eclisse (The Eclipse)*, or *Il Mare (The Sea)*. A title like *Last Year in Marienbad* indicates a lack of discipline.

The Actors: Engage Italians if possible – preferably Italians of the new, non-voluble generation. They must be good at saying nothing for long stretches of the film. If you cannot afford Marcello Mastroianni, Monica Vitti and Alain Delon (who now passes for Italian), hire people as much like them as possible. *Il Mare* has Umberto Orsini, Françoise Prévost (who can pass for Italian) and Fino Mele.

The Characters: You *may* get by with two, but you *must* have no more than three – preferably two males, one female. The whole purpose of the film is to tell the audience as little as possible about the characters, so pay attention to:

Their Names: You *may* give each character one first name (no more), but it is better to call them simply 'A', 'B' and 'X', as in *Last Year in Marienbad*. In *Il Mare* a compromise has been reached: they are called simply The Man, The Woman and The Boy. Quite enough to be going on with, for if you reveal more about them you risk having:

A Plot: Leave this strictly to the filmgoers. They don't want to know what *you* think is going on between The Man, The Woman and The Boy in *Il Mare*. Let *them* ask themselves, Is The Man deserting The Boy in favour of The Woman? Is The Boy coming between The Man and The Woman? Is The Woman trying to attract The Man and The Boy? Audiences will enjoy themselves figuring out what such relationships are at any given moment. It is as stimulating as geometry. But of course even a plot like this must have:

A Setting: Very, very important. As empty and devoid of life as possible. If you don't favour city suburbs between the rush hours – as in *La Notte* and *L'Eclisse* – the very next best thing is an island. *Il Mare* is set on Capri – *but in wintertime*. Grey skies. Weak sun. Not a tourist in sight. You never get the idea that Gracie Fields is anywhere in the vicinity. This would be fatal to:

The Action: The essential part of this is known as THE WALK. People take minutes to walk to their table from the restaurant door. They trail each other down Capri's alleyways, up street steps, along hotel corridors – the tempo may be varied by the odd violent action, such as spitting in the sea, but nothing should be too definite. Take great care over such an element as LOVE. Keep your head. You may show close-ups of ear-lobes and knee-caps. But skip the night of frustrated passion: enough to show The Man retrieving his socks at dawn. Impress on your cast that this will confer on them tremendous advantages when it comes to:

The Acting: Since nothing is explained for sure in the film, critics approaching it will have nothing to check the acting against. Dialogue should be spoken flatly like a recorded language-course – e.g. 'What time does the express connect with the Naples boat?' To some, the acting may look like sleep-walking, but there will always be the critic who will call it 'brilliantly understated'. Your leading lady's face may look as if it has been set in plaster-of-Paris, but some critic is sure to describe her as 'Garbo-esque'.

The Golden Rule is: *Make the audience work*. 'Less is more' should be your guiding aesthetic; and the less people have to go on, the more they can assume the function of the film-maker. After all, Do-It-Yourself has invaded practically every other human activity: it is about time it took over the cinema.

In 1978 significant gloom was still alive and well in the cinema. John Wells, temporary film critic for the *Spectator* in April (which was bad luck on the films showing then) went to see the much praised Bresson film *The Devil, probably*. It sounds better in French: *Le Diable, probablement*. His main impression was that the cameraman on the film must have been very short because of the number of shots of feet and legs. Wells' own legs carried him out of the cinema before the end, but he has left us a vivid impression of what he did see:

The film, or the hour or so I saw of it – I left immediately before the depressive hero's interview with the psychiatrist Dr Mime – suggests that the seventy-year-old Bresson as a fashion-crazed old fart – the film's production company is called Sunchild and its ideas spring or rather stagger from an *Observer Magazine* consciousness of the post-flower-power era – is at the end of his tether.

Quite apart from the content of the picture – gloomy, non-acting, Pre-Raphaelite youth in early seventies' haircut lopes through druggy Paris of Alienated Generation in world menaced by much over-used film-clips of pollution, baby seal clubbers, policemen, insecticide etc. – the style of the film suggests that Bresson has dozed off in his wheelchair, leaving the nuts and bolts of script-writing, directing, shooting, editing and sound-recording to gloomy Pre-Raphaelite amateur film-makers.

The camera is set up in front of a lift: sound of lift approaching, lift arrives and after a longish pause opens, gloomy Pre-Raphaelite lopes slowly out and leaves shot, footsteps heard retreating, lift doors eventually close. The wit, the narrative skill, the life of the picture lies in the editing, in taking ten seconds out of the lift doors, a lift being a lift being a lift, but it is not the way of the amateur film-makers to let you off without seeing the lift doors closing. Lift doors closing are a truly meaningful image of the great mechanical you know doom that is threatening civilization, have a puff of this stuff from Acapulco, etc. and the projector whirrs on.

The film in any case deserves some sort of Mental Cruelty to Audiences award for the non-acting Pre-Raphaelites' delivery of their lines: the lines in themselves are not all that special, consisting in the main of 'I am here'; 'You are here?'; 'Now I am going'; 'You are going?' etc. but delivered with the arrogant monotony, as they are, of a bad-tempered travel agent reading out a list of trains to a client he suspects is wasting his time, the effect on me at least, and I hope I have made it clear as your temporary critic that I can speak only for myself, is to depress and crush the spirits.

'Cinema', observed François Truffaut, 'is an improvement on life.' However, it seems that there are a number of cinematic examples around to demonstrate the reverse of this proposition.

Telly

Reviewing the telly must be a thankless task and indeed a certain weariness often creeps into the columns of the reviewers. Some of the freshest writing on television, however, is provided by Nancy Banks Smith in the *Guardian*; often one suspects that the programme was decidedly inferior to her review of it. Here are a few samples; fiction first:

THE SURVIVORS

If 'The Survivors' (a new BBC1 series) weren't done in electronic spots on a screen, it could be done in cross-stitch on a sampler. It has a moral, an admonition something like: 'And God destroyed the world and said to Adam – dig that.'

The premise is that mankind is almost wiped out by a mutant virus. A phrase which silences awkward questions. The sickness seems to be affiliated to bubonic plague, though judging by the discreet way sufferers feel their armpits it might be body odour. And the lesson (enunciated appropriately enough by a schoolteacher) is that 'we survivors must learn again all the old crafts and skills'. Like, he suggests – rather wildly, surely – blowing light bulbs. All this is a pertinent, not to say fashionable theme nowadays.

In 'The Survivors' things fall apart, the centre cannot hold and mere anarchy (three yobs, for the sake of economy) is loosed upon the world. Just how the world would come to pieces is an interesting intellectual exercise. Railway stations might dry up like river beds and city streets log-jam with cars as they do here. And birds would begin to sound noisy, except to the deaf, who would run out of hearing-aid batteries (a small touching point made by the schoolmaster).

It is directed with some flair, but as yarns go you couldn't accuse it of being ambitious. Are you sitting comfortably? Then I'll begin with a woman playing against that most expendable of machines, a contraption for throwing tennis balls. And end with a girl walking away from a pile of useless £5 notes.

'We'll manage,' says one man, and immediately the lights go out. 'Go. You still have a chance,' says another and hands a survivor a candle.

You see? Good, I thought you might.

However, pedagogically speaking, the science programmes provide the real meat of television:

'Horizon' (BBC2), may its long face never grow shorter, went off for the summer hols in downright merry mood. 'Horizon' normally bears an endearing resemblance to Eeyore. 'Good morning,' said Eeyore gloomily. 'If it is a good morning,' he said, 'which I doubt,' said he. If it is normally a little short of hey-nonny-no this is not surprising in a programme which takes its subject, man and science, seriously. I felt almost cheated when it reported with moderate optimism on the subject of food additives. There was, however, one very characteristic scene when Dr Magnus Pike, in the sort of hat that brooks no back answers, worked his way along a greengrocer's display, commenting in a carrying voice on the benzole cyanide in cress, the oxalic acid in rhubarb, and the afflictions which can follow unreasonable indulgence in onions and cabbage. How many men, one wonders, were sitting on the greengrocer to prevent him felling Dr Pike with a convenient cucumber. 'I don't,' Dr Pike added kindly, 'want to frighten people.'

Royal occasions bring out the BBC in hot but loyal flushes; even the most bizarre events like the Royal Variety performance. The 1980 one was said by Richard Ingrams in the *Spectator* to have 'taken on a geriatric air. People you assumed were dead totter on the stage to wild applause. Perhaps the idea is to show the Queen Mother she is not the only old stager who is still going strong. As well as nonagenarians, sagging busts were a feature of this year's show . . .'

And Clive James paid tribute to the Queen Mother's sporting spirit in sitting through several hours of bilge and sycophance:

She also once volunteered to be bombed by the Luftwaffe, but that was some time ago, and perhaps nowadays she should be more careful about exposing her august and beloved person to mechanized outrage. David Jacobs recited a poem in her honour. Miserably composed, it referred to 'a Scottish larse'. I tuned out when a rabbit in a red spangled suit started playing the piano.

But a Royal Wedding, or better still, a Jubilee, provides the commentators (some of whom also you might have thought were long since dead) with their finest hours. The clichés and the useless information are retailed with an air of religious awe. Nancy Banks Smith describes one Jubilee programme:

Tom Fleming is not my favourite royal event commentator, being given to pomp and much circumstantial detail. He knows the State Coach weighs 4½ tons and was delivered at five in the morning, and the names of all the horses: Budapest, Beaufort, Rio, Santiago, and so forth. So forth not being a horse, of course.

They are greys because it shows the red and gold harness so well and that must be one reason why London, grey in style and stone, lends itself so well to pageantry. When most truly moved Fleming is barely rational: 'One wonders what the conversation will be in the stable tonight when these horses get home.'

However, let joy be unconfined and criticism minimal. The walk-about was a genuinely gay and pretty business with the Queen being handed a painting here, a posy there. I watched with close attention and fed my findings into a computer. The conclusion is that the Queen is likeliest to stop and talk to you if you are a young, male foreigner in a funny hat sitting in a wheel-chair near a Boy Scout; the Duke if you are a nun with a periscope.

Bearskins do not count as funny hats, though Prince Charles was committed to wearing one which rendered him unrecognizable.

The best way to see St Paul's is to be a bat. The remarkable aerial shots from the dome were as round as a gunsight with the crimson carpet crossing exactly where the Queen knelt. Her vulnerability throughout the procession was both a worrying and yet a defence in itself. Her face in church and perhaps off-guard seems to fall into lines for which grief would hardly be too strong a word.

However, the Archbishop of Canterbury is always good for a laugh. He quoted Jesus, adding with episcopal emphasis: 'How right He was!' I cannot explain even to myself why I find that so funny.

The drive back was a relaxed affair with boys in jeans running to keep up with the landau, pigeons surprised by the joy and not a car in sight except on sufferance. The whole heart of London was what planners are pleased to call a pedestrian precinct. Just people, how pleasant.

Royal occasions of a different kind are the expensive show-cases for egomaniacal stars. They get applause for doing very little, or nothing at all – sometimes more applause for nothing at all. Probably the worst ever of these was a Charles Azna-vour/Liza Minnelli mutual admiration show in 1974. Clive James reviewed it in the *Observer*. If you missed it then, enjoy the full flavour now:

HI! I'M LIZA

Bad Sight and Bad Sound of the Week were twin titles both won by 'Love from A to Z' (BBC1), a river of drivel featuring Liza Minnelli and Charles Aznavour. Right up there beside the Tom Jones specials in the Bummer Stakes, this grotesque spectacular was fascinating for several reasons, none of them pleasant.

To begin with (and to go on with and end with, since the pheno-menon was continuous), there was the matter of how Charles had contrived to get himself billed above the normally omni-dominant Liza. Not only was his name foremost in the opening titles, but the between-song lectures, instead of being delivered by Charles on the subject of Liza's talent, were mainly delivered by Liza on the subject of Charles's genius. 'Hi!' Liza would yell intimately, her features suffused by that racking spasm of narcissistic coyness which she fondly imagines looks like a blush, 'I'm Liza.' (Such a *coup* is supposed to stun you with its humility, but in the event it is difficult to choke back the urge to belch.) She would then impart a couple of hundred words of material – supplied by someone going under the name Donald Ross – on the topic of Charles Aznavour, with particular reference to his creativity, magnanimity and vision.

This would be followed by a lengthy and devastating assault on 'My Funny Valentine' by Charles himself, in which the song's subtlety would be translated into the standard emotional intensity of the French cabaret ballad, leaving the viewer plenty of oppor-tunity to note how the tortured singer's eyebrows had been wrinkled by hard times, lost loves and the decline of the franc. Or else, even worse, Liza in person would pay a tribute to Lorenz Hart by singing 'My Romance' as if her task were to put significance into the lyric instead of getting it out. 'You know,' she announced at one point, and I had a sinking sensation that I did, and didn't agree, 'the most that you can ever hope for an entertainer is to *touch* people.'

Liza, who can't even walk up a flight of stairs sincerely (a flight
of stairs was wheeled on for the specific purpose of allowing her to
prove this), is more touching than she knows. She began her career
with a preposterous amount of talent, the shreds of which she still
retains, but like her mother she doesn't know how to do anything
small, and, like almost every other young success, she has embraced
the standards of excellent proposed by Showbiz, which will agree
to love you only if your heart is in the right place – where your
brain should be.

Liza can't settle for being admired for her artistry. She wants to
be loved for herself. Charles, to do him the credit he's got coming
as the composer of the odd passable song in the relentlessly up-
and-down-the-scale French tradition, is less innocent. In fact he's
so worn by experience he's got bags under his head. He knows the
importance of at least feigning to find his material more interesting
than his own wonderful personality – a key trick for prolonged
survival, which Liza will have to learn, or go to the wall. The show
was recorded at the Rainbow. It was pretty nearly as bad as anything
I have seen in my life, and deepened the mystery of why it is that
it is always the BBC, and not ITV, which brings us these orgies of
self-promotion by dud stars: package deals which consist of nothing
but a wrap-up.

Permissions

Nicholas Parsons and the publishers are grateful to the following authors, agents and publishers for permission to quote the extracts in the book. Extracts are listed below alphabetically by author, and page numbers refer to their positions in this book. Asterisks indicate copyright holders.

James Agate pp. 7–8, 9 from *Immoment Toys* courtesy of the Estate of James Agate★ and Jonathan Cape Ltd pp. 10–11 from *The Agate Anthology* (ed. Van Thal) courtesy of Granada Publishing Ltd★ pp. 140, 156 from *Red Letter Nights* courtesy of the Estate of James Agate★ and Jonathan Cape Ltd

Kingsley Amis pp. 91–2 courtesy of the *Spectator*★

Ros Asquith pp. 170–71 courtesy of *Time Out*★

Paul Bailey★ pp. 117–18 courtesy of Deborah Rogers and the *Observer*

Nancy Banks Smith★ pp. 210–11, 212 courtesy of the *Guardian*

Beverley Baxter pp. 137–9, 141, 158–9 from *First Nights and Noises Off* courtesy of Hutchinson Publishing Group Ltd★ p. 168 from *First Nights and Footlights* courtesy of Hutchinson Publishing Group Ltd★

Max Beerbohm pp. 133, 136 from *Around Theatres* courtesy of Mrs E. Reichman★ and William Heinemann Ltd pp. 160, 169 from *Last Theatres* courtesy of Mrs E. Reichman★ and William Heinemann Ltd

Philip Bergson p. 203 courtesy of *The Times Educational Supplement*★

Edward Bond★ p. 149 courtesy of the author

Richard Boston★ pp. 93–6 from *Baldness Be My Friend* courtesy of David Higham Associates Ltd and Elm Tree Books
p. 186 courtesy of the *Guardian*

Alan Brien★ pp. 162–3 courtesy of *Punch*

Hugh Brogan★ pp. 40–42 courtesy of the author and the *Listener*

Richard Buckle★ pp. 46–7 courtesy of Dance Books Ltd

Peter Bull p. 152–3 from *I Know the Face But. . .* courtesy of Peter Davies Ltd

Cyril Connolly p. 10 from *Previous Convictions* courtesy of Deborah Rogers★ and Hamish Hamilton Ltd

Bernard Crick★ pp. 55–6 courtesy of the *Guardian*

Bosley Crowther pp. 184–5 courtesy of the *New York Times*★

Daily Mail reviewer p. 119 courtesy of the *Daily Mail*★

Daily Telegraph reviewer p. 115 courtesy of the *Daily Telegraph*★

D. J. Enright★ pp 20–21 from *Conspirators and Poets* courtesy of Bolt & Watson Ltd and Chatto & Windus Ltd

James Fenton pp. 172–4 courtesy of the *Sunday Times*★
p. 198 courtesy of the *New Statesman*★

Penelope Gilliat★ pp. 188–90 from *Unholy Fools* courtesy of
      Secker & Warburg Ltd

Gerald Gould p. 15 courtesy of the *Observer*★

Graham Greene★ pp. 183–4 from *The Pleasure Dome*
      courtesy of Lawrence Pollinger Ltd and
      Secker & Warburg Ltd

Geoffrey Grigson★ pp. 21, 99 from *The Contrary View*
      courtesy of Macmillan, London and
      Basingstoke
      p. 30 courtesy of the *Observer*

Guardian review p. 150 courtesy of the *Guardian*★

Alex Hamilton★ pp. 99–101 courtesy of the *Guardian*

Robert Herring★ pp. 186–7 from *Garbo and the
      Nightwatchmen* (ed. Alistair Cooke) courtesy
      of Secker & Warburg Ltd

Peter Heyworth pp. 130–31 courtesy of the *Observer*★

Anthony Howard p. 57 courtesy of the *New Statesman*★

Robert Hughes pp. 47–9 courtesy of the *Sunday Times*★

Aldous Huxley pp. 83–4 from an essay entitled 'Document'
      out of *Music at Night and other Essays*
      courtesy of Mrs Laura Huxley★ and Chatto
      & Windus Ltd

Clive James★ pp. 211–12 from *The Crystal Bucket* courtesy
      of Jonathan Cape Ltd
      p. 213 from *Visions Before Midnight* courtesy
      of Jonathan Cape Ltd

Paul Johnson p. 84 courtesy of the *New Statesman*★

Mervyn Jones p. 72 courtesy of the *New Statesman*★

James Joyce p. 176 from *James Joyce: The Critical Heritage*
      (ed. Robert Deeming) courtesy of the *Observer*★
      and Routledge & Kegan Paul Ltd

Carl Jung p. 15 from the *Collected Works of Jung* vol. 15, courtesy of Routledge & Kegan Paul Ltd★

Pauline Kael★ pp. 193–4 from 'Apes must be remembered, Charlie' (*New Yorker*, 17 February 1968) reprinted in *Going Steady* and quoted here courtesy of Little, Brown & Co. (Boston, Massachusetts)

George Kaufman pp. 31–2 from *By George* courtesy of Anne Kaufman Schneider★ and Angus & Robertson Ltd

Jonathan Keats pp. 67–8 courtesy of the *New Statesman*★

Bernard Levin p. 8 courtesy of the *Sunday Times*★
pp. 80–82 courtesy of *The Times*★
★pp. 113, 179–81 from *Taking Sides* courtesy of Jonathan Cape Ltd

Peter Lomas p. 71 courtesy of the *New Statesman*★

Gavin Lyall pp. 88–90 courtesy of the *Spectator*★

Kenneth McClellan★ pp. 164–6, 167–8, 175 from *Whatever Happened to Shakespeare?* courtesy of Vision Press Ltd

Dwight Macdonald★ pp. 4–5, 12–13, 29, 74–6 from *Against the American Grain* courtesy of Victor Gollancz Ltd

Alasdair MacIntyre★ p. 54 courtesy of the *Listener*

Norman Mailer★ pp. 51–2 from *Cannibals and Christians* courtesy of André Deutsch Ltd

Rodney Milnes pp. 126–7 courtesy of the *Spectator*★

Sheridan Morley pp. 141–2 courtesy of *Punch*★
★pp. 142–3 from *Review Copies* courtesy of Robson Books Ltd

John Mortimer★ pp. 45–6 courtesy of the *Sunday Times*

Raymond Mortimer p. 27 from *Try Anything Once* courtesy
of Hamish Hamilton Ltd★

Malcolm Muggeridge★ pp. 39–40, 57–9 from *Tread Softly Or
You Tread On One Of My Jokes*
courtesy of William Collins Sons &
Co. Ltd

David Nathan p. 149 courtesy of the *Sun*★

New York Times reviews pp. 182–3, 185 courtesy of the
New York Times★

Benedict Nightingale p. 172 courtesy of the *New Statesman*★

Philip Oakes p. 199 courtesy of the *Sunday Telegraph*

Observer 'Daylight' reporter p. 145 courtesy of the *Observer*★

George Orwell p. 69 from *Collected Journalism and Letters –
vol. 1* courtesy of Estates of the Late George
Orwell★ and A. M. Heath & Co. Ltd

John Osborne★ pp. 156–7 courtesy of the author

Dorothy Parker pp. 8–9, 73 from *The Collected Dorothy
Parker* courtesy of Duckworth & Co. Ltd

William Plomer★ p. 36 from *Electric Delights* courtesy of
Jonathan Cape Ltd

J. B. Priestley pp. 27–8, 29, 206 from *Thoughts in the
Wilderness* courtesy of William Heinemann
Ltd

Punch review pp. 62–5 courtesy of *Punch*★

Robert Rhodes James★ p. 56 courtesy of the author and the
Sunday Telegraph

Bryan Robertson p. 154 courtesy of the *Spectator*★

Kenneth Robinson p. 202 courtesy of the *Spectator*★

Richard Schickel p. 202 courtesy of *Time* magazine

Bernard Shaw pp. 17, 123–4, 132–3, 135 courtesy of the
                    Society of Authors on behalf of the Bernard
                    Shaw Estate★

Colin Simpson pp. 111–13 courtesy of the *Sunday Times*★

Spectator – pp. 60–61 courtesy of the *Spectator*★
            – 'Pharos' pp. 124–5 courtesy of the *Spectator*★
            – 'Strix' pp. 77–80 courtesy of the *Spectator*★

Sir John Squire pp. 3, 36–8, 176–9 taken from *Books in
                    General* courtesy of Mr Raglan Squire and
                    Secker & Warburg Ltd

A. J. P. Taylor pp. 70–71 courtesy of the *Observer*★

Paul Theroux pp. 65–7 courtesy of the *Sunday Times*★

Time Out review p. 201 courtesy of *Time Out*★

Times reviews pp. 148, 149 courtesy of *The Times*★

Barry Took pp. 204–5 courtesy of *Punch*★

Gore Vidal ★pp. 1–3, 18–19, 25–6 from *Matters of Fact and
                    Fiction* courtesy of William Heinemann Ltd
                    pp. 26–7, 42–4 from *Collected Essays 1952–1972*
                    courtesy of Curtis Brown Ltd

Alexander Walker★ pp. 191–2, 194–6, 207–8 from *Double
                    Takes* courtesy of the author and Elm
                    Tree Books
                    p. 200 courtesy of *Evening Standard*

Alan Watkins pp. 72, 85 courtesy of the *Spectator*★

Auberon Waugh★ pp. 22–4 from *Books and Bookmen*
                    p. 85–7 courtesy of the *New Statesman*

Stuart Wavell p. 144 courtesy of the *Guardian*

H. G. Wells pp. 6–7 from *H. G. Wells's Literary Criticism*
                    edited by Patrick Parrinder and Robert M.
                    Philmus (The Harvester Press, Sussex, 1980)
                    courtesy of the Estate of H. G. Wells★

John Wells pp. 208–9 courtesy of the *Spectator*

Edmund Wilson p. 3 from *Classics and Commercials* courtesy
of W. H. Allen★

Tom Wolfe★ pp. 104–7 from *The Painted Word* (Farrar,
Straus and Giroux) courtesy of Tom Wolfe c/o
International Creative Management

Robert Wraight★ pp. 107–9 from *The Art Game* (Leslie
Frewin, 1965)

Illustration Credits

Bibliography

Margot Asquith – *Lay Sermons*. Thornton Butterworth, London, 1927.

James Henry Stanley Barlow – *Goodbye England*. Hamish Hamilton, London, 1969.

Clifford Bax – *Whither the Theatre? A letter to a young playwright*. Home & Van Thal, London, 1945.

Anthony Burgess – *Urgent Copy*. Jonathan Cape, London, 1958.

Frances Eliza Hodgson Burnett – *A Lady of Quality: Being a most curious, hitherto unknown history etc*. F. Warne & Co., London, 1896.

Mary Butts – *Death of Felicity Taverner*. Wishart and Co., London, 1932.

Carolino – *English as she is spoke* (edit. James Millington). Field & Tuer, London, 1883. Reprinted by Dover Publications, London, 1970.

Barbara Cartland – *Love at the Helm*. Weidenfeld & Nicolson, London, 1980.

Dennis Chapman – *The Home and Social Status*. Routledge & Kegan Paul, London, 1955.

Alex Comfort – *The Joy of Sex*. Quartet Books, London, 1974.

James Gould Cozzens – *By Love Possessed* in Reader's Digest Condensed Books, vol. 22. 1960.

Lloyd C. Douglas – *The Robe*. P. Davies, London, 1954.

Lord Drogheda – *Double Harness*. Weidenfeld and Nicolson, London, 1978.

Sir Edwin Durning-Lawrence – *Shakespeare Myth*. Gay & Hancock, London, 1912.

Lawrence Durrell–Henry Miller: A private correspondence (edit. George Wickes). Faber & Faber, London, 1963.

Ian Fleming – *Dr No*. Jonathan Cape, London, 1958.

Atherton Furlong – *Echoes of Memory*. Field & Tuer, London, 1884.

Richard Gilman – *The Confusion of Realms*. Weidenfeld & Nicolson, London, 1970.

Edward Heath – *Sailing*. Sidgwick & Jackson, London, 1975.
Music. Sidgwick & Jackson, London. 1976.
Travels, People and Places in My Life. Sidgwick & Jackson, London, 1977.

Ernest Hemingway – *Across the River and into the Trees*. Panther, London, 1977.

Marjorie Holmes – *Two From Galilee: a love story of Mary and Joseph*. Hodder & Stoughton, London, 1973.

Tony Honoré – *Sex Law*. Duckworth, London, 1978.

Lyndon Baines Johnson – *My Hope for America*. Corgi, London, 1964.

James Joyce – *Finnegans Wake*. Faber & Faber,

London, 1964.
Ulysses. Bodley Head, London, 1960.
Anna Livia Plurabelle. Faber & Faber, London, 1930.
Portrait of the Artist as a Young Man. Jonathan Cape, London, 1968.
Dubliners. Jonathan Cape, London, 1967.

Joseph Wood Krutch – *Samuel Johnson*. Cassell and Co. Ltd, London, 1948.

Timothy Francis Leary – *The Politics of Ecstasy*. MacGibbon & Kee, London, 1970.

F. R. Leavis – *Literature in Our Time and in the University*. Cambridge, 1979.

Laurie Lee – *A Rose for Winter*. Hogarth Press, London, 1961.

Lord Longford – *Richard Nixon*. Weidenfeld & Nicolson, London, 1980.
The Grain of Wheat. William Collins, London, 1974.

Arnold Lunn – *Spanish Rehearsal*. Hutchinson & Co., London, 1937.

Norman Mailer – *The Naked and the Dead*. André Deutsch, London, 1960.

Benito Mussolini – *The Cardinal's Mistress* (translated by Hiram Motherwell). Cassell & Co., London, 1929.

Richard Neville – *Playpower*. Paladin, London, 1971.

Pornography: The Longford Report. Coronet, London, 1972.

Rosenberg – *Idylls of the King: A Study of Tennyson's 'Fall of Camelot'*. Harvard, USA, 1974.

A. L. Rowse – *Shakespeare the Man*. Macmillan, London and Basingstoke, 1973.

George Barnett Smith – *Poets and Novelists*. New York, 1875.

Arianna Stassinopoulos – *The Other Revolution*. Michael Joseph, London, 1978.

William Nathan Stedman – *Sonnets, Lays and Lyrics*. Sydney, Australia, 1911.

Eleanor Turton – *Virgin Soil*. Hutchinson & Co., London, 1938.

Theodore H. White – *The Making of the President 1960*. Jonathan Cape, London, 1962.

Colin Wilson – *The Outsider*. Victor Gollancz, London, 1956.

Harold Wilson – *The Labour Government 1964–1970: A Personal Record*. Michael Joseph, London, 1971. *The Governance of Britain*. Michael Joseph, London, 1976.

The Wit of President Kennedy (compiled by Bill Adler). Leslie Frewin, London, 1964.

Writers at Work, 4th series (edit. George Plimpton). Secker & Warburg, London, 1977.

Selected Bestsellers

☐	**Gone with the Wind**	Margaret Mitchell	£2.95p
☐	**Robert Morley's Book of Worries**	Robert Morley	£1.50p
☐	**The Totem**	David Morrell	£1.25p
☐	**The Alternative Holiday Catalogue**	edited by Harriet Peacock	£1.95p
☐	**The Pan Book of Card Games**	Hubert Phillips	£1.50p
☐	**The New Small Garden**	C. E. Lucas Phillips	£2.50p
☐	**Food for All the Family**	Magnus Pyke	£1.50p
☐	**Everything Your Doctor Would Tell You If He Had the Time**	Claire Rayner	£4.95p
☐	**Rage of Angels**	Sidney Sheldon	£1.75p
☐	**A Town Like Alice**	Nevil Shute	£1.50p
☐	**Just Off for the Weekend**	John Slater	£2.50p
☐	**A Falcon Flies**	Wilbur Smith	£1.95p
☐	**The Deep Well at Noon**	Jessica Stirling	£1.75p
☐	**The Eighth Dwarf**	Ross Thomas	£1.25p
☐	**The Music Makers**	E. V. Thompson	£1.50p
☐	**The Third Wave**	Alvin Toffler	£1.95p
☐	**Auberon Waugh's Yearbook**	Auberon Waugh	£1.95p
☐	**The Flier's Handbook**		£4.95p

All these books are available at your local bookshop or newsagent, or can be ordered direct from the publisher. Indicate the number of copies required and fill in the form below

3

Name

(block letters please)

Address

Send to Pan Books (CS Department), Cavaye Place, London SW10 9PG
Please enclose remittance to the value of the cover price plus :

25p for the first book plus 10p per copy for each additional book ordered to a maximum charge of £1.05 to cover postage and packing
Applicable only in the UK

While every effort is made to keep prices low, it is sometimes necessary to increase prices at short notice. Pan Books reserve the right to show on covers and charge new retail prices which may differ from those advertised in the text or eleswhere